TYRANIDS

THE GREAT DEVOURER

CONTENTS

PRODUCED BY GAMES WORKSHOP IN NOTTINGHAM
With thanks to the Mournival for their additional playtesting services

Games Workshop Ltd, Willow Rd, Lenton, Nottingham, NG7 2WS

games-workshop.com

INTRODUCTION

The book you hold is the ultimate guide to the planet-devouring xenos menace known as the Tyranids. Within, you'll find everything you need to assemble your own host of these nightmarish alien organisms, complete with rules for representing several unique and voracious hive fleets, and equipping your creatures with a variety of lethal weapon symbiotes.

The Tyranids are a race of alien predators who seek to devour every scrap of life in the galaxy. For aeons they drifted through the intergalactic void, hibernating as they made their long journey. Now, they have awakened, and the tendrils of their vast hive fleets reach ever further into populated space, consuming world after world as they advance. Within these pages you will discover the true, horrifying scale of the Tyranid incursion, and the untold carnage they have already wrought upon the races of the galaxy.

The Tyranids offer tremendous options for the avid collector, as many of their models come with an impressive variety of horrific biomorphs and organic weapons of war from which to choose. You can let your imagination run wild when it comes to assembling and painting such a collection, as the colours and patterns of the Tyranids are endlessly varied; you could choose vibrant, aggressive colours, or opt for a dark and ominous aesthetic. Alternatively, you could take inspiration from the gruesome histories presented in this book, and paint your army in the colours of one of the major hive fleets ravaging the galaxy. Whether you wish to assemble a sky-darkening swarm of winged horrors, a living tide of vicious warrior-organisms or a ground-shaking stampede of towering monsters covered in thick chitinous plate, this book will give you the options you need to amass a truly intimidating alien host.

Contained within this book you will find everything you need to assemble your own unique Tyranid army, and unleash it upon the battlefield.

THE DESTROYER OF WORLDS: This section provides a grim history of the Tyranid threat, as well as an analysis of the predatory methods unique to the galaxy's most ravenous hive fleets.

COLOURS OF THE HIVE FLEETS: Here you will find a showcase of gorgeously painted miniatures and example armies, to inspire your own Tyranid collection.

THE TYRANID SWARM: In this section you will find datasheets for every model in the Tyranids range.

THE SHADOW IN THE WARP: Finally, this section will provide you with additional rules, including Warlord Traits, Bio-artefacts, Stratagems and psychic powers unique to the Tyranid hive fleets. You will also find matched play points costs for every unit.

To play games with your army, you will need a copy of the Warhammer 40,000 rules. To find out more about Warhammer 40,000 or download the free core rules, visit warhammer40000.com.

When the Tyranid hive fleets clash with the Daemons of Chaos, neither race is granted succour. The inconstant warp-stuff from which Daemons are made offers the Tyranids no sustenance, while the unknowable entity of the Hive Mind is immune to terror and daemonic corruption. Thus, these two super-predators instead battle for the right to consume or despoil the galaxy's vast stocks of

THE DESTROYER OF WORLDS

The Tyranids are unlike any other race to be encountered by Humanity. They are the ultimate predators; to them, all living things, from the lowliest insect to the most advanced civilisation, are mere prey. Only now are the inhabitants of the galaxy realising the scale of the threat; unless the Tyranids can be stopped, it will mean nothing less than the extinction of all.

The Tyranids are likened to a galactic swarm consuming everything in its path, feeding on entire worlds and leaving only dead husks in their wake. Their threat is such that an unprotected planet can be infested and stripped clean of all its organic material in a matter of weeks without even slowing down the advance of the hive fleet.

THE INTERGALACTIC PREDATOR

The Tyranids are not native to the galaxy; they have journeyed across the unspeakable cold of the void, where time and space conspire to hold the stars apart with inconceivable distances. Yet the Tyranids crossed this expanse nonetheless, moving through the empty darkness for countless millennia to reach the rim of the Segmentae Majoris. Who can say for sure what could compel an entire race to make such a venture? Perhaps the Tyranids have already consumed everything of worth in their home galaxy and must find new feeding grounds or starve. It is possible that the Tyranids have been preying on galaxies since time immemorial and this is but the latest to feel their predations. Some have even speculated that the Tyranids are in flight from an even greater threat, be it a cosmic disaster or another fearsome race, and have risked the nothingness between galaxies rather than face extinction. Whatever the truth, for the Tyranids to have endured such a voyage must have required utter single-mindedness and unimaginable energy. During their journey, the Tyranids slumbered in a state of frozen hibernation, but now they have arrived, they have awoken and they are hungry.

THE HIVE FLEETS

The Tyranids are a space-borne race that have inveigled their way into the realms of Man, as well as those of other xenos, like a disease spreading through a healthy body. The Tyranids travel in great fleets of gigantic organisms grown in the bubbling organ-sacs of the vessel's reproductive chambers. All of these creatures are born to serve the single entity that is the ship, and the ship itself exists only as part of the entity that is the hive fleet.

When a hive fleet encounters a prey world, it does not invade for territorial gain or out of a sense of pride or vengeance. Indeed, it is doubtful the Tyranids even comprehend such concepts. Rather, they invade to harvest valuable biomass and feed their insatiable hunger. The Tyranids require an endless supply of food, not only to nourish the hive fleets, but to grow new organisms. Therefore, when a hive fleet invades a planet rich in life, every action of every Tyranid creature is honed to a single goal – the total and rapid absorption of that world's population, ecosystems and bio-resources. To this end, the hive fleet creates an army with the express purpose of overcoming the prey world's defenders before it is stripped of every scrap of biomatter and devoured.

CREATURES OF THE SWARM

Tyranid warrior-organisms are creatures of visceral horror, implacable monsters with razor-sharp claws which can tear a man apart in the blink of an eye, and grotesque bio-cannons that fire hungry, parasitic missiles into their prey's flesh.

Every weapon and projectile used by the hive fleets is a living organism, grown from the reconstituted biomatter of previous invasions. The Tyranids have no form of mechanical technology and, instead, harness an advanced form of biotechnology to create organic equivalents of the tools, weaponry and ammunition used by other races. These creatures live in a highly symbiotic fashion, fusing into each other's flesh so that it is often impossible to say where one Tyranid creature ends, and another begins. In this way, Tyranid warrior-beasts wield living weapons that are literally extensions of their own bodies, each

'There is a cancer eating at the Imperium. With each decade it advances deeper, leaving drained, dead worlds in its wake. This horror, this abomination, has thought and purpose which functions on an unimaginable, galactic scale, and all we can do is try to stop the swarms of bioengineered monsters it unleashes upon us by instinct. We have given the horror a name to salve our fears; we call it the Tyranid race, but if it is aware of us at all, it must know us only as Prey.'

- Inquisitor Czevak at the Conclave of Har

The bio-construct nature of the Tyranids makes them a terrible foe to face, for their armies contain a creature specialised for every conceivable facet of warfare, which can be altered and regrown to suit a battle's needs in a short span of time. Thus can a hive fleet adapt to generate a force capable of overwhelming any opposition, unleashing a vast throng of ferocious alien monsters that can fly, run, burrow and stalk through the defences of any foe.

THE HIVE MIND

The Magos Biologis of the Imperium categorises each Tyranid hive fleet as a separate force, an individual entity that competes with other hive fleets for resources. Indeed, each is self-sufficient, appearing to exhibit different strategies and developing unique creatures to overcome its prey. However, the truth is more complex, for each hive fleet is but a splinter of one greater assemblage. The Tyranids' numbers are vast beyond counting, swarms so large that they block out the very stars, yet each and every creature is but a single cell in the living body of a single super-organism.

Every thought and action, every spark of life in the Tyranid race, is bound and interlinked into a single unfathomable consciousness, a great entity that stretches across hundreds of light years of space. This gestalt sentience is known as the Hive Mind. It holds all Tyranids in a psychic bond that enables them to act in perfect synchronicity. Under the influence of this ancient consciousness, the Tyranids have fed on countless planets and devoured civilisations since time immemorial.

The majority of Tyranid organisms have no distinct mind as a human would understand it, having been created to perform a single task to the exclusion of all else. Unless the implacable will of the Hive Mind instructs them to do otherwise, these organisms simply fulfil the functions for which they were created, acting on nothing more than instinct. Larger, more complicated, Tyranid beasts have been grown to make limited decisions appropriate to current stimuli and situations, but even these actions are subordinate to the goals of the Hive Mind.

The Hive Mind's influence is strongest in the vicinity of creatures such as Tyranid Warriors and the feared Hive Tyrants. These beings are able to communicate with their kin, not through language, but by a synaptic form of telepathy through which they relay and channel the will of the Hive Mind. Under the command of such creatures, the Tyranids operate in perfect unison, slaved to the psychic imperatives of a single communal intelligence. However, should the synapse creatures be slain, the link between individual creatures and the Hive Mind will be severed – many of the lesser organisms will revert to their baser, animalistic behaviours. For this reason, the Tyranid swarms do not have only a single commander, but many, to ensure the Hive Mind's synaptic control is maintained across the entire Tyranid race.

THE SHADOW IN THE WARP

The coming of a Tyranid hive fleet is preceded by a smothering psychic signal that envelops entire star systems and disrupts all forms of warp travel and communication. Swallowed up by psychic static, whole worlds suddenly go deathly silent, giving no clues as to what is unfolding on the surface below, or of what terrors are about to befall. This is the Shadow in the Warp, and it heralds imminent invasion and horror.

It is unknown if the Shadow in the Warp is created deliberately by the hive fleets, or if it is simply a byproduct of the Hive Mind's innate synaptic control. In any case, the Shadow in the Warp creates fear and panic wherever it falls, instilling a pervasive dread into the minds of a prey world's defenders, plunging entire planets into misery and despair. For highly psychic races, such as the Aeldari, or for luckless psykers caught within this enervating effect, the malaise is magnified tenfold. Should a psyker attempt to use his otherworldly abilities, the cerebral cacophony worsens even further; the psychic sound of a billion alien thoughts scratches at his mind, and unless he is particularly strong-willed he will be pitched into an insanity where he will repeatedly utter phrases in a tongue impossible to properly pronounce.

For races such as the Imperium of Man, whose means of interstellar communication and travel rely upon highly specialised psykers such as Astropaths and Navigators, the Shadow in the Warp is one of the deadliest facets of the Tyranid menace. Bereft of their means to call for reinforcements or safely navigate surrounding space, the worlds of the Imperium are easily isolated from the wider galaxy. By the time the Shadow in the Warp falls, it is already too late; these beleaguered planets are effectively on their own. They must fend for themselves and face the Tyranid swarm with the weapons they have to hand, or die in the attempt.

DESTROYER OF WORLDS

The Tyranids do not communicate with other races, and why should they do so? Tyranids are as far above other life forms, such as Mankind, just as Mankind is above the domesticated livestock it consumes. The Tyranids cannot be reasoned with, appeased or surrendered to. There can be no hope of mercy from such a foe. To face the Tyranids is simply a matter of survival: kill or be consumed.

Vast swathes of the galaxy have already been stripped of life, and with every passing year the hive fleets push deeper into regions of populated space. Even as the prey races direct their forces to repel these threats, still more Tyranid fleets approach from the intergalactic void and emerge from their aeons-long slumbers. The thought processes of the Hive Mind are gathering pace as more Tyranids wake and recall the age-old purpose of their kind – feed, grow, survive.

A GALAXY IN FLAMES

In the latter days of the 41st Millennium the galaxy-wide cataclysm of the Great Rift tore a ragged wound across realspace, signalling the beginning of a new age of darkness. Further warp storms followed, rippling across the galaxy, spilling the raw matter of Chaos into the material realm in ever-increasing quantities.

This ongoing corruption of the galaxy spells potential disaster for the Hive Mind. Tyranid hive fleets require vast stockpiles of organic matter to power their galactic assaults. The mutable, inconstant stuff of Chaos provides none of this vital sustenance. With every passing season, more planets and systems are swallowed up by the roiling tide of empyric madness, denying the Tyranids the precious biomass that sustains them.

Yet the Tyranid race is defined by its ability to adapt in the face of disaster. The timeless sentience of the Hive Mind has already developed new organisms and hunting patterns in the face of this peril. That which is edible shall be consumed, and all else shall be obliterated with murderous efficiency.

THE DEATH OF TYRAN

The first recorded contact with Tyranids happened in early 745.M41, on the eastern outskirts of the Imperium. Up to this point, Mankind was wholly unaware of the new threat on its borders, and if any of the galaxy's older empires were aware of the oncoming swarm, they did not see fit to warn the upstart Imperium.

'We cannot live through this. Mankind cannot live through this. In a single day they have covered this planet with a flood of living blades and needle-fanged mouths. Kill one, and ten take its place. If they are truly without number, then our race is doomed to a violent death before every shred of our civilisation is scoured away by a force more voracious than the fires of hell themselves.

Death! By the Machine God, Death is here!'

- Magos Varnak, last words

Yet the hive fleet had left evidence of its approach for those with the wit to see it. Over the course of the preceding decade, Imperial explorers had performed a census of the planetary systems surrounding the far-flung outpost of Tyran Primus. In the course of their survey, these explorers discovered whole worlds scoured of life. Verdant planets known to have been teeming with flora and fauna were now reduced to scorched and barren rock. Not one creature, not even the simplest of bacteria, remained. Though this was reported to the Explorator General of the Administratum, little more was done – the galaxy is a huge place, mysteries commonplace and the Administratum as slow to act as only a massively labyrinthine bureaucracy can be.

As the Tyran outpost dutifully continued to file reports of dead worlds, the Tyranid hive fleet drew inexorably closer. Thus far the Tyranids had consumed only isolated worlds with no intelligent life, replenishing the reserves of biomatter expended during the long, slow crawl through the interstellar void. Now reinvigorated, the aliens descended upon Tyran Primus – the first of Mankind's worlds to feel their wrath, and the invasion for which the Imperium would name their race. That the Tyran outpost had any warning at all was due to sheer chance. A survey ship, returning from cataloguing another devoured world, encountered a cloud of unidentified objects on the edge of the Tyran System. Though crippled by peculiar fleshy mines on the edge of the cloud, the survey ship managed to escape and limp back to the Tyran Primus base, carrying with it a dire warning. A handful of days later, the invasion began.

The outpost of Tyran Primus was no easy prey. Nestled deep in the ruins of an ancient chain of volcanic islands, this base was heavily fortified to resist the fearsome storms and sea creatures of Tyran's wild oceans, and its defences did not end there. Given Tyran's position on the edge of known space, and its extreme separation from the Imperium's other worlds, it had been founded with armament deemed adequate to deter the attentions of piratical raiders or repel an aggressive alien presence.

Four giant defence lasers stood guard over the Tyran Primus base, themselves protected by hardened ceramite silos and void shield generators. This already formidable firepower was further complemented by three dozen autocannon and lascannon interceptor emplacements, an overlapping network of defence bastions and Proteus-class bunkers.

Nor could the planetary garrison be found wanting. In addition to the Skitarii bodyguard of the outpost's commander, Magos Varnak, Tyran boasted three full wings of Thunderbolt fighters, three Endeavour-class cruisers and an entire infantry regiment of the Imperial Guard. Such was the standard for a frontier outpost of the Imperium, a design that had proven itself against a hundred adversaries. Yet here, against this new alien menace, this formidable arsenal would prove woefully insufficient.

THE FIRST ASSAULT

Tyran's defence lasers opened fire the moment the first alien ships made orbit. For more than an hour, the storm-wracked skies of Tyran were split again and again by incandescent blasts as the base's gunners desperately fended off the descending invaders. Then, just as the cooling systems of the defence lasers began to glow white and overheat, the invaders withdrew.

Perhaps buoyed by false confidence, Magos Varnak immediately ordered his small fleet to harry the withdrawing vessels, but this strategy soon proved to be folly. Penetrating the spore cloud that masked the alien fleet, the pursuing vessels discovered that fewer than a dozen of the strange vessels had been destroyed out of a fleet of several thousand. Having lured the cruisers away from Tyran, the leading edge of bio-ships suddenly changed direction, and fell upon the Imperial vessels with a vengeance. The *Emperor's Fist* was the first to be destroyed, its hull shredded by a voracious swarm vomited forth by a much smaller vessel. The *Righteous Destiny* lasted scarcely longer – a cluster of tendrils drew its prow into a hive ship's gaping maw. Only the *Sword of Warriors* lasted long enough to convey a warning to the Tyran outpost, but before the transmission was complete, leech-like pods gnawed through

the starship's adamantium hull, unleashing hundreds of Genestealers directly into the vessel's bridge and decks. The crew were slaughtered within minutes, leaving the unhelmed cruiser adrift in space.

With the Imperium's cruisers destroyed, the hive fleet returned to Tyran, and this time the defences could not hold them back. Thousands of Tyrannocytes descended on the world and, though the laser defences destroyed many, countless hundreds more crashed into the seas. All around the base, the seas thrashed and boiled as the invaders burst from their pods and tore their way through the ferocious inhabitants of Tyran's oceans. Then the first invaders scaled the walls. At first, the disciplined volleys of the Imperial Guard drove the creatures back. Amongst their ranks were veterans from Catachan, well used to combating alien monsters, and they would not easily yield. Officers bellowed orders through the pouring rain, and torrents of firepower scythed deep into the alien ranks. The hides of the smaller beasts were of scant protection against the torrent of lasgun fire, and offered no defence at all from the booming autocannons of the interceptor grid. Wave after wave of Hormagaunts and Genestealers was torn apart, their corpses choking the rain-lashed killing zones between the bastions. Thunderbolts darted through the skies above, expertly jinking through the lightning-chased skies, blasting apart incoming pods with precision fire before turning to intercept new targets.

Then the northern defence laser fell silent. Thousands of Gargoyles had mindlessly thrown themselves into its throat, clogging the massive beam projectors with their incinerated corpses. Moments later, the eastern defence laser complex ceased firing as an enormous Carnifex rammed through the reinforced steel wall, trampled over the defenders and hurled itself at the coolant lines. One by one, the Thunderbolt fighters tumbled from the skies, their engines choked by spores, or their cockpits torn apart by shrieking Harpies. As more and more of the defence network went dark, the Tyrannocytes began to fall onto the base itself.

THE SWARM TRIUMPHANT

An hour later, and the Tyran outpost was as good as lost. The bastions were overrun or destroyed, the defence laser complexes fallen silent. Even the Guardsmen tempered on the harsh death world of distant Catachan, men and women who had reckoned themselves amongst the toughest, most stalwart of warriors, abandoned their posts and fled into the driving rain in search of an escape that did not exist. Here and there pockets of resistance still held out under the watchful gaze of a brave or foolhardy officer, but one by one these were extinguished. Only the command bunker remained, and its walls began to crack under the impact of massive blows. Through the few functioning displays, Varnak saw the flood of aliens rampaging through his once impregnable base, destroying everything they found. Finally, the adamantium gate of the bunker crashed inwards, and the Tyranids poured into the command complex. Guardsmen and Skitarii fought back with flamers, but the aliens swarmed through the searing fires and hacked their way onwards.

As Hormagaunts poured into the command centre, Varnak whispered a final prayer to the Emperor and triggered a switch, sending a data-codex plummeting into the depths of the base. This codex would be Tyran's enduring legacy, for it would be recovered many months later by one Inquisitor Kryptman, a man who would dedicate his life to opposing the Tyranid menace. But for Kryptman's arrival, Tyran's fate might have gone unnoticed by the wider Imperium for millennia. He found a blasted and sterile planet, unrecognisable as the teeming ocean world it had once been. The planet had been sucked dry, every scrap of vegetation and every drop of water consumed.

As Kryptman reviewed the auto-logs contained within the data-codex, the full horror of Tyran's downfall was revealed. Wasting not another moment, the Inquisitor set forth to warn the rest of the galaxy of the oncoming horror from beyond the stars, a horror Kryptman named 'Tyranids' for the world they had consumed. The Tyrannic Wars had begun.

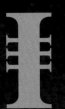

INVASION SWARMS

When a Tyranid hive fleet descends upon a prey world to strip it of life, it does so in a series of distinct stages. Each wave of the invasion unleashes a fresh menagerie of biological nightmares, perfectly designed to sow despoilment and death. In mere days, a once-thriving planet is scoured of every drop of organic matter. Hunger briefly satiated, the hive fleet drifts away in search of its next meal, leaving nothing but an airless tomb behind.

001 ELAPSED CHRONOSEGMENTS
Subject:Vanguard
File:1283853M
- Genestealers
- Broodlords
- Lictors
- Deathleaper

Even before the hive fleet makes orbit, vanguard organisms have infested the prey world, sowing confusion and terror ahead of the invasion.

021 ELAPSED CHRONOSEGMENTS
Subject:Assault
File:3526834M
- Carnifexes
VARIANTS
- Old One Eye
- Screamer-Killers
- Thornbacks

In the event of heavy resistance, crusher-broods of Carnifexes are unleashed to smash apart armour and fortified positions.

009 ELAPSED CHRONOSEGMENTS
Subject:Skyswarm
File:1475835X
- Gargoyles
- Harpies
- Hive Crones

Shadows fall across the prey world, and the air is filled with the sound of beating wings. The planet's terrified populace look up to see the hive fleet's skyswarms descend, overwhelming isolated defenders and screening onrushing ground swarms.

017 ELAPSED CHRONOSEGMENTS
Subject:Subterranean Assault
File:2999161S
- Raveners
- Red Terror
- Trygons
- Trygon Primes
- Mawlocs

Burrowing bioforms carve subterranean tunnels through the bedrock of the planet, undermining fortifications and civilian centres. They burst from the ground in the midst of such structures, slaughtering defenders unprepared for such an assault.

024 ELAPSED CHRONOSEGMENTS
Subject:Leader-beasts
File:386123N
- Hive Tyrants
- Winged Hive Tyrants
- The Swarmlord

The greatest of the hive fleet's synaptic commanders are deployed to the surface to ensure the obliteration of any particularly stubborn resistance. Their aeons of battlefield experience inevitably assures a swift and bloody massacre of the prey.

010 ELAPSED CHRONOSEGMENTS
Subject:Gaunts
File:1872531L
- Hormagaunts
- Termagants

A tide of warrior-organisms known as gaunts floods towards the planet's major defences, sweeping over any resistance with sheer weight of numbers. This relentless assault divides the prey world's defenders into isolated pockets.

013 ELAPSED CHRONOSEGMENTS
Subject:Synapse
File:2242581/3
- Tyranid Warriors
- Tervigons
- Zoanthropes
- Maleceptors

With the major sites of resistance identified, the Hive Mind deploys highly advanced synapse creatures to facilitate their destruction.

015 ELAPSED CHRONOSEGMENTS
Subject:Sporecasters
File::273671/S
- Venomthropes
- Toxicrenes

Sporecasting bioforms spit clouds of spores into the prey world's skies, denaturing the environment and eliminating non-Tyranid life.

014 ELAPSED CHRONOSEGMENTS
Subject:Spores
File:2543141G
- Spore Mines
- Mucolid Spores
- Sporocysts
- Tyrannocytes

The hive fleet's bio-ships expel clouds of spores into the upper atmosphere. Ranging in size and function from enormous bio-transports to microscopic toxins, these spores begin the process of altering the prey world to suit the Tyranids' needs.

024 ELAPSED CHRONOSEGMENTS
Subject:Guards
File:389234N/X
- Hive Guard
- Tyrant Guard

In order to protect its most valuable leader-beasts and vital infestation sites, the Hive Mind deploys heavily armoured bioforms created solely for their protection. Any attempted enemy assault faces an impervious wall of hardened chitin.

036 ELAPSED CHRONOSEGMENTS
Subject:Feeders
File:529346DW
- Ripper Swarms
- Pyrovores
- Haruspexes

With every last pocket of resistance crushed, living tides of feeder organisms sweep across the world's surface, consuming every last scrap of biomatter.

029 ELAPSED CHRONOSEGMENTS
Subject:Bio Artillery
File:4246188R
- Biovores
- Exocrines
- Tyrannofexes

Artillery beasts are deployed in vast numbers to destroy any buildings and indigenous organic structures, as well as any surviving inhabitants. The desolation they leave behind expedites the gradual consumption of the planet.

HIVE FLEET BEHEMOTH

Having scoured Tyran Primus of biomass, the alien hive fleet codified 'Behemoth' moved on in search of other worlds to feed upon, pushing its tendrils ever deeper into the galaxy whilst the death screams of an entire world went unheard.

By the time Inquisitor Kryptman reached Tyran, a year had passed since the attack. At first, the Inquisitor could not equate the husk of a planet he found to ocean-bound Tyran Primus. The world had been sucked dry; every scrap of vegetation and every drop of water was gone. A crater was all that remained of the Adeptus Mechanicus outpost, and all that could be found of the planet's cruiser fleet were acid-eaten hulks – icy shells devoid of life and adrift in space. After a long search, Inquisitor Kryptman recovered Magos Varnak's data-codex, the knowledge contained within it bought with the life of an entire planet. What Kryptman saw when he reviewed the fragmented data was a dire prophecy of doom: static-laced images of scythe-limbed aliens, footage of the skies over Tyran darkening with swarming monsters, and orbital pict-views of a fleet of living ships so vast that the stellar horizon was veiled in inky blackness.

THE FATE OF THANDROS

Kryptman ordered his Astropath to send a warning to the Imperium, but the psyker could not penetrate the warp turmoil left by the passing of the alien fleet. Even the nearby Thandros telepathica booster matrix was obscured. In desperation, Kryptman set course for the Thandros System in the hopes of re-establishing communications with the Imperium there. It was on this voyage that Kryptman realised the scale of the Tyranid threat. Following in the hive fleet's wake, Kryptman discovered a string of barren worlds that records indicated should be verdant and lush.

Reviewing a decade's worth of planetary survey data from that region of space, Kryptman saw a pattern emerging. He was able to plot the hive fleet's course by the trail of dead and lifeless worlds it had left behind. There was no subtlety to the hive fleet's approach, no sense of strategic genius. It merely ploughed through the galaxy without stopping, devouring everything in its path with a rapacious hunger that would become its defining feature. As dictated by tradition, Kryptman codified the new alien threat with an ancient and forbidding name from legend: Behemoth.

Though Kryptman's ship made good speed, the Tyranids had attacked the Thandros System and moved on long before his arrival. Thandros was not as well protected as Tyran, and was likewise overwhelmed by the seemingly endless numbers of bio-horrors that flooded its cities and fortifications. The telepathica matrix was found to have emptied all of its turret magazines and burned out its defence laser crystal before being overrun. It was evident that Thandros had fought bravely, but its populace had nonetheless been slaughtered and consumed.

A VOICE IN THE DARK

With Thandros lost, Kryptman's quest became critical. The next system in Hive Fleet Behemoth's path was Ultramar, and unless it was forewarned, the Imperium might lose its best chance to halt the progress of the Tyranid onslaught. With haste, Kryptman and his agents salvaged what remained of Thandros' telepathica matrix, and through a herculean effort, his Astropath finally managed

to pierce the Shadow in the Warp to contact the unsuspecting Imperium. The Astropath, nose and ears streaming blood from the effort, broadcast Kryptman's warning. A single voice spoke back from the darkness, and it came from Macragge, the heart of Ultramar and the home world of the Ultramarines Chapter of Space Marines.

By the grace of the Emperor, Inquisitor Kryptman arrived at Ultramar ahead of Hive Fleet Behemoth, and met with Marneus Calgar, Chapter Master of the Ultramarines, beneath the portico of his white marble palace. Lord Calgar stood as a giant before the Inquisitor, his stature grand even among the superhuman warriors of the Space Marines. Calgar listened intently to the man's words, but Kryptman's terrible discoveries did not disturb his noble demeanour. A true heir of Primarch Guilliman's genius, and one of the most accomplished military leaders in the Imperium, nothing escaped Calgar's notice, not one detail about the foe that could be turned into an advantage. Hive Fleet Behemoth was fast approaching, and the Ultramarines Chapter prepared for the greatest battle in their history.

> 'An alien threat has risen from beyond the abyss, a swarm so vast that it blots out the stars. This horror fights neither for power nor territory, but rather to feed a hunger so insatiable that it will eventually devour the entire galaxy.'
>
> - Inquisitor Kryptman

ULTRAMAR BESIEGED

Behemoth had spent countless aeons travelling through the infinite blackness of the interstellar void before its emergence into the galaxy, and the hive fleet was unable to contain its ravenous hunger. Driven onwards by this incessant need to consume, Behemoth's route towards Macragge was straightforward, even predictable. However, this did not make it any less deadly a threat. Prandium, the paradise world known as the Jewel of Ultramar, was the next obstacle in Behemoth's inexorable path. Even Prandium's prodigious orbital defences and well-equipped, highly motivated regiments of Ultramar Auxilia could not hold back the tide of invading xenos. Utterly unprepared for the single-minded ferocity of the Tyranid race, these mortal soldiers were annihilated by wave after wave of swarming gaunts and looming weapon-beasts. Ill-fated Calth fell next, ravaged by a smaller force of Tyranids seeded by the hive fleet's bio-ships.

Yet it was upon Macragge, heart of the Ultramarines' stellar empire, that the fate of the sons of Guilliman would be decided. Bristling with orbital gun platforms and guarded by the imposing Ultramar Defence Fleet, this was a far more formidable target than anything Behemoth had previously faced. On the ground, the entire Ultramarines Chapter stood ready to repel the xenos assault. However, as Behemoth drew near, the sheer immensity of the threat facing Macragge became forebodingly clear.

THE RAVENOUS BEAST

Hive Fleet Behemoth was the first tendril of the Tyranid invasion to awaken after the long journey though the void. Its brutal, headlong charge through the eastern Imperium was driven by a ravenous hunger that had smouldered for countless aeons; a hunger it could never satiate or fully control. In the years since its emergence, this most savage of hive fleets has come to be defined by untrammelled ferocity. Even the might of the entire Ultramarines Chapter could not see Behemoth destroyed. In the years since the hive fleet's defeat at the Battle of Macragge, scattered tendrils of the Behemoth have ground countless worlds to dust beneath their crushing stampedes.

Behemoth attacks as a clenched fist, unleashing its full might upon a prey world with little thought to subtlety or strategy. Swarms of gaunts sweep across the earth, searching for large clusters of biomass; on occupied worlds, this will inevitably draw them towards cities and fortified complexes. As these advance swarms encounter resistance, the Hive Mind will deploy more advanced organisms into the fray. Where more adaptive and experienced hive fleets will seed their invasion swarms with highly specialised organisms in order to exploit identified weaknesses in their prey, Hive Fleet Behemoth typically fields the strongest and largest warrior-forms, hulking beasts that can smash their way through any defence.

This juggernaut of charging flesh and tearing claws is all but unstoppable. Packs of hunting Carnifexes will barrel towards fortifications and gatherings of enemy troops, battering their way through rockcrete and armour, crushing all before them to bloody paste. Behemoth Hive Tyrants will launch themselves into the thick of the fighting, laying about themselves with eviscerating swipes of their organic blades.

+++CLASSIFIED+++
Subject:8/2/Behemoth
File:1283853M
Auth:CX25oA
Source:Tnipr Prime
Access:Viridian

The organisms of Tyranid splinter fleets often develop unique markings that differentiate them from their ancestor host.

Organisms of the Kordex Strain, known for the frenzied bellowing they make in combat, bear a distinctive dotted carapace.

Brightly coloured armour crests identify Tyranid Warriors from the splinter fleet known as the Crimson Maw.

BATTLE FOR MACRAGGE

When Hive Fleet Behemoth arrived at Macragge, the Tyranids found it fortified against them. This was no isolated frontier world, neither was it an ill-defended relay system to be overwhelmed in a brief but vicious struggle. This was Macragge, the Imperium's bulwark on the eastern rim and home world to an entire Chapter of Space Marines.

Thanks to Inquisitor Kryptman, Macragge had been warned of the Tyranids, and Marneus Calgar bent his legendary strategic skills to buttressing Macragge's already formidable defences. Space Marine Strike Cruisers and Battle Barges loomed like gigantic azure monoliths amongst the Ultramar Defence Fleet and the planet's orbital weapon platforms; Macragge was surrounded with a ring of firepower. Another foe would have been daunted by the assemblage of might that now guarded the capital world of Ultramar, but the Tyranids came on without delay. The first waves of bio-ships swept past the defences, intent on reaching the planet below. Each vessel was targeted and eliminated in turn by massed firepower, but not before delivering clusters of bio-organisms to Macragge's surface.

Tyranids swarmed over the planet's frozen landscape, and the Ultramarines were quick to respond. For a time, Calgar's forces slowed the tide, trading territory for time as they whittled down the oncoming swarm, staining the snow with alien ichor. Yet even under Calgar's leadership, these tactics could only last for so long against such numbers, and the Ultramarines were soon forced into making a stand at Cold Steel Ridge.

THE SWARMLORD STRIKES

The Hive Mind had learnt from the Ultramarines' tactics, and having identified Calgar as the main threat to the Tyranid advance, it unleashed its deadliest servant to bring about his end – the Hive Tyrant later classified in Imperial records as the 'Swarmlord'. Under the influence of the Swarmlord, the Tyranids' primal fury was coupled with keen strategy. Instead of mindlessly charging at their prey, the Tyranids circumvented fire zones, ambushed enemy counter-attacks and concentrated on weak points in Calgar's line that could only have been perceived by a military genius. The Ultramarines were in danger of being overwhelmed.

With the foe reeling, the Swarmlord extended its will and ten thousand alien minds answered. Raveners and Trygons burst from the chill ground in the midst of manned trenches, separating the beleaguered defenders from Calgar's main force. By the time the Ultramarines cut through the subterranean swarms, the trench network was a charnel of gore overrun with Tyranids. The Ultramarines purged them with fire, but in so doing left the Swarmlord's true target – the mighty Baneblade *Pride of Hera* – without infantry support. A wave of Carnifexes tore the super-heavy tank apart. With its destruction, the western flank was lost.

On the eastern flank, Calgar cursed himself for underestimating his foe. Under the Swarmlord's dominion, the swarm was adapting to defeat Calgar's tactics as quickly as he could conceive them. Knowing that staying on Cold Steel Ridge would waste more lives, Calgar ordered his forces to fall back to the orbiting Battle Barge *Octavius*. With luck, they could hold out long enough for Thunderhawk Gunships to arrive and extract them.

Somehow, the Swarmlord sensed Calgar's intent to escape, and with an alien shriek, it plunged into the fray. Beside the Swarmlord came a host of elite warrior-organisms, and together they cut a path directly towards their quarry. Seeing the danger heading towards their Chapter Master, the Ultramarines hastened to his aid but found themselves assailed from all sides as the Swarmlord urged hordes of lesser creatures to intercept the would-be heroes. The swarm fell upon the Ultramarines with blind fury, undaunted by the roar of boltguns. Their deaths did little more than delay the Space Marines, but it would prove enough; Calgar would have to face the Swarmlord and its bodyguard alone.

Calgar fought like a hero of legend, but there were simply too many foes and he was finally laid low, his body rent and torn. Calgar's last strength was expended in mortal combat with the Swarmlord itself, and the Hive Tyrant towered over the Space Marine, blades raised to deliver the killing blow. But the fatal strike never fell. Calgar's Honour Guard broke through the mass of Tyranids to throw themselves in front of their wounded Chapter Master, axes of Ultramar flashing in the cold light as they slowly drove the Swarmlord back and shielded their lord with their own bodies. Through valour and sacrifice, they held the swarm back until the Thunderhawks arrived to evacuate the surviving Ultramarines. Marneus Calgar would not die this day, but Cold Steel Ridge was lost.

THE WAR IN SPACE

Yet if the battle on the ground fared poorly, the war in space was proving disastrous. The first Tyranid assault wave had claimed the mighty Battle Barge *Caesar*. The third wave saw the destruction of the better part of Ultramar's Defence Fleet. By the time the ninth wave was launched, Macragge's orbital defence stations were bloody tombs, mere hunks of debris left spinning in space. Macragge now lay undefended, and the Tyranid invasion intensified.

A fresh wave of bioforms landed on Macragge, bringing a new stage of the planetary assault directly to the prey world's polar fortresses. However, the war in space was not yet concluded. Refusing all but the most vital medical aid, Calgar took command of the remaining ships and turned their firepower to the orbiting hive fleet. The Hive Mind responded as it had done before at Tyran Primus, withdrawing its bio-vessels from the planet to lure the prey world's defending fleet into a deadly trap. Calgar took the bait, and pursued the hive fleet to the ringed world of Circe on the edge of the Macragge System, but not without a plan of his own.

As Calgar approached Circe, a second shoal of bio-ships concealed in the planet's rings launched themselves at the battered fleet. However, the first salvoes had scarcely been exchanged when Battlefleet Tempestus entered realspace on the far side of Circe – it was the Tyranids' turn to be caught in the jaws of a trap. Even so, the fighting was fierce, and only the desperate sacrifice of the *Dominus Astra* swung the battle in the Imperium's favour, the great Emperor-class battleship detonating its mighty warp engines and creating a cataclysmic vortex that dragged many hive ships to oblivion. Caught between the guns of two Imperial fleets, nearly all of Hive Fleet Behemoth's bio-ships were destroyed. A scant few, scarred and battered, slipped away into the depths of space. Though it had suffered a grievous defeat, the galaxy had not heard the last of Behemoth.

THE BEHEMOTH FALLS

In truth, the war was won at Circe. The only question that remained was whether Macragge would be lost in the process. Whilst battle raged in space, the valour of the Ultramarines was being tested as never before on the surface. The veterans of the 1st Company led a tenacious defence of the polar fortresses, holding every wall and battlement. When their boltguns ran dry, the Space Marines switched to their pistols; when they too ran out of ammunition, they fought with chainswords and combat blades. Not once did they yield. Only at the last possible moment did the veterans fall back to their fortresses' hearts, prepared to sell their lives dearly.

When the fleet-bound Ultramarines returned to Macragge, they found a landscape subsumed by carnage. Though a few survivors were found in the ruin of Macragge's southern fortress, none were discovered in the north. The 1st Company had died there to a man, fighting back-to-back against the full fury of the swarm, their bodies swamped amongst mounds of Tyranid dead. Though the Ultramarines had prevailed, they had been dealt a blow that would take centuries to recover from.

The body of a Hive Tyrant believed to be the Swarmlord was found on the corpse-littered ice fields outside the northern polar fortress, but the damage it had sustained made it impossible to identify with certainty. Rumours persist that the beast had somehow escaped death and that the Tyranids would one day return. It would be decades before the truth was revealed.

'As I looked into its dead black eyes, I saw the terrible sentience it had in place of a soul. Behind that was the steel will of its leader. Further still, I could feel its primogenitor coldly assessing me from the void. And looking back from the deepest recesses of the alien's mind, I perceived what I can describe only as an immortal hunger.

We can slay the Tyranids on our worlds, blast their fleets from space, grind their armies to torn and ruined fragments. But their hunger? That is beyond our ability to slay.'

- Varro Tigurius,
Ultramarines Chief Librarian

Upon Cold Steel Ridge the Ultramarines stood against the endless swarms of Hive Fleet Behemoth, unleashing blistering volleys of bolter fire that ruptured chitin carapaces and splattered torrents of corrosive ichor across the tundra.

THE FIRST TYRANNIC WAR

The Sin of Damnation

The Genestealer-infested space hulk, *Sin of Damnation*, is cleansed in a close-fought series of assaults by the Blood Angels 1st Company. At the time, none are aware that the Genestealers are the vanguard of an imminent galactic invasion.

The Behemoth Arrives

A vast fleet of alien bio-ships enters the galaxy on the Eastern Fringe.

The Flight of Malan'tai

Warned of the Tyranid onslaught by far-flung bands of Rangers, the Farseers of Craftworld Malan'tai opt to remove themselves from Behemoth's approach whilst there is still time to escape.

The Death of Tyran

Kryptman's Quest

Whilst investigating the mysterious silence of Tyran Primus, Inquisitor Kryptman learns the horror of the alien threat. Kryptman names the aliens 'Tyranids' and races to warn to the Imperium.

The Thandros Incident

The binary worlds of Thandros offer little resistance to the oncoming Tyranids, and their citizens are slaughtered in the darkness of their own mines.

Behemoth Advances

Imperial Explorator Fleet Dorsari, the world of Helmont and the Moons of Ra'pson all fall before Behemoth's inexorable advance.

The Jagga Waaagh!

Behemoth falls upon Jagga, pirate base of Kaptin Blackgit. The Ork Kroozers that form Blackgit's fleet launch boarding parties to storm the encroaching bio-ships. The tide soon turns when the rampaging Orks awaken the Tervigons within each ship, which spawn countless broods of Termagants. The Orks are swamped and the Termagants then flood back through the Orks' own boarding tubes to slaughter the Kroozers' crews. Blackgit, sensing defeat as the communications from his fleet abruptly end, attempts to escape by ramming his ship through a lone bio-vessel blocking his path, only to fatally discover it is a starship-sized spore mine.

Prandium Devoured

Prandium, the jewel of Ultramar, proves an easy and bountiful conquest for the Tyranids. The barren rock left in Behemoth's wake is scarcely recognisable as the once verdant paradise of yore.

The Sybari Slaughter

The Chaos Renegade warband known as the Death Shadows musters at Sybari in preparation for a secret strike against Ultramar. They are isolated when the Shadow in the Warp envelops the system, and their warlord, the Sorcerer Malafor, is driven to insanity by the Tyranids' psychic presence. Leaderless and in the midst of preparing for an assault of their own, the renegades are unprepared to defend Sybari from the swarm. Though they reap a high tally, the entire warband is annihilated in less than an hour.

The Purge of Ymgarl

The Salamanders conduct a xenocidal campaign to purge the moons of Ymgarl of Genestealer infestation. Though the Salamanders suffer heavy casualties, the moons are finally declared scoured, or so they believe…

Assault on Calth

Bio-ships seed Calth with invaders before rejoining the hive fleet at Circe. Though few in number, the Tyranids are led by a great Carnifex that wreaks havoc until it is shot in the skull by a Commissar.

Battle for Macragge

The full might of Hive Fleet Behemoth falls upon Macragge. There it faces the entire Ultramarines Chapter. Ultimately the Tyranids are defeated by the Adeptus Astartes and Macragge saved, but the Ultramarines' victory comes at a terrible cost. The entirety of the Chapter's veteran 1st Company is slain. It is a disaster that will take the Ultramarines centuries to recover from.

A Monster Reawakens

The body of a one-eyed Carnifex is discovered encased in ice on Calth. Though believed to be dead, the creature awakens and butchers everything in its path. Hundreds of Tyranid creatures that had been lurking in Calth's labyrinthine cave systems emerge and flock to the Carnifex's side. As tales of its rampage reach Macragge, the Ultramarines despatch Sergeant Telion to hunt down the monster terrorising Calth's populace, a beast they have entitled 'Old One Eye'.

The Belly of the Beast

Mortifactors Space Marines board an isolated hive ship believed to have survived Behemoth's destruction. The Space Marines suffer ninety per cent casualties, but eventually slay the giant bio-vessel.

The Old Hunter

Sergeant Telion of the Ultramarines leads the Chapter's next generation of Scout recruits on hunt-and-destroy missions across Ultima Segmentum, seeking remnants of Hive Fleet Behemoth.

The Anphelion Project

An Imperial taskforce, sent to investigate a covert project which studied captured Tyranid life forms, is ambushed and decimated by monstrous alien organisms.

Blackthorne's End

The Freeblade Knight known as Blackthorne seeks the head of the Hive Tyrant responsible for the fall of his Noble house. After smashing through the living wall formed by the monster's bodyguard organisms, Blackthorne finally cleaves his reaper chainsword though its torso. His oath remains unfulfilled however, as the monster's ravaged exoskeleton knits back together with frightening speed. Blackthorne screams one final curse upon his nemesis as the Hive Tyrant sends a devastating pulse of psychic feedback through the neural circuitry of his Throne Mechanicum, ending the lone hunter's anguish.

PARADISE DESPOILED

The Aeldari would first encounter the Tyranids amidst the paradise worlds of the Ybaric Cluster. There they would discover the dreadful losses that must be suffered in order to repel these extragalactic invaders.

A New Threat

Hive Fleet Naga, a relatively small Tyranid fleet, descends upon the Ybaric Cluster and consumes several minor races on the edge of Ulumeathi space. Its progress does not noticeably slow.

A Cry for Help

A string of Aeldari Exodite worlds and maiden worlds fall under the shadow of Hive Fleet Naga. The Aeldari craftworlds of Idharae, Iyanden and Malan'tai despatch fleets to their aid.

The Serpent Wounded

The leading elements of Hive Fleet Naga are caught between the warfleets of Idharae and Malan'tai. With an efficiency born of instinct, Naga splinters into two tendrils.

The War for Halathel

The flagship of Iyanden's fleet is destroyed whilst attempting to pierce the Tyranid blockade on Halathel. Prince Yriel assumes command and defeats the remaining bio-ships, but it is too late to save Halathel's Exodite protectors. Overwhelmed by rage and grief, Yriel orders the planet to be scoured of all life lest a single Tyranid survive, before rushing to rejoin his kin at Eth-aelas.

Eth-aelas Besieged

Cornered and outgunned, the second, smaller tendril of Hive Fleet Naga is destroyed by Aeldari pulsar fire, but not before its bio-ships seed Eth-aelas with warrior-beasts. The Aeldari forces make planetfall to seek and destroy the remaining Tyranids on the surface.

The Sound of Doom

A mind-wracking psychic scream reverberates through the caverns of the webway as all contact is lost with Craftworld Malan'tai.

Naga Defeated

Yriel's forces arrive at Eth-aelas and immediately join the Aeldari already fighting on the planet's surface. After a string of bloody victories, the last Hive Tyrant is slain at the battle of Sorrowforge Pinnacle.

The majority of Hive Fleet Naga is destroyed, though there will be many further battles before all of its constituent parts are wiped out. The Aeldari learn first-hand the horrifying strength of the Tyranid race.

The Lure

By subtly diverting pilgrim convoys into its path, operatives of the Alpha Legion lure a splinter fleet of Behemoth towards the forge world of Ammunheim. As the Adeptus Mechanicus diverts its forces to fend off the impending invasion, the Traitor Marines launch dozens of raids into now unguarded Imperial territory, spiriting thousands of Astropaths away into the void for some dark and unknown purpose.

Death Comes to Nephilim

A splinter of Hive Fleet Behemoth draws ever closer to the galactic core, skirting the western border of the Ultima Segmentum and preying upon remote systems and frontier worlds. Eventually this tendril reaches the Nephilim Sector, where it encounters the Ravenwing of the Dark Angels Chapter. The Space Marines' swift harrying tactics, which had proved so vital against mass Tyranid swarms, are ineffective against the towering bio-horrors that the splinter fleet hurls into the fray.

Monster Against Machine

The menace of Nephilim next descends upon the world of Rakkor IX, sworn to the Knights of House Raven. The Knights encounter a foe that has markedly changed its tactics since Behemoth first battered its way across Ultramar. Rather than unleashing vast swarms of lesser organisms, this splinter fleet deploys nodes of advanced organisms – synapse creatures and monstrous warrior-forms who are able to fight with far greater autonomy than a typical Tyranid invasion force. At the heart of this xenos host lurks the dread Hive Tyrant known as the Nephilim King.

Recognising a dark mirror of their own feudal structure, the Knights of House Raven name the splinter fleet the Court of the Nephilim King. The Court adapts with astonishing speed to every tactic and strategy the Knights employ, preying upon their pride and aggression to isolate and destroy individual war machines. Rakkor IX is lost. The House Raven survivors swear an oath of vengeance upon the Court of the Nephilim King.

Bane of Shau-Yor

When a fragment of Behemoth threatens the Aeldari maiden world of Shau-Yor, Craftworld Biel-Tan unleashes the engines of Vaul. The pristine surface of Shau-Yor plays host to a titanic clash of towering bio-monstrosities and graceful Aeldari grav-tanks. Stalking through the carnage comes the Tyrannofex that the Aeldari name the Bane of Shau-Yor, its colossal bio-cannon obliterating enemy vehicles with every peristaltic blast. Their losses mounting, the warriors of Biel-Tan are forced to abandon Shau-Yor to the Great Devourer.

Phrixis Erupts

The world of Phrixis and its precious, city-sized promethium refinery are threatened by a large Tyranid splinter fleet. The 33rd and 91st Mordian Iron Guard are deployed to hold this vital strategic location at all costs. The Mordians hold out for months, refusing to give ground in the face of endless waves of Tyranid assaults. In a cruel twist of fate, a dying bio-titan, blasted apart by barrages of lascannon fire and high-explosive rounds, discharges its bio-cannon directly into a fuel intake valve, setting off a cataclysmic chain reaction. The resultant detonation obliterates the entirety of the 91st Iron Guard. The surviving 33rd Mordian, guarding the perimeter, stubbornly hold out until their ammunition reserves run dry, at which point they are encircled and torn apart.

Drakeslayer

On the frontier mining world of Kernov, Watch Sergeant Dramus of the Deathwatch slays the subterranean terror known as the Obsidian Drake, ending the Trygon Prime's decades-long reign of terror.

HIVE FLEET KRAKEN

For more than two hundred years after Hive Fleet Behemoth's rampage, the Imperium was relatively untroubled by the Tyranids. Though several smaller hive fleets passed into the galaxy in that time, they primarily vented their fury on alien worlds, leading many to believe the Tyranid menace was all but spent. Nothing could have been further from the truth.

By early 990.M41, a new Tyranid invasion had descended upon the Imperium, and it was named Kraken. Where Hive Fleet Behemoth had fought as a single massive wave that advanced and fought as one, Kraken was actually a series of smaller fleets that moved to attack many worlds concurrently. Not only did this compound the Imperium's difficulty in opposing the hive fleet, it spread the Shadow in the Warp tenfold. Whole sectors were silenced simultaneously, isolated by the Hive Mind's choking influence. Only months after the onslaught had begun did accounts begin to reach the wider Imperium – grim tales of entire sectors sown with poisonous spores, of hulking monsters bursting forth from the shadows, ripping and slashing with murderous claws. Reports filtered in of billions of creatures swarming across the face of defenceless worlds, devouring everything in their path.

THE TENDRILS OF KRAKEN

Seen on a galactic scale, Hive Fleet Kraken was attacking across a front that covered thousands of light years, making a cohesive defence impossible to mount. The Imperium was forced to concentrate its forces on the most strategically important worlds, whilst others were evacuated or simply abandoned to their fate. For the first time the Imperium was exposed to the predatory intellect of this seemingly bestial race. Kraken employed cunning vanguard tactics that Behemoth had largely eschewed in favour of an overwhelming assault. Previously unseen bioforms struck ahead of the hive fleet, assassinating key military and civilian officials, whilst sowing fear and confusion across entire sectors.

There were some glimmers of light in the darkness. Several Space Marine Chapters endeavoured to save those worlds the Imperium had abandoned. Some, such as the Lamenters and the Scythes of the Emperor, paid for their boldness with heavy losses, their once proud Chapters reduced to a few scattered remnants, whilst the Knights of Eternity were entirely wiped out. Others carried the battle to the Tyranids in the manner that only Space Marines could, boarding hive ships and blowing them apart from the inside. Yet no matter the effort the Imperium made, the Tyranids were too many, and they drove ever onwards into the galaxy.

ICHAR IV

Fortunately for Mankind, Hive Fleet Kraken did not remain spread out indefinitely, and many of its tendrils converged on Ichar IV, a hive world that some years earlier had been the site of a Genestealer infestation. Thousands of clawed attack-beasts burst from the underhives in support of the invaders. Defence perimeters were quickly overrun by the scuttling horrors that had lurked patiently in hiding for so long. Ever more Tyranids made planetfall – not merely the Termagants and Gargoyles common to the vanguard of Hive Fleet Behemoth's assaults, but monstrous Exocrines and Tyrannofexes by the score. Worse still, giant bio-titans now stalked across the surface of the beleaguered planet. Hive Fleet Kraken had descended on Ichar IV with everything at its disposal.

Despite its woes, Ichar IV was not yet lost. Forewarned by the previous infestation, Marneus Calgar led the Ultramarines to save the Ichar System, inflicting crushing losses on the Tyranid armada in space and in the claustrophobic environs of the towering hive cities. Veterans of the First Tyrannic War scoured Ichar IV's hives in a series of close-quarters battles that lasted almost a full year.

In a replay of history, Marneus Calgar faced none other than the Swarmlord – a reincarnation of the same beast that had laid him low on Macragge – during the final battle for Ichar IV. This time, however, it would be Calgar who emerged triumphant, slaying the beast in an epic duel. Without the Swarmlord to counter Calgar's military strategy, the Ultramarines and their Astra Militarum allies finally cast the Tyranids from the world. Victory had come too late to save Ichar IV, which was now little more than a smoking charnel house – a world sacrificed so that thousands more might endure. Perhaps worse for the Imperium, the Hive Mind absorbed the Swarmlord's consciousness again, and having learned from its own death, its next reincarnation would prove the most dangerous yet encountered.

THE SPLINTER FLEETS

The scattered remnants of the Tyranid attack on Ichar IV fled towards the galactic core, driving well within the defence perimeters drawn against Hive Fleet Kraken. These splinter fleets have, if anything, become an even greater threat as they feed upon unsuspecting and ill-defended worlds far from the major war zones. Running battles with the splinter fleets have continued for many years since Kraken's passage, draining the galaxy's defences against later incursions. It is doubtful if the true extent of the devastation caused by the hive fleet will ever be known.

Splinter fleets can comprise as few as a dozen hive ships, but even a dozen bio-ships are more than capable of overrunning a planet and harvesting its biomass to become a yet greater threat. Some have become so large as to be classified as a new, distinct hive fleet. Indeed, Hive Fleet Magalodon is grown from one of Kraken's sundered tendrils, and continues to ravage the Imperium to this day. So too does the Court of the Nephilim King, a splinter of Hive Fleet Behemoth, continue to devour world after world.

Doubtless, the Tyranids have learnt much about the inner galaxy's defences from these splinter fleets. Every battle the Tyranids engage in, won or lost, adds to the Hive Mind's ever-growing understanding of its prey. Was this the true goal all along? Who can say? It is perhaps preferable to believe that the Hive Mind had this very eventuality planned from the onset, rather than to entertain the only other possibility: that the Hive Mind has the strategic wit to turn even its defeats into victories elsewhere…

Ghostly pale skin is the mark of the Kraken splinter fleet named the Fangs of Vanthel by the Aeldari of Craftworld Saim-Hann. This host has rampaged across several maiden worlds, and thus far evaded all attempts to encircle it.

Medgar's Razor emerged on the coreward border of the Segmentum Pacificus several Terran years ago. How the splinter fleet travelled so far across Imperial space is unknown.

THE LURKING MENACE

An Imperium that had only experienced the sector-smashing battering ram of Hive Fleet Behemoth was caught completely off guard by the next stage of the Tyranid invasion. Where Behemoth hurtled on a direct path towards the galactic core, crushing all in its path with the sheer ferocity of its advance, Hive Fleet Kraken employed a level of cunning and strategy that threw its opponents into terrified confusion. The tentacles of the Kraken attacked from multiple sides at once, outflanking and trapping its prey. As the fractured Imperium rushed its navies to defend one sector, another tendril of the hive fleet would sweep in to devour unguarded territory.

Even now, scattered and greatly reduced in size, the hive fleet devours its way through the galaxy, having learned the tactics of its prey and formulated devious adaptations to counter them. Tendrils of the Kraken sweep towards worlds left unstable by Genestealer Cult uprisings and sprees of violent slayings, falling upon their vulnerable quarry with predatory cunning.

Upon the battlefield, the Kraken's victims are cut apart by flanking manouevres, or scattered as chameleonic horrors rush from hidden lairs into their midst, slicing and tearing with razor-sharp claws. Lictors and Genestealers are particularly favoured by the hive fleet for their stealth and swiftness, and broods of these monsters will be unleashed in hunting packs, slaughtering commanders and eliminating key threats to the greater swarm. Rarely will the Kraken engage a foe head-on. Instead, its questing tendrils of vanguard organisms will strike and fade, probing for vulnerabilities. Once such a weakness is found, the hive fleet will exploit it with ruthless precision, concentrating its swarms to harry and pull enemy formations apart, where one by one they can be picked off and devoured.

DOOM OF IYANDEN

At around the same time that one tendril of Hive Fleet Kraken was battling the Imperium on Ichar IV, another was approaching Iyanden, one of the largest and most populous of the Aeldari craftworlds. It would be here, amidst eldritch architecture and within wraithbone halls, that the most bloody conflict yet between Aeldari and Tyranid would occur.

Though Iyanden's rune-casting Farseers had foreseen echoes of doom upon the future, the first proof of the Tyranid threat was reported by the craftworld's Rangers. A large tendril of Hive Fleet Kraken was headed directly towards Iyanden. It was too vast to outrun and no mere battle line could contain it. Farseer Kelmon, spiritual leader of Iyanden, declared that all would have to fight together if they were to stand a glimmer of hope. The entire craftworld made ready for war, and in a sacred ritual, the Avatar of the Bloody-handed God was awakened.

THE WALKING DEAD

Even with every Aeldari on Iyanden armed, the swarm that approached still vastly outnumbered the defenders. With a heavy heart, Kelmon ordered the ghost warriors to be brought forth. In an act considered by many Aeldari to be akin to tomb robbing, the spirit stones of Iyanden's ancestors were plucked from their resting places and placed in the wraithbone shells of war-constructs to fight alongside their still-living children. It is a testament to the terrible threat Hive Fleet Kraken posed that it forced the Aeldari to commit such a distasteful act. Without the ghost warriors, the Tyranids would have overwhelmed the craftworld, but by waking them from death, Kelmon risked the accumulated wisdom and cultural memories of Iyanden itself.

THE SHADOW DESCENDS

The first Tyranid swarms attacked Iyanden twenty days later. By then, the craftworld had already been isolated for over a week by the Shadow in the Warp, and a dark malaise hung heavy in every Aeldari heart. The Tyranids approached the giant craftworld like a vast shoal of sharks, thousands of bio-ships attacking in unrelenting waves. Iyanden's formidable space fleet destroyed each wave in succession, but the ability of the craftworld's forges to repair and replace lost spacecraft was outstripped by the viciousness of the deep-space battles. The Aeldari do not fight wars of attrition by choice, and slowly, craft by craft, the Aeldari succumbed and the jaws of the Great Devourer closed in on the craftworld. Then, Iyanden was hit by two huge attack waves in quick succession, swarms that dwarfed all the other assaults combined, and the remaining flotilla of Aeldari vessels was swept aside. The bloated Tyranid craft blotted out the stars as they descended onto their quarry, vomiting forth armies of hideous creatures into Iyanden's unspoilt havens. A horrific psychic scream resounded around the craftworld's infrastructure as seething hordes of clawed, scuttling aliens were disgorged into its heart.

THE KRAKEN STRIKES

Battles erupted all over Iyanden, the fighting bitter and close ranged, with

Amidst the wondrous halls of Iyanden was fought a battle of unsurpassed horror. Every citizen of the craftworld took up arms to repel the Tyranid onslaught, but against the cunning swarm tactics of Hive Fleet Kraken, even their skill and bravery was not enough.

enemy forces often only separated by the width of a corridor or wall. Aeldari Guardians fought bloody battles with vast numbers of Termagants, shuriken fire and fleshborer maggots screeching through the air with equal lethality. Aspect Warriors and Wraithguard attempted to slice their way through massed swarms of Genestealers and Tyranid Warriors that blocked the arterial corridors like a vile cancer. Above curved halls, Swooping Hawks and Gargoyles fought a deadly aerial dance whilst sleek Aeldari jetfighters and bat-winged Crones exchanged roles of hunter and prey at breakneck speeds amidst alabaster spires. Carnifexes wrestled with ancient Wraithlords as Trygons battled towering Wraithknights. Graceful Phantom Titans duelled with grotesque bio-titans, slaying each other over a spore-choked surface. War even raged beyond the material realm as Zoanthropes and Warlocks engaged in mighty psychic duels. The Aeldari had no place to hide, no sanctuary the Tyranids could not breach and no warrior or weapon of war that the aliens could not match. Soon, the Aeldari's Walking Dead outnumbered the living.

The Aeldari warriors sold their lives dearly, exacting a terrible toll in Tyranid corpses, but it was not enough. First the Fortress of Tears fell, then the Shrine of Asuryan was destroyed. Most terrible of all, the deeply spiritual Forests of Silence were ravaged by the Tyranid hordes. It is said that many of the Aeldari wept tears of rage and sorrow to see the damage inflicted on their precious forest shrine, realising that they now stood on the brink of extinction.

THE PRODIGAL SON

Word of Iyanden's peril managed to reach Prince Yriel, despite the psychic barriers isolating the craftworld. Though Yriel, exiled long ago from Iyanden, had vowed never to return to the place of his birth, he could not abandon Iyanden in its darkest hour. Tempering his indignation, Yriel and his fleet made best speed to the battle.

Like the burning spear of Khaine, Yriel's forces thrust through Hive Fleet Kraken's blockade and struck deep into the bio-fleet enveloping Iyanden. The renegade prince was an admiral without peer, and upon joining forces with the battered survivors of Iyanden's fleet, the Aeldari ripped the heart out of the Tyranid swarm. Yriel prevented any more of Kraken's spawn from reaching the wounded craftworld, whilst simultaneously coordinating

counter-strikes on the largest bio-vessels. Kraken launched two further waves but both were destroyed. Bloodied but unbowed, Yriel's forces prepared to sell their lives dearly, for surely another wave would overwhelm them. Minutes passed into hours as the Aeldari ships scanned the runes of their scanners awaiting the next assault, but it did not come. The space-borne hive fleet had been defeated.

> 'My loyal warriors. My kin, by deed and bond. Our home faces obliteration. Our people are dying. The light of Iyanden fades.
>
> But it is not yet extinguished.
>
> Outcasts and exiles, follow me to war. Like a spear of flame we shall pierce the darkness. We will bring ruin to the void-spawned filth that seeks to defile the Shrine of Asuryan.
>
> If we are to die, let it be here. Let it be with blades in hand, amidst the spirits of our ancestors and the bodies of our foes. What say you, exiles of Iyanden? Are you with me?'
>
> – Prince Yriel, High Admiral of the Eldritch Raiders

TO SLAY A MONSTER

Under Iyanden's skies, the battle for the craftworld's soul still raged. The Tyranids now turned like cornered rats and hurled themselves at the Aeldari with renewed ferocity. A massive Hive Tyrant led the frenzied horde, and neither shuriken nor sword blade could pierce the monster's hide. Wherever the beast attacked, the Aeldari were butchered, and across the craftworld, the Tyranids were breaking through, sweeping aside pockets of resistance. The final confrontation was at hand, and victory was within the Hive Mind's grasp.

Amidst the carnage, the Avatar stepped forward. With a growl akin to an erupting volcano, the fiery warrior roared a challenge to the Hive Tyrant, but instead of meeting the iron-clad figure, the monster urged its minions to attack. Not one, but a dozen Carnifexes stampeded towards the flame-wreathed Avatar. Under such an assault, not even the embodiment of the Bloody-handed God could prevail.

With the Avatar lost, the last vestiges of hope ebbed from the Aeldari. But, in an act of loyalty that restored Yriel as a hero of his people, the Raider Prince and his forces disembarked from their ships to reinforce Iyanden's survivors. The Tyranids were on the verge of overrunning the Aeldari lines when Yriel himself plunged into the fray wielding the cursed Spear of Twilight. This ancient weapon, locked in stasis by Iyanden's seers, was a weapon of such power that it would eventually burn out the life-force of any who wielded it. That Yriel was willing to sacrifice not only his life, but also his immortal soul, was a testament to the drastic measures that had to be taken in order to defeat the Tyranids.

With one fluid motion, Yriel thrust the Spear of Twilight into the Hive Tyrant's gaping maw and out through the back of its chitinous skull. With a howling scream, the Tyrant collapsed and died at Yriel's feet. The last echoes of the monster's death shriek signalled the defeat of the alien horde. With their synaptic conduit severed, the remaining Tyranids ceased to attack as a united wave as they reverted to their base instincts. The scattered alien invaders were systematically hunted and eliminated in a series of vicious one-sided battles. The Tyranid attack on Iyanden was over.

THE COST OF VICTORY

The victory on Iyanden was a hollow one indeed, for though Kraken had been defeated, Iyanden stood in ruins. Four-fifths of Iyanden's population lay dead – a terrible blow for the declining Aeldari race. Amongst the slain lay Farseer Kelmon, surrounded by the bodies of a dozen Tyranids whose forms bore the marks of psychic fire. Worse still, all the souls within those spirit stones that had been destroyed by the Tyranids were lost forever; Iyanden would never truly recover. The Aeldari had learned a painful lesson and would never again underestimate the threat of the Great Devourer.

Hive Fleet Kraken was now little more than splintered fragments of its former might, yet credit lay neither entirely with the defenders of Iyanden nor the actions of the Ultramarines on Ichar IV. The Aeldari and the Imperium had been fighting as unwitting allies – had Kraken not struck Iyanden, the Ultramarines' victory at Ichar IV would have been impossible, and vice versa. Had either Ichar IV or Iyanden fallen, Kraken would have been unstoppable.

THE SECOND TYRANNIC WAR

THE GORGON STRIKES

Hive Fleet Gorgon invades the space of the T'au Empire, thrusting the young race into a deadly battle for survival.

THE KRAKEN AWAKES

Hive Fleet Kraken awakens from its long slumber and invades the Eastern Fringe. The Diatan, Salem and Veridian Sectors fall silent as the Shadow in the Warp envelops them.

RAVENS AND KRAKENS

Originally despatched to rescue the remaining population of the planet of Idos, the Raven Guard 4th Company are instead ordered to launch a desperate surgical strike in an attempt to defeat the Tyranid swarm ravaging the world.

TERROR FROM THE SHADOWS

Over the course of several weeks, the prosperous trading world of Tareska is ravaged by a series of brutal slayings. One by one, the planet's key governmental and military figures are slaughtered by a 'living shadow' that appears as if from nowhere to carve its victims apart. Terrified, the few remaining officials flee to underground bunkers and fortified strongholds, locking themselves away from the world above. Ungoverned, and without an organised military to enforce order, Tareska begins to fall apart. At the height of the food riots, the bio-ships of Hive Fleet Kraken loom into orbit, obliterating the planet's meagre defence fleet.

THE MARTYRDOM OF SALEM

Confronted with the horror of Hive Fleet Kraken, the monks of the asteroid-monastery of Salem choose to poison themselves and their carefully tended ecosystem with necrotising rotweed, rather than allow their purified flesh to be consumed by the advancing Tyranids.

THE ICHAR REBELLION

The planet of Ichar IV erupts into rebellion as a faction known as the Brotherhood overthrows the planetary governor. Soon after the fighting breaks out, Inquisitor Agmar, despatched from the Inquisitorial fortress on Talasa Prime, leads his battle forces into the planetary capital of Lomas and discovers that at its heart, the rebellion is harbouring a massive Genestealer infestation. Realising the forces under his command are insufficient to combat the threat, Agmar sends an urgent plea for assistance.

CLEANSING OF ICHAR IV

Responding to the Inquisitor's report, the Ultramarines Battle Barge *Octavius* arrives in orbit, carrying two full companies of Space Marines alongside elements of the newly founded, but understrength 1st Company. The Ultramarines lead the attack into the heart of Ichar IV's planetary capital whilst regiments of the Imperial Guard advance in support. The planet is brought back under the heel of the Imperium within three weeks of bitter fighting, and the victors report all trace of the Genestealer infestation has been cleansed from Ichar IV.

THE PRICE OF COURAGE

As part of a century-long crusade of penitence, the Lamenters launch an attack against Hive Fleet Kraken, fighting a series of hopeless battles. Whilst their heroics slow Kraken's advance for a while, the Chapter is brought to the edge of extinction by the horrendous casualty rate inflicted upon it.

MORTREX OVERRUN

The Imperial world of Mortrex is overwhelmed by unrelenting tides of Ripper Swarms. The dread beast known as the Parasite of Mortrex spawns thousands of these mindless feeder-beasts from the still-living bodies of its victims.

THE LOSS OF CERES XIV

THE JAWS OF DEFEAT

Kraken sinks its teeth into the mining world of Devlan. The Imperial Guard's carefully prepared defences prove useless against assaults from beneath by tunnelling Tyranid creatures, spearheaded by a monster known to the populace as the Red Terror. Due to the sacrifice of Lamenters Space Marines, the Tyranids are held back long enough to evacuate a few million colonists before Devlan is consumed.

THE DEATH OF SOTHA

Kraken invades Sotha, home world of the Scythes of the Emperor, who are overrun by the Tyranids. The Chapter is decimated and the few survivors reluctantly evacuate to Miral Prime to regroup with their off-world forces.

MYSTERY OF ADRI'S HOPE

A refugee ship from Devlan arrives in orbit around Adri's Hope, ominously silent. Those investigating the ship find it to be an abattoir, all aboard mercilessly butchered. Though a breach of quarantine is suspected to have allowed a Tyranid organism to get aboard, nothing is found. Three weeks later, all contact is lost with Adri's Hope.

GOETHE'S LAST STAND

Princeps Goethe of the Imperator Titan *Mettalum Olympus* single-handedly manages to hold back a tendril of Hive Fleet Kraken on the ash-choked plains of Horst Prime. The mighty war engine is finally destroyed when a brood of Hierophant bio-titans pounce on the noble machine like a pack of wild dogs. In the frenzied attack, *Mettalum Olympus*' plasma reactor is breached and the resultant explosion vaporises everything for a mile around, leaving behind a crater that is still visible from orbit – a testament to the sacrifice needed to fight the Tyranids.

THE DEFENCE OF MIRAL

Imperial Guard regiments and the Space Marines of the Scythes of the Emperor Chapter barely hold out against Tyranids on the death world of Miral Prime. Against the onslaught, the Imperium's forces are forced to fall back to a huge rock mesa known locally as the 'Giant's Coffin' to make a defiant last stand. Here, they fight daily against raging hordes of Tyranids. Despite their heroics, the Scythes of the Emperor suffer catastrophic casualties. Faced with the total destruction of their Chapter, the Space Marines reluctantly retreat, leaving Miral Prime to the Kraken.

The Trophy Hunter

Eager to add to his burgeoning collection of skulls, Roghax Bloodhand, warlord of a World Eaters warband of Chaos Space Marines, leads his maniacal host into a headlong attack against a tendril of Hive Fleet Kraken.

To Strike a Blow

Though too late to save the rain-drenched bastion world of Eorcshia from a splinter fleet of Hive Fleet Kraken, Space Marines of the Deathwatch successfully plant nucleonic charges within the innards of the massive Tyranid bio-ship at the centre of the fleet as it feeds upon the dying planet. Upon the charges' detonation, the entire splinter fleet falls into disorder.

The Fall of Iyanden

The Aeldari craftworld of Iyanden is subjected to a series of massive Tyranid attacks. The once mighty craftworld musters every warrior at its disposal, living and dead, and is soon embroiled in desperate fighting against wave after wave of Tyranid organisms.

After a long and bloody battle Iyanden is saved, though the cost is unbearably high. Within the craftworld's halls, the dead now greatly outnumber the living. Little more than a remnant of its former glory, Iyanden remains as a solemn testament to the Hive Mind's hunger.

The Kraken Strikes

Several tendrils of Hive Fleet Kraken converge on the world of Ichar IV. The full might of the Ultramarines answers Ichar IV's call to arms, and once again, the Hive Mind responds by unleashing the Swarmlord. The experience of Ultramarines Veterans from the First Tyrannic War proves decisive, and slowly but surely, Kraken's grip on Ichar IV is severed and the Tyranids are scoured from the world.

The Splinters of Kraken

Following the twin defeats at Ichar IV and Iyanden, the scattered remnants of Hive Fleet Kraken flee towards the galactic core, driving well within the defensive lines drawn to combat the Tyranid threat. Though the Kraken as a single entity is defeated, these splinter fleets, varying in size from a few dozen to a few hundred bio-ships, continue to be a dire threat, preying upon ill-defended worlds and vulnerable supply lines.

The Anvil

Forewarned of the approach of a large splinter tendril of Hive Fleet Kraken, the Imperial Fists turn the world of Heugen's Anvil into a killing field of tripmines, razor-wire and interwoven gun emplacements. As the Tyranids swarm forth, the Space Marines cut them down with blistering fusillades of bolter fire. Soon, the battlefield is littered with great piles of xenos dead, and the orbiting bio-ships slowly retreat into the void, pursued by Battle Barges of the sons of Dorn.

It is only after the fleeing Tyranid vessels are rounded up and eliminated that the Imperial Fists receive distress calls from the neighbouring system of Poltiskyne. Soon, the disturbing truth dawns upon the Space Marines – Hive Fleet Kraken had split its fleet in two before making landfall upon Heugen's Anvil, and its surviving xenos vessels were at that very moment descending upon several undefended worlds.

Deadly Cargo

Drukhari corsairs of the Flayed Skull Kabal return to Commorragh with a valuable cargo – several dormant Lictors, gathered from the burned-out remnants of a Kraken bio-ship. Before the crew can sell these priceless specimens, the Tyranid life forms awaken from their slumber, breaking loose and falling upon their captors in a gore-splattered frenzy. Temporarily sated, the chameleonic horrors slip away into the underwarrens of Commorragh.

Maw of the Magalodon

Born from the ashes of the Kraken, the splinter fleet known as Magalodon terrorises Imperial space, spreading terror and confusion before it like a bow wave. Secreted aboard cargo vessels and interstellar transports, the Magalodon's vanguard organisms spread like a cancer through sector after sector, birthing fanatical cults, assassinating planetary governors and sowing the seeds of discord and mayhem. The crystal mining belt of Hyrdos XII is one of the first Imperial holdings to feel the Magalodon's maw close around it. In the space of a single week, the splinter fleet's Lictors slaughter every single void-miner in the complex.

Death in the Webway

Utilising illusions, feints and the sacrifice of an oblivious Imperial battlefleet, Harlequins of the Reaper's Mirth lure a splinter of Hive Fleet Kraken away from vulnerable Exodite worlds and deep into the webway. There, amidst the maddening pathways and non-Euclidean geometry of that mysterious realm, they exterminate the Tyranids, though the masque pays a high price in blood for its victory.

The Grand Coalition

An isolated tendril of the Kraken reaches towards the T'au sept world of Dal'yth, a prosperous trading hub frequented by countless alien races. Water caste diplomats make earnest pleas to their trading partners, imploring them to lend their naval strength to a coalition armada that will intercept the Tyranid menace. This fleet sails forth, and is almost entirely destroyed. Fortunately, the T'au's own losses are comparatively minimal, and precious time is bought for Dal'yth to ready its defences.

Season of Unrest

Across the Ultima Segmentum, reports emerge of previously docile worlds erupting in violent riots and uprisings. This unrest coincides with the emergence of several previously unidentified Tyranid splinter fleets, though Imperial high command deems this little more than unfortunate happenstance.

Purging of Ghosar Quintus

Deathwatch Chaplain Ortan Cassius leads a Kill Team to the mining world of Ghosar Quintus, and there encounters a cult that worships the Tyranids as a saviour race. Cassius and his warriors slay the Genestealer Patriarch at the heart of the cult, but discover that the ruling Trysst Dynasty of Ghosar Quintus has spread its demented faith across the Segmentum, and possibly beyond. The implications for the Imperium are staggering, and grim beyond measure.

HIVE FLEET LEVIATHAN

At the close of the 41st Millennium, the largest and greatest of the Tyranid hive fleets descended upon the galaxy. The Hive Mind had learnt well the lessons of its earlier invasions, and this new fleet, Leviathan, employed these teachings to the detriment of all other life it encountered.

Once again, it was Inquisitor Kryptman who alerted the High Lords of Terra to the new Tyranid hive fleet, one of terrible size that he named Leviathan. Where the other hive fleets had attacked the Eastern Fringe, striking the galaxy edge-on as they emerged from the intergalactic void, this new hive fleet appeared to have skirted the galactic rim, and was now attacking upwards through the galactic plane.

As with Kraken before, Leviathan did not focus its forces into a single killer blow, but attacked across a broad front. Leviathan's tendrils stretched across the Segmentums Ultima, Tempestus and even Solar. By the time Inquisitor Kryptman could raise the alarm, Leviathan had already advanced far, and the Shadow in the Warp that heralded its coming had orphaned dozens of worlds. The worlds of Valedor and St. Capilene had already been lost, the forge world of Gryphonne IV – home of the mighty War Gryphons Titan Legion – had fallen ominously silent and the agri world

of Tarsis Ultra was embroiled in a bloody battle for survival. The morale of the Imperium's forces began to plunge as more worlds were consumed, and with every planet devoured, Leviathan grew stronger.

A DRASTIC MEASURE

With a grim finality, Inquisitor Kryptman ordered that a galactic cordon be established. His plan was that a band of worlds should be evacuated across the path of Leviathan's main advance, with many of them razed to the ground in order to deny the hive fleet any further raw materials for its ships. This would slow its advance long enough for Battlefleets Solar and Tempestus to muster. Any worlds already under invasion within the bounds of this cordon were to undergo Exterminatus just at the point when the Tyranids descended to feed upon the doomed populace. Kryptman theorised that, using this method, the swarms would expend great resource to claim a world, only to have every living thing upon it reduced to ash by barrages of cyclonic torpedoes and virus bombs. With one stark and callous decision, Kryptman had condemned billions of souls to extermination. To this

day, it remains the single largest act of genocide ever inflicted upon the Imperium by its own forces since the Horus Heresy.

Kryptman's decision to abandon hundreds of Imperial worlds in the face of the alien advance was met with howls of outrage by his peers. His butcher's bill was deemed intolerable, and many influential Inquisitors called for Kryptman to be declared Excommunicate Traitoris. When dozens of the cleansed worlds were claimed by the ever-expanding Orks of Octarius, Kryptman's detractors cursed him for a radical, a traitor and a fool. A Carta Extremis was issued, stripping Kryptman of his title and forcing him into exile as a criminal of the worst kind

However, the fact remained that the inexorable advance of Leviathan had slowed to a crawl. Kryptman had bought the Imperium time, that most valuable of commodities, at the expense of a hundred worlds. He had resolved that the many lives he had to sacrifice would not be lost in vain, and had put into action a plan aimed not merely at slowing the advance of Hive Fleet Leviathan, but at dealing it a fatal blow.

KRYPTMAN'S GAMBIT

Despite being cast out of the Inquisition, Kryptman could not abandon his fight against the Hive Mind. As Leviathan continued to spread its tendrils into the Imperium, he took it upon himself to harness the power of the swarm. The former Inquisitor claimed that he could not only defeat Leviathan, but in doing so, he could rid the Imperium of the galaxy's native enemies. Though many of his few remaining allies labelled him a reckless menace, it could not be denied that he understood the Tyranids as no other did. But, as the Imperium would learn, understanding an enemy such as the Tyranids, and controlling it, are two equally impossible things.

Determined to prove his theories right, Kryptman planned to use a tendril of Leviathan to eliminate the Ork empire of Octarius. The Imperium had long been embroiled in an ever-escalating war against the Orks in this region of space, and despite huge influxes of reinforcements – resources that Kryptman deemed would have been better served fighting the Tyranids – the Orks were dominating the war. Kryptman's gamble was to change the balance of power forever.

Enlisting aid from a squad of Deathwatch Space Marines who still had faith in him, Kryptman captured a live brood of Genestealers and then loaded them onto *Perdition's Flame*, a space hulk that had emerged from warp space ahead of the approaching hive fleet. As the Tyranids awoke from stasis, Kryptman destroyed the moon of Gheist, and in doing so, diverted the hulk's trajectory towards the Orks. Within weeks, the Tyranid infestation had spread to dozens of worlds. The Hive Mind had sampled a new feeding ground, and in response, a tendril of Leviathan veered towards Octarius. At first, it appeared that Kryptman's gamble had succeeded.

As Tyranids and Orks fought an endless war across the sector, the Imperium was content to let the alien forces wipe each other out. However, both Orks and Tyranids are races that thrive on war. Greenskins flocked to join the fight from light years around, and every Ork devoured provided yet more biomass to feed the growing Tyranid swarm. It soon became apparent that Kryptman had only delayed the inevitable, for whichever aliens emerged from the conflict as victors would do so stronger than ever before.

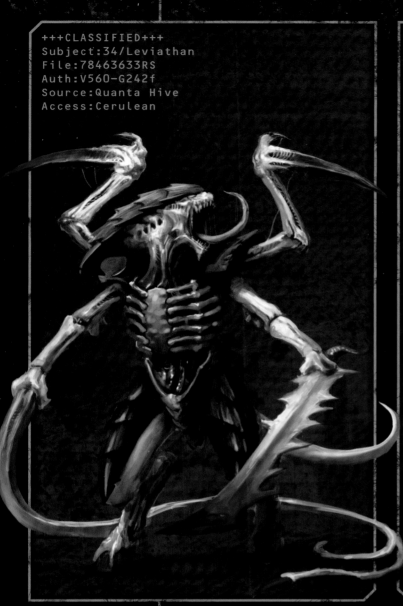

THE ULTIMATE EVOLUTION

The Leviathan is the greatest Tyranid threat to assail the galaxy thus far, the largest and most fearsome hive fleet ever recorded. So vast is its reach that seemingly no corner of the Imperium is safe, and with every passing year it thrusts more and more tendrils through the void, devouring entire sectors and civilizations, adding to its prodigious stocks of biomass.

Yet it is not merely the size of Leviathan that makes it such a formidable threat, but the accumulated lessons that the Hive Mind has learned, bolstered by every previous Tyranid incursion into the galaxy. There are few foes that can surprise the hive fleet, few tactics that will take it unaware, for the Tyranids have encountered them all. Leviathan's synaptic network is also more sophisticated than those of previous incursions, allowing the Hive Mind to conduct uncannily coordinated combined assaults on land and from the skies. Attacking simultaneously on all fronts, with every organic tool at the Hive Mind's disposal, Leviathan chokes and crushes the life from its prey, before feasting on the ruined remains.

The sheer scale of the advancing hive fleet poses another dilemma for its targets. Where Leviathan approaches, the Shadow in the Warp is magnified and its reach extended, for the hive fleet's synaptic network is far stronger than that of any other Tyranid host. The Imperium has suffered greatly due to this phenomenon, as communication is broken across vast swathes of its territory. When Hive Fleet Leviathan's super-swarms enter the battlefield, broods of Zoanthropes and towering Maleceptor organisms ensure that its nullifying aura stretches far indeed, smothering the latent abilities of any psykers who are sent against it and leaving its prey isolated and terrified.

The Ghosts of Phol were a host of Tyranids who boarded the grand battleship Bellerophon and slaughtered its entire crew.

The Tyranid Warrior brood known as the Silent Murder slaughtered thousands in the war for Forge World Cadamine.

The Praxima Strain survived Leviathan's defeat at Baal, and was spat out of the warp in the heart of the Segmentum Obscurus.

WAR IN OCTARIUS

Kryptman had lured Hive Fleet Leviathan into the Ork-held Octarius Sector in the hope that the two alien species would annihilate each other. Where another race would have been terrified at the approaching swarm, the Orks were jubilant – after all, they live for a good fight. Only time would tell if the warlike creatures had finally met their match.

The first world of the Octarius Sector to feel Leviathan's hunger was Orrok. Above the Orks' settlements, thunder rumbled and the skies turned from blue to black as bio-ships entered orbit. Weirdboy psykers began to gibber in fear – something was clawing at the backs of their brains, something with an infinite hunger focused upon the Orks like the eye of a starving predator. Then the storm broke.

THE DEMISE OF ORROK

Millions of warrior-organisms swarmed across Orrok. To the Ork mind, the best form of defence is to beat the enemy to death, so it was not long before a tide of greenskins crashed headlong into the oncoming Tyranid swarm. Thousands of aliens of both races died in a matter of seconds as blades and fangs sank home. All semblance of strategy was lost, replaced by blind fury, but the Orks' enthusiasm for war could not defeat the Tyranids' overwhelming numbers. By nightfall, every single greenskin on Orrok was dead, their bodies reconstituted and channelled back to the orbiting bio-ships to create yet more Tyranids. Death had come to the Octarius Sector.

THE WAAAGH! WITHOUT END

Dozens of worlds were soon crawling with Tyranids, and every time the skies darkened, the Orks planetside would give a great roar of delight, slapping each other on the back and grinning fiercely as for once, the fight came to them. The greatest battle centred on the planet of Octaria itself, heart of the Ork empire. Billions of Orks and Tyranids clashed over Octaria's mountainous terrain, both forces sending a near constant stream of reinforcements into a grinding war of attrition. The ground underfoot turned into a crimson mulch of spilt blood and alien ichor. It was total, unremitting, endless violence, and the Orks loved it.

The battle for Octaria continued to escalate, and neither side had a shortage of numbers. Orks streamed in from distant sectors to join the fight of the century, and

Tyranid bio-ships produced fresh waves of warriors as quickly as they could assimilate biomass. So it was that, as the war on Octaria raged, Leviathan was forced to seek out nearby prey worlds whose biomass could be fed into the meatgrinder.

THE GHORALA SWARM

In their search, a handful of Leviathan's scout ships happened across the world of Ghorala, a planet rich in biomass and base to Skarfang, Pirate-Warboss of the dreaded Skar Fleet. This mighty, if ramshackle, armada fell upon the bio-ships before they could react. The Tyranid fleet was all but destroyed under Skarfang's guns. However, amidst the carnage, a single bio-ship broke through the Ork blockade, pouncing on the planet as a starving man might snatch at a scrap of bread. Alien blood and viscera spilt into the vacuum of space, but in its death throes the bio-ship delivered several broods of Tyranids to the world's surface. Skarfang grew glum as he realised the battle was over, and he resolved to join the fight on Octaria, as the few Tyranids that had made planetfall were soon stomped out.

THE SWARM SURVIVES

For the first time since the Tyranids had invaded the Octarius Sector, they found themselves embroiled in a war where they were vastly outnumbered by their prey. Skarfang's horde was mighty, and somehow, the Tyranids sensed that a war of attrition would only end in their demise.

In response, the Ghorala swarm adapted in order to survive. At first, the Tyranids stalked and preyed upon isolated Ork patrols, but the greenskins soon took to scouring the landscape in mobs too large for the fledgling swarm to face. Forced to abandon their guerrilla war, the Tyranids adopted an altogether more cunning strategy and engaged the Orks in the open. The Tyranids attacked without thought of survival, every action aimed at maximising the carnage. Despite the Tyranids' frenzied attacks, the Orks' superior numbers gave them the advantage in these brutal skirmishes. Whenever the Tyranids were on the verge of being overrun, they would, in eerie unison, switch from hyperactive slaughter to hasty retreat. The Tyranids lurked in nearby cavern complexes or else burrowed beneath the soil to shelter from pursuant search parties. In the dead of night, synapse creatures re-mustered the scattered swarms to the corpse-choked battlefield. There, the Tyranids fed on Ork cadavers and Tyranid carcasses alike, before returning to digestion pools secreted in the planet's rocky mesas. Slowly but surely, the Tyranids' numbers started to grow.

SKARFANG'S FURY

As the Tyranid forces swelled, they changed their methodology yet again, growing more aggressive and seeking out ever larger concentrations of Orks. Though the Tyranids' reward for their victories was ever-increasing masses of bio-resources, the increased violence soon attracted the bored Skarfang to the surface to join the fray. Wherever Skarfang's guttural war cries were heard, the Orks attacked with renewed vigour. Even when the Tyranids looked to be on the cusp of victory, the Warboss was able to turn the tide, bellowing blood-curdling threats that encouraged his Boyz to get stuck back in. The Tyranids were being pushed back by the resurgent Ork front; slowly the swarm was being trampled to death. Despite the Tyranids' earlier success, there was little chance that they could face a united Ork force of such magnitude and survive. Whilst Skarfang lived, the Ghorala swarm was doomed.

DIVIDE AND CONSUME

In response, the Tyranids created Lictors with the express purpose of eliminating the Ork Warboss. Within days, the Lictors had tracked their eminent quarry, but Skarfang's packs of squig hounds foiled all attempts to get close enough to assassinate their target. Although eternally patient, lying in wait for a chance to strike down their target was a luxury the starving swarm could ill afford. So instead, they created an opportunity.

Following pheromone trails, a scuttling tide of Hormagaunts was thrown at the Ork lines. As the Orks roused to man their rusty barricades, Tyranid Warriors willed the scuttling masses to withdraw. Skarfang's frustration rose to infuriation as the Tyranids repeated these feints, approaching from different directions to within an arm's length, then withdrawing before the Orks could retaliate. On the tenth such retreat, Skarfang's temper could take no more. With a roar, the Warboss ordered his mobs to pursue the retreating swarms. Soon, black smoke was belching skywards as Battlewagons and Trukks rumbled after the swarm. The Tyranids had succeeded in goading the Warboss, separating him from the bulk of his forces and luring him into an ambush.

The Tyranids had spawned broods of Venomthropes to blanket the greenskins in a thick, toxic fog. As the Orks pursued their quarry, they rode headlong into the sudden, blinding mist. The entire convoy ground to a halt as vehicles skidded into rocky outcrops or else lost control and ploughed into each other. Coughing and hacking, those Orks that hadn't choked on their own blood pulled themselves from the wreckage. Skarfang himself stumbled across the battlefield and happened across the tentacled beasts responsible for creating the noxious cloud. As he vented his anger on the venomous creatures, the fog receded and the eviscerated corpses of Orks surrounded the Warboss. Lictors had stalked through the blinding cloud and despatched the unwary greenskins one at a time until only Skarfang remained. The Lictors closed on their true quarry, surrounding the Warboss in deathly silence. Revving his chainblade into life, Skarfang charged the nearest with a roar of defiance. He managed two steps before a dozen mantis-like claws pierced his form and tore him asunder.

With Skarfang dead, it was not long before vying Ork bosses started fighting amongst themselves to fill the power vacuum. The Orks were soon divided, and the disparate bands became easy prey to the united Tyranid swarm. Each was isolated and destroyed in quick succession, and within days, the Orks on Ghorala had been slaughtered like cattle. The Tyranids gorged themselves on their flesh.

> *'Dis ain't no stinkin' scrap against puny gits dat run and hide behind walls when da killin' starts, dis is proper fightin'!'*
> - Pirate-Warboss Skarfang

THE SWARM REBORN

From the digested remains of Ghorala, the swarm created new bio-ships and set forth to rejoin the hive fleet at Octaria, the biomass it had consumed destined to fuel the next phase of planetary invasion.

Though the war for Octaria rages still, one thing is already clear: despite the machinations of Kryptman and the ferocity of the Orks, Leviathan shows no signs of stopping. The Tyranids are not only surviving the Octarian War, they are thriving in it.

Indeed, the vast quantities of biomass that the war has generated are already being put to use by the Hive Mind. Having already consumed the resources necessary to power its inexorable push towards the galactic core, Leviathan has begun to leave prey worlds behind for the next wave of the Tyranid invasion to consume. These pre-digested planets provide essential feeding grounds for nascent hive fleets such as Hydra and Kronos. Even worse for the galaxy's warring races, tendrils of formidable Octarian Tyranids spawned from the most potent Ork biomass are beginning to detach from the main host and push into new territories.

Finding its super-swarms ineffective against the numberless Ork hordes of Octarius, Leviathan deployed specialised organisms: colossal bio-titans and gun-limbed horrors.

THE BATTLE OF BAAL

In the final days of the 41st Millenium the largest tendril of Hive Fleet Leviathan ever recorded descended upon Baal, home world of the Blood Angels Space Marines, and its twin moons of Baal Prime and Baal Secundus. The battle which followed would be the bloodiest and most costly in the noble history of the sons of Sanguinius.

SHADOW OF LEVIATHAN

Chapter Master Dante, Lord of the Blood Angels and one of the most honoured and respected warriors in the Imperium, had long known of the Tyranid menace approaching Baal. Only months ago the Cryptus System, the shield of fortified worlds guarding the approach to the Blood Angels' home world, had fallen, overwhelmed by the sheer immensity of Hive Fleet Leviathan. Baal was next, and though its guardians were amongst the mightiest warriors in the galaxy, the Blood Angels could not stand alone.

Knowing that the fate of his Chapter, and perhaps of the Imperium itself, would rest upon the defence of Baal, Dante sent out the call to the Blood Angels' successor Chapters, telling of the doom that was approaching the home world of their beloved progenitor, Sanguinius. All came to the Blood Angels' aid, from the ferocious Flesh Tearers to the noble Blood Drinkers, and even the savage, insular warriors of

the Carmine Blades. Every single battle-brother would be vital in the upcoming war, for the oncoming Tyranid fleet was enormous, by far the largest Tyranid host ever recorded by the Imperium.

Hundreds of thousands of bio-ships, in clusters so thick that the invasion fleet seemed to be one vast, many-limbed organism, surged towards Baal. The Blood Angels' own fleet met them head-on, its numbers bolstered by the presence of several spaceborne successor Chapters. The sky above Baal erupted in a violent firestorm as the rugged vessels of the Space Marines slammed their way into the midst of the approaching Tyranids, launching devastating broadsides and storms of nuclear-tipped warheads. Valorous as this naval action was, it was also hopeless. One by one, Space Marine Battle Barges and Cruisers were isolated and overwhelmed, battered by organic missiles and enveloped by swarms of smaller bio-ships. Entering low orbit over Baal and its moons,

Leviathan's vessels began to disgorge clouds of spores and organic transports into the atmosphere. As the space battle raged overhead, the defenders of Baal awaited the first waves of Tyranids, taking up positions amidst Heresy-era fortifications that had been unearthed and rebuilt by Chapter serfs and servitors. Baal and its twin moons had been transformed into killing fields, dotted with artillery redoubts, mine-laced choke points and criss-crossing fire zones.

AGAINST THE SWARM

The first few Tyranid swarms to make planetfall were obliterated by pre-ranged artillery bombardments and a blistering fusillade of bolter rounds long before they reached the defensive lines. Yet with each passing moment, more Tyrannocyte spores rained down from low orbit, their bulging flesh-sacs bursting open to disgorge warrior-organisms into the fray. By the tenth wave, the ground was barely visible beneath a stampede of chitin-armoured

The Battle of the Dome of Angels was amongst the most fiercely contested engagements of the Baal conflict. Three Chapter Masters gave their lives as the Blood Angels and their successor Chapters repulsed wave after wave of slavering Genestealers.

bodies. Amidst this carpet of living flesh loomed colossal synapse creatures – Hive Tyrants and giant Tervigons which spewed out gaunts by the score. These monsters directed the swarms around them even as they unleashed salvoes of burning plasma, or tore great rents in the fortifications with massive weapon-limbs. Genestealer broods swept into these breaches, where the fighting descended into frantic hand-to-hand slaughter. At the rear of the Tyranid swarms, a hulking creature surveyed the carnage, observing the Blood Angels' strategies, directing its lesser kin to counter their every move with a cunning born of aeons-long warfare. The Swarmlord, herald of the Hive Mind, had been spawned anew to ensure the Blood Angels' demise.

Over the course of weeks the scions of Sanguinius hurled back nineteen waves of Tyranid assaults, fighting with a valour and skill that honoured the memory of their fallen Primarch. Blood Drinkers fought back to back with Angels Encarmine, forming a circle of blades and bolters against phalanxes of advancing Tyranid Warriors. Blood Angels Assault Marines leapt into the heart of the enemy swarm, hunting the largest and most ferocious monsters. Amidst rad-scorched desert valleys, massed formations of tanks and artillery clashed with stampedes of charging Carnifexes in a grinding, churning maelstrom of metal and flesh. As brave as the defence of Baal was, it could not last. With every Tyranid attack, more battle-brothers were slain. Five Chapter Masters amongst the Blood Angels' successor Chapters gave their lives to hold back the surging tide, but as the bodies piled higher it seemed such selfless sacrifice would be for naught. Baal was ready to fall.

THE GREAT RIFT OPENS

It was at this dark hour that a fresh calamity was unleashed upon the Baal System. In a cataclysmic eruption of empyric energy, the galaxy-spanning warp storm known as the Great Rift tore open. The skies above Baal burned with aetheric fire, and within the roiling depths of the immaterium, ancient, malevolent beings turned their dread gaze upon the material realm. Upon Baal Prime, the Blood Angels' successors unleashed the full measure of their hatred against the Tyranid swarms. It was as the fighting upon the moon was at its most ferocious that reality tore open, and the scent of brimstone and burning blood filled the air. With a bellowed chorus of praises to

the Blood God Khorne, daemonic legions boiled from the widening rift. At their head came a creature drawn from the blackest of nightmares, a bat-winged monstrosity wielding a rune-marked axe in one clawed fist, and a barbed whip in the other. This was Ka'Bandha, Bloodthirster of Khorne. No foe was more hated by the sons of Sanguinius, for thousands of years ago Ka'Bandha had stoked in them the Red Thirst, the genetic curse which had so ravaged the Chapter. Ka'Bandha sought the sole honour of slaughtering the Blood Angels, and had no intention of allowing the Tyranids to interfere before the time of his triumph was at hand.

The Bloodthirster's legions fell upon both Tyranids and defenders of Baal, and xenos and transhuman blood was spilled in torrents. Tyranid Warriors hacked and tore at leering Bloodletters, while stampedes of Bloodcrushers swept across the gore-splattered earth, smashing Termagants beneath their brazen hooves. Ka'Bandha stalked through the madness of battle, reaping a devastating toll upon all in his path with great swipes of his dread weapons. The Space Marine defenders, led by Chapter Master Gabriel Seth of the Flesh Tearers, fell back, harried on all sides. Only the sacrifice of the Knights of Blood, an excommunicated successor Chapter who had nonetheless been accepted as allies by Chapter Master Dante, allowed the survivors to board their vessels and escape, as Baal Prime was overwhelmed by warp-spawned monstrosities. As Seth's forces retreated, they caught one last glimpse of the Knights of Blood, hurling themselves into the thick of close combat with mindless ferocity, fully enveloped by the madness of the Black Rage.

In Baal's orbit, thousands of Hive Fleet Leviathan's bio-ships were snatched into the warp by coils of empyric energy or swallowed by rifts in space. Soon, only the burning remnants of gutted hive ships remained, drawn in by Baal's gravitic pull to rain down upon its ravaged surface.

Below this raging inferno, Chapter Master Dante led his few remaining warriors in a fighting retreat to the walls of the Blood Angels' fortress monastery. Time itself was a victim of the surging empyric insanity – it seemed as if the carnage stretched on for years, as xenos and Space Marine fought and slew, racing towards a mutual annihilation. Forward strode the Swarmlord, entering the fray at this vital juncture, carving Space Marines apart

with every slice of its jagged boneswords. Exhausted and filled with sorrow, yet defiant as ever, Dante hacked his way through the press of xenos flesh with the Axe Mortalis, seeking the Swarmlord's head. Under the burning sky, the two duelled, until Dante, bleeding from a dozen mortal wounds, cut the creature down. As Dante collapsed, his anguished warriors straining to reach his prone body, the tortured skies finally cleared. The storm had passed, and where before the Tyranid armada had blotted the sky, not a single xenos vessel remained. In their place were majestic Imperial ships. Primarch Roboute Guilliman, the resurrected Avenging Son, had arrived, at the head of the Indomitus Crusade.

FURY OF THE PRIMARCH

Now it was Drop Pods and Stomraven Gunships which dotted the skies above Baal, as Guilliman and his warriors crashed down into the midst of the Tyranid swarm. Hive Fleet Leviathan's remaining ground force still outnumbered the Space Marines, but the death of the Swarmlord and the destruction of the Tyranid fleet left it reeling, as Hormagaunts and Termagants reverted to their frenzied, predatory instincts. With the Primaris Space Marines – a new breed of genhanced warriors, birthed from the vaults of Mars – fighting at Guilliman's side, unleashing devastatingly accurate salvoes from their bolt rifles, the mighty host of Leviathan was cut to pieces. Individual clusters of organisms fled into Baal's radioactive wastes. It would take many months to hunt down and eliminate them all, but Baal had been saved. Gravely wounded but still alive, Chapter Master Dante bent the knee before Primarch Guilliman. In Dante and the surviving Blood Angels, Guilliman recognised a noble spirit, a flickering flame kept alive from the Imperium's glorious past. His gift to them was mighty indeed: formations of Primaris Space Marines with which to bolster their devastated ranks, derived from the bloodline of Sanguinius.

Of Hive Fleet Leviathan's bio-ships, there was no sign. Upon Baal Prime, not a scrap of life remained. The Daemons had vanished back into the warp, leaving behind an ominous warning; mountains of Tyranid skulls, piled impossibly high. These ziggurats formed the reviled symbol of Ka'Bandha, a grim message to his eternal nemeses. For now the menace of Leviathan had been defeated, but the trials of the Blood Angels were far from over.

THE THIRD TYRANNIC WAR

THE COILS OF PYTHOS

The Red Talons Space Marines hold the fortress world of Orask on the edge of the Ghoul Stars from an invading splinter of Hive Fleet Pythos.

THE LEVIATHAN ARISES

Hive Fleet Leviathan strikes at the underbelly of the Imperium, sinking its tendrils into Segmentums Tempestus, Ultima and Solar.

SLAUGHTER OF ST. CASPALEN

Blood stains the cloisters as Leviathan invades the shrine world of St. Caspalen. The world's leaders are slain and terrorised by a Tyranid assassin and, riven with panic, the planet's defence forces are easy prey. The only true resistance comes from a force of Sisters of Battle who hold out bravely for weeks, but even they are overwhelmed when Deathleaper lures Trygons to excavate beneath their holy bastion and swarms of Hormagaunts use the tunnels in their wake to flood the fortification. The loss of St. Caspalen is a blow to the Imperium, and a manifest warning that faith alone is no defence against the Tyranids.

THE SWARMLORD RETURNS

Leviathan's swiftest victories occur along a spine of worlds in the Hodur Sector. In the span of a single year, the Swarmlord oversees the absorption of dozens of worlds, including Talon – home world of the Storm Falcons Space Marines Chapter.

THE FOLLY OF PRIDE

The supposedly impenetrable Iron Warriors fortress world of Forgefane falls to the Tyranids in less than a week.

BATTLE OF BLOODSTAR

Battlefleet Ultima concludes a disastrous campaign against Leviathan when it is ambushed and entrammelled by two separate Tyranid fleets in the Bloodstar Sector and the celebrated flagship, Imperial Glory, is destroyed.

A WORLD ABANDONED

The Adeptus Mechanicus abandon the world of Tesla Prime, choosing to use its military forces to bolster Gryphonne IV, one of the principal forge worlds in the galaxy, in preparation for a defiant stand against Hive Fleet Leviathan.

DEFENCE OF TARSIS ULTRA

Leviathan invades Tarsis Ultra as the first snows of winter begin to fall. Despite the presence of the Ultramarines and the Mortifactors, the tide of battle turns against the armies of the Imperium due to the Tyranids' sheer numbers. Tarsis Ultra is saved not by force of arms alone, but through a biological plague created by Magos Locard and delivered into the very heart of the hive fleet by Uriel Ventris of the Ultramarines 4th Company. All attempts to replicate a similar contagion have thus far resulted in failure.

MASS EXTERMINATUS

Inquisitor Kryptman orders the extermination of all life on hundreds of worlds to create a cordon to slow the advance of Hive Fleet Leviathan.

THE BATTLE FOR GRYPHONNE IV

Skies darken with bio-ships over the forge world of Gryphonne IV, home of the War Gryphons Titan Legion. Combined with the planet's Skitarii legions and the military forces of Tesla Prime, the Adeptus Mechanicus prepare for war.

When Tyranid warrior-organisms reach the planet's surface, a battle of truly epic scale unfolds. The landscapes of metal and girder run black with ichor as heavy weaponry takes a fearsome toll on the invaders. Within an hour, the ground shakes to the tread of Titans, emerging from their cathedral hangars to engage the huge monstrosities stalking through the manufactorum.

However, for every bio-titan that falls to the fury of the Mechanicus' guns, one of the Imperium's giant war machines is torn apart by enormous bladed claws, volleys of bio-cannon fire and gouts of hissing pyro-acid. The ground reverberates to the tread of duelling giants for days on end, the Adeptus Mechanicus and the swarms of the Hive Mind both refusing to give.

Despite the resolve of the Tech-Priests and the toll their machines reap on the Tyranids, the Tyranid invasion gathers pace. Slowly but surely, the defenders of Gryphonne IV are overwhelmed by the unending swarm, and even the mighty Titans of the War Gryphons are brought crashing down.

Within days, the world is scoured. Though the loss of Gryphonne IV is a calamity of unprecedented scale for the Imperium, the Tyranids are uncaring of their victory and Hive Fleet Leviathan simply moves on in search of fresh feeding grounds.

A BLOODY HARVEST

A lone bio-ship launches an invasion against the planet Stormvald. The Phoenix Lord Maugan Ra stands alone against the swarm, and triumphs.

THE FALL OF SHADOWBRINK

Hive Fleet Leviathan descends upon the cathedral world of Shadowbrink, annihilating the prey world's defenders. The sheer scale of the carnage rips open an ancient daemonic rift, and legions of warp-spawned horrors boil forth to fall upon the Tyranid swarms. Unwilling to abandon the reserves of biomass it has gathered, the Leviathan unleashes its full might upon the Daemon aggressors.

Though the Hive Mind is unused to fighting creatures of the empyrean, it adapts to these new foes with startling speed. Vast hordes of Hormagaunts and Termagants clash with legions of Bloodletters and Plaguebearers, as colossal bio-titans and Greater Daemons stalk through the fray. Ultimately, even this vast daemonic host cannot beat back the numberless swarms of the Tyranids. One by one the Daemons of Shadowbrink are slain, and their raging spirits banished to the warp.

Stuck in the Craw

Hive Fleet Leviathan fights the Imperial Guard regiments of Catachan on the death world of Jorn V. Though outnumbered, the Catachan Jungle Fighters prove stubbornly resourceful and slow the Tyranids' advance long enough for additional Imperial Guard and Space Marine reinforcements to arrive planetside and strike a vital blow against the hive fleet.

Kryptman's Gambit

Kryptman undertakes a dangerous mission on the labyrinth world of Carpathia. Leading several specially equipped Deathwatch teams into the heart of the planet's caverns, Kryptman succeeds in capturing a live Genestealer brood in a stasis field, though many of the Space Marines die in the attempt.

The Crusader Thwarted

High Marshal Helbrecht of the Black Templars, in pursuit of the Ork Warlord Ghazghkull Thraka, leads a fleet forged from fifteen Space Marine Chapters against a splinter tendril of Hive Fleet Leviathan which is barring his path. Despite employing every strategy and ploy at his disposal, Helbrecht's fleet is continually forced to fall back before the Tyranid advance. His mounting ire matches the rising numbers of the Space Marines lost to the Leviathan.

Perdition's Flame

Kryptman and his allies board the space hulk *Perdition's Flame* and lodge his clutch of captured Genestealers within. Kryptman then orders the destruction of the moon of Gheist, diverting the space hulk's path into the sector-wide Ork empire of Octarius.

The Octarian War

Octaria burns as Tyranids and Orks engage in bloody battle across the sector. Hive Fleet Leviathan gluts itself upon vast deposits of biomass, even as more and more greenskins rush to the front lines, drawn by the promise of a proper fight. Ultimately, both violent species prosper in this hellscape of unending violence; Inquisitor Kryptman's plan may have bought the Imperium valuable time, but it also forges Leviathan into a far stronger and more formidable foe.

Gorgo's End

A tendril of Leviathan reaches from beneath the galactic plane to encircle the prosperous agri world of Gorgo. Invaluable due to its precious yields of spider-vine, Gorgo is protected by a garrison of the Cadian 23rd, highly experienced and well-equipped warriors. Yet even these veterans are unprepared for the nightmare that approaches. Battle cannons and anti-air missiles thin the oncoming waves of Tyranid organisms, but the Cadians are quickly forced back to the Obsidian Line, a defensive ring of Imperial Bastions. It is then that Leviathan unleashes its siege-breaking swarms: Broodlords and their Genestealer packs, accompanied by massive biological battering rams. These specialised organisms smash great breaches in the Obsidian Line, forcing their way inside and massacring the defenders. Within a matter of hours, Gorgo falls.

The Battle of Baal

The single largest concentration of Hive Fleet Leviathan yet recorded descends upon Baal, home world of the Blood Angels.

The Galaxy Burns

Summoned into being by a series of Chaos-engineered catastrophes, the colossal warp storm known as the Great Rift tears the galaxy in half. Daemons pour into realspace, and entire civilisations are devoured. Swallowed by violent aetheric tempests, many tendrils of the Tyranid hive fleets are dragged into the immaterium. Most are lost forever in the roiling madness of that realm, but others are vomited back into reality thousands of light years away.

Return of the Primarch

As the Great Rift tears open reality, empyric storms ravage the Baal System. Upon Baal itself, the battle between Blood Angels and Tyranids rages on, but the vast Leviathan fleet orbiting Baal is pulled apart by empyric storms and devoured by the madness of the warp. Daemons invade the moon of Baal Prime, annihilating a great portion of Leviathan's invasion swarms. They are led by Ka'Bandha, ancient nemesis of the Blood Angels. The Bloodthirster slaughters the entire Tyranid host upon Baal Prime, and piles their skulls high in the shape of his dread sigil, leaving a chilling message for his hated foes, before vanishing back into the warp.

As the empyric insanity begins to wane, Roboute Guilliman's Indomitus Crusade arrives at Baal, assisting the few surviving Blood Angels in the extermination of the isolated Tyranid ground forces. Baal is saved, but at the cost of almost the entire Blood Angels Chapter.

Scattered to the Stars

Leviathan's enormous Baal invasion fleet is torn into a thousand fragments, and spat out across the vast expanse of the galaxy. Several hundred bio-ships tumble out of the void in the heart of the Maelstrom, and there fall upon the piratical fleet of Huron Blackheart, master of the Red Corsairs. Another, larger host emerges in the midst of the Velis System, fearfully close to the heart of Segmentum Solar. Garbled distress calls received from Velis Prime speak of frenzied, shrieking swarms of Tyranids covered in bizarre, fungoid growths and wielding previously unrecorded bio-weapons. It is unknown how many more of these splinter fleets survived the cataclysm at Baal intact.

Fury of Leviathan

In the wake of its defeat at Baal, Leviathan launches a vast offensive along the southern border of the Segmentum Solar. The Tyranid assault reaches as far into the galactic core as Bloodfall, home world of the Red Wolves. Recently reinforced with Primaris Space Marines, the Red Wolves prove stubborn and deadly foes, until Leviathan unleashes its most fearsome weapons: broods of monstrous bio-titans, spawned in the brutal furnace of the Octarian War and glutted upon potent greenskin biomass.

Diverted from the ongoing war with the Orks, these monsters are formidable siege organisms. With colossal, hooked fore-limbs they smash great rents in the Red Wolves' fortifications, and swarms of Genestealers flock into the breaches. Their fortress monastery hopelessly compromised, their losses horrific, the Red Wolves are forced to retreat, securing vital stocks of gene-seed and evacuating upon their remaining Battle Barges.

The Last Wall

As Leviathan pushes ever further towards Holy Terra, Primarch Guilliman despatches dozens of newly founded Primaris Chapters to the front lines of the Third Tyrannic War.

GALACTIC FEEDING GROUNDS

As Hive Fleet Leviathan pushes every further towards the galactic core, entire worlds are being scoured of life, and hundreds more are embroiled in a desperate fight for survival. Yet despite its colossal reach, Leviathan is but a fraction of the Tyranids' true number, and more horrors seep forth from the interstellar void with every passing year.

The Great Devourer has sunk its tendrils deep into the galaxy, and thus far, it has shown only the first hints of its true strength. Hive Fleet Leviathan's encroachment could not have happened at a worse time for the Imperium, for the emergence of the galaxy-spanning warp anomaly known as the Cicatrix Maledictum has thrown Mankind's domain into turmoil unmatched since the bleakest hours of the Horus Heresy. The war fleets of Chaos pour forth on every front, and thousands upon thousands of worlds have already been lost, burned or fallen eerily silent. Yet the Imperium can ill afford to leave its back unguarded against a foe as powerful as the Tyranid hive fleets, even as it struggles to react to the impending apocalypse pressing on its every border.

Roboute Guilliman, Primarch of the Ultramarines and Lord Commander of the Imperium, has put his peerless tactical mind towards solving this dilemma. Several Primaris Space Marine Chapters raised in the Ultima Founding have been directed to the front lines of the Tyrannic Wars, specifically tasked with holding Hive Fleet Leviathan at bay and, if possible, exterminating it entirely. Meanwhile, the military juggernaut of the Imperium's armed forces ramps up its own production, deploying fresh regiments of infantry and thundering tank battalions into the grinding horror of the front lines. The Imperium of Man will not submit to the Great Devourer without a fight.

EVER-EMERGING THREATS

Unfortunately for the Imperium and the other races of the galaxy, it is not only Leviathan that is assailing their realms. New hive fleets are even now beginning to emerge from their cold sleep through the intergalactic void. Hive Fleet Hydra snakes its way towards the galactic core, feasting upon both Imperial worlds and the drifting husks of defeated hive ships. Hive Fleet Moloch's inexorable advance from the galactic north is also gathering momentum as it has devoured the Kiltor Sector and now the Tarellian civilisation. Hive Fleets Scylla and Charybdis carve parallel paths up through the Segmentums Pacificus and Solar, the closest known Tyranid threat to Holy Terra. Though the Imperium might have a little time left to prepare its defences against these twin threats, Craftworld Saim-Hann is caught in the jaws of the two hive fleets, and cannot easily navigate a path to avoid one without risking falling into the clutches of the other.

None know for sure how many other hive fleets still lie dormant within the void, slowly approaching the galaxy to wake and feed. Nor are the threats of previous Tyranid invasions truly over. The splintered fleets of Hive Fleet Kraken are regaining their strength as they feast on a bounty of worlds ill prepared to defend themselves whilst the galaxy looks to supposedly greater threats. Long-dormant remnants of Hive Fleet Jormungandr stir to life, bringing several Imperial worlds to the brink of destruction. The resurgent remnant

> *'Tyranids are creatures from our darkest nightmares. But remember this: they can bleed and they can die...'*
> *- Inquisitor Kryptman, prior to his excommunication*

FRESH HORRORS

The rate at which new hive fleets are identified has increased dramatically in recent years, and shows no sign of slowing despite the warp turbulence ravaging the galaxy. As fast as the races of the galaxy can raise new armies to combat the Great Devourer, fresh nightmares emerge from the inky depths of the intergalactic void.

Hive Fleet Scitalis winds its way into the Eastern Fringe, embedding itself deep into sectors held by the T'au Empire. Hive Fleet Arachnae has found itself embroiled in a long war against the Necrons of the Novokh Dynasty, as it attempts to consume and despoil planets that the Overlords have long claimed as their own. Hive Fleets Garmr and Ladon are drifting toward the borders of Imperial territory, devouring the ravaged death worlds of the Vultis Sector and consuming vast quantities of monstrous fauna in the process.

of Behemoth, thought slain over two centuries ago, continues to ravage populations and settlements within Ultima Segmentum, with scattered reports of Tyranid attacks on worlds from Calth to Macragge and beyond. Worse still, the violent breaches in reality ravaging the galaxy have devoured several splinter fleets and tendrils of larger hosts, vomiting them forth far behind the front lines of the Imperium, in the midst of vulnerable sectors.

A GLIMMER OF HOPE

However, as the ongoing Octarian War is proving, the Tyranids are encountering ever greater levels of resistance from their prey. Whilst the Imperium reinforces whole star systems, raising thousands of Imperial Guard regiments and dozens of Space Marine Chapters solely to combat the Tyranid threat, several Aeldari craftworlds have begun to burn entire worlds to cinder, employing ancient weapons of destruction not used in millennia. The T'au Empire, having learned well at the claws of Hive Fleet Gorgon, are developing new technologies and weaponry to fight the Tyranids and field-testing experimental prototypes to defend their realm. Even the Necrons and forces of Chaos are turning their attentions towards a foe that is slowly devouring a galaxy that both believe is theirs alone to rule over or despoil as they see fit.

Yet, despite the forces arrayed against them, the Tyranids still push relentlessly towards the galactic core. The Third Tyrannic War has already claimed trillions of lives, and the carnage is escalating on all fronts. With every lost battle, the hive fleets create new breeds of warrior-organisms and bio-constructs to counter and defeat their foes. With every victory, another world dies, devoured to feed the insatiable hunger of the Hive Mind.

WAR ZONE VALEDOR

There have been times when the starfaring bio-fleets have fallen foul of warp storms, never to appear again. Some, like the splinter fleet of Kraken that was sent headlong into the empyrean by the seers of Craftworld Iyanden, face an even stranger fate. This Tyranid host's bio-ships later emerged from a dimensional rift into the Valedor System, deep in the Segmentum Solar. The splinter fleet had crossed the span of the galaxy in a matter of years. Worse still, it had emerged right in the path of Hive Fleet Leviathan.

When Iyanden's seers learnt of this, panic gripped them. If the bio-matter from Hive Fleet Kraken were to merge with that of Leviathan, the resultant strains of Tyranids would be all but unstoppable, for they would combine the genetic secrets of Ork, Aeldari and human alike. Dreading the repercussions that this unholy union would have upon the craftworlds of the Aeldari, the Iyanden council implored their allies on militant Biel-Tan to intercede. Yet despite its swift and deadly attacks, even the Swordwind was unable to keep the hive fleets apart.

If it were not for a shadowy bargain struck with the Drukhari, the paradise planet of Valedor – or Dûriel as the Aeldari called it – would have been the birth site of a new doom for the galaxy. By using the Fireheart, a Commorrite artefact of incredible power, the combined forces of the Aeldari destroyed Dûriel in a storm of fire and violence just as the Tyranids were about to seize their vile prize. In the process they averted disaster – for a time, at least…

TENDRILS OF THE GREAT DEVOURER

The many Tyranid hive fleets roaming the galaxy have each formulated their own predatory behaviours and unique adaptations with which to master the battlefield.

HIVE FLEET JORMUNGANDR

Hive Fleet Jormungandr is the Great Serpent, an insidious menace that has plagued Imperial space for centuries. The Imperium has claimed to have destroyed the hive fleet on several occasions, only to discover that Jormungandr has burrowed deep beneath the infrastructure of its worlds like a flesh-eating parasite, lying in wait for the perfect moment to re-emerge.

Jormungandr favours a unique method of planetary invasion. Initially, it keeps its bio-ships as far away from enemy defences as possible. Instead, its hive vessels utilize gigantic, whip-like dorsal growths to hurl space debris at the targeted world. Orbital guns may destroy many of these objects, but at least a few will reach the surface. Should that happen, the planet's doom is sealed, for Jormungandr has sown each asteroid with Tyrannocyte clusters and Ravener broods, and larger bioforms such as Mawlocs and Trygons. Upon landfall, these burrowers dig deep in into the earth, creating vast underground tunnels beneath key fortifications.

When the invasion begins, swarms of hidden horrors burst forth from these ambush sites, emerging amidst the unaware foe and tearing them apart. Should this assault somehow be repulsed the threat is still not over, for the hive fleet will go to ground in the tunnel network it has created, digging in with grim resolve. Once ensconced, it is almost impossible to dislodge. It may take a few months, or several years, but Jormungandr will always rise again.

Hive Fleet Jormungandr's warrior-organisms hunch low to the ground as they advance, utilising the tunnel networks they have torn through the earth as cover from enemy fire.

THE GREAT SERPENT RISES

Hive Fleet Jormungandr's endless patience and unique method of assault make it a formidable foe to contend with. Even when it appears routed and broken, the hive fleet is doubtless sowing the seeds of its inevitable return.

Awakening

Hive Fleet Jormungandr winds its way into the galaxy. Unlike its predecessors, this latest tendril of the Tyranid menace does not immediately fall upon heavily defended worlds. Instead, it preys upon outlying trade hubs and frontier worlds, building up a huge reserve of biomass.

Coils of the Great Serpent

Less than two years after its first appearance, Jormungandr coils itself around the Imperial-held Thalassi Sector. Slowly, it begins to constrict.

Deadly Rain

Jormungandr appears in the skies above Gedron II, and hurls thousands of meteors into its atmosphere. The vast redoubt fortresses that protect the planet's hive cities destroy many of these rocks. The remainder fall into the ocean.

Jormungandr's bio-ships retreat, and Gedron II's governor declares the invasion over. Several months later, hosts of many-limbed Tyranid creatures burst into the lower halls of Gedron II's fortifications, slaughtering all in their path. As planetary defence forces scramble to react, long-range scans pick up a colossal body of vessels entering orbit. The Great Serpent has returned.

The Trap is Sprung

Battlefleet Gammek responds to a garbled distress call from Sarposia. Its ships emerge from the warp amidst the ruins of the planet's vast orbital shipyards, but there is no sign of Tyranid vessels, only scores of large asteroids and scattered debris. It is only when the fleet drifts into the asteroid field that tacticae officers report movement from within the clusters of rock. Glistening, molluscoid vessels

had been using the asteroids as protective shells, and now they launch a blistering assault upon Battlefleet Gammek. Caught in a storm of biological missiles and hurled meteoroids, not a single Imperial ship escapes the ambush.

Battle of the Black Nebula

High Admiral Hanroth's vast armada defeats Jormungandr in a long and costly naval battle, scattering it to the stars.

Jormungandr Returns

Several years after Jormungandr's apparent defeat, reports begin to drift in from the Thalassi Sector and beyond, telling of Tyranids bursting forth from the earth, overrunning defences and killing at will. Contact with several patrol fleets is lost, and fleeing trade hulks tell of bizarre organic vessels embedded in drifting comets.

Hive Fleet Hydra's prodigious generative capability stretches to the very least of its bio-organisms. Even lowly slimer maggots possess the capability to multiply with terrifying speed, infesting the flesh of their victims.

HIVE FLEET HYDRA

A recent tendril of the Tyranid invasion, Hive Fleet Hydra drifts along in the wake of Leviathan, seeking out defeated splinters of previous hive fleets in order to cannibalise them and absorb their genetic memory. Though Hydra appears to be relatively small in size, this impression is deceiving; it is capable of unleashing vast hordes of bioforms, burying its prey under sheer weight of numbers.

When approaching a prey world, Hydra seeds its atmosphere with thousands upon thousands of spore clusters, each containing scores of dormant Hormagaunts and Termagants. When its initial invasion swarms encounter resistance, each slain organism releases a powerful synaptic pulse. Upon sensing this psychic death cry, the embedded spore clusters immediately release their living cargo. Instinctively these reinforcements converge upon the kill-signal, driven to a frenzy by the echo in their predatory consciousness. Thus, a single pack of slaughtered gaunts swiftly becomes a cluster of swarming xenos bodies, which soon becomes a living tidal wave of chitin and flesh.

On several occasions Hive Fleet Hydra has swept into sectors of space that have only recently repelled a Tyranid assault, falling upon and consuming both weary survivors and the carcasses of fire-gutted bio-ships, before disappearing into the void once again. Whether Hydra's unnerving generative capacity is related to this pattern of feeding upon members of its own race is a subject of heated debate amongst Imperial scientists. Many experts, most notably the famed Magos Xenobiologis Echros Van-Zendrech, have theorised that this development may signal the next stage in the Tyranid invasion – an autophagic cycle that will unleash a new, more resilient wave of Tyranid bioforms upon the fractured galaxy.

THE CEASELESS SWARM

There are seemingly no limits to the swarms that Hive Fleet Hydra can bring to bear against its prey. To do battle with this nightmare is to drown beneath a tide of surging xenos bodies.

THE HYDRA STIRS

Drukhari of the Poisoned Fang encounter the still-dormant Hive Fleet Hydra. Instead of destroying it, the Kabalites board the largest bio-vessels, intent on bringing specimens back to the Haemonculi. However, they are unprepared for the rate at which the bio-ships awaken. Every pirate that sets foot inside one of the vessels is killed, butchered by a tide of rapidly spawned Tyranids. Those Drukhari still aboard their vessels attempt to escape, but for every drone ship they destroy two more take its place. Prematurely awakened from its slumber, Hive Fleet Hydra accelerates its advance into the galaxy to slake its hunger.

A GRIM ANALYSIS

Magos Xenobiologis Echros Van-Zendrech leads several survey ships to the Locis System, where Hive Fleet Hydra is in the final stages of devouring the mining world of Korstock. Van-Zendrech watches the consumption of the civilian population with keen interest, noting Hydra's unique attack patterns.

THE HUNTERS HUNTED

A strike force of White Scars hunts the Hydra across the sand dunes of Haadekh. Veterans of countless xenos wars, the Space Marines know that the best method of fighting Tyranids is to cut the head from the beast, sending the swarm into confusion. However, each synapse creature the White Scars slay sends out a psychic scream, attracting fresh swarms of Tyranids to their location. Soon they are surrounded. Warriors to the end, the White Scars sell their lives dearly. Their sacrifice draws Hydra's swarms away from Haadekh's equatorial cities, giving the Imperium time to evacuate key personnel.

TRIUMPH TO DISASTER

After months of campaigning, the armies of Lord General Syvar Daeus turn back a tendril of Leviathan from the borders of the Corilanus System. In his honour a great Imperial Triumph is held on the planet of Ollfyre. Just as Daeus' legions reach the Plaza of Fallen Heroes, shadows begin to fall across the millions of onlookers. Looking up, the terrified populace sees its doom approaching – countless spores darken the skies, and beyond that vast, organic shapes drift into orbit, blocking the light from Corilanus' binary suns. The Hydra has come, drawn by the death throes of its defeated kin.

HIVE FLEET GORGON

The T'au know well to fear the Gorgon, for this voracious hive fleet has scoured the Eastern Fringe for many centuries, wreaking hideous losses upon their prized colonies. Its toxic hosts despoil and denature as they sweep across a world, spitting a miasma of polluting spores into darkening skies, and agonising their prey with a potent blend of necrotic poisons.

Hive Fleet Gorgon possesses a remarkable ability to adapt at a biological level to new threats, beyond any hive fleet seen before or since. Nowhere is this adaptability more notable than in the lethal bio-weapons unleashed by the fleet's invasion swarms. Since the First Battle of Sha'draig, where the T'au Empire deployed their ever-evolving technology against the Gorgon to spectacular effect, every single organism spawned within the hive fleet's bio-ships – from mindless drone to towering synapse creature – has contained a toxin gland filled with a blend of semi-sentient spores. These microscopic particles can rapidly develop and adapt to any genetic makeup. As the Gorgon engages its prey, consumed bio-matter is broken down within the spore chimneys of Toxicrenes and Hive Tyrants, its chemical composition transmitted throughout the swarm via the synaptic network. In mere moments, spores across the fleet restructure themselves in order to produce toxins specifically designed to incapacitate the hive fleet's chosen prey.

Gorgon relies upon this lethal malleability to break down the defences of targeted worlds. Its invasion swarms contain particularly large numbers of sporecaster organisms, which pour clouds of toxins into the atmosphere ahead of the opening assault. As the defenders choke on their own blood or paw at their decaying flesh, swarms of gaunts and more complex warrior-forms rip and tear at the twitching bodies, toxin sacs pulsing as their venom-dripping fangs sink deep into flesh.

Even a minor graze from the claw of a Gorgon warrior-form can prove lethal. A single spore can wreak horrific damage upon a host, rupturing organs and turning blood to caustic black slime.

ADAPT AND DEVOUR

Hive Fleet Gorgon's ability to rapidly adapt to new threats is beyond even that of its ever-evolving kin. There is no battlefield which the Gorgon cannot master, and no foe that its sentient spores cannot bring low.

First Encounters

The T'au Empire first encounters Hive Fleet Gorgon upon the forest world of Sha'draig. Initial T'au victories swiftly give way to attrition, as the Tyranids adapt to counter their opponent's every single weapon and tactic. The Empire desperately rushes experimental rail weapons and prototype macro-missiles to the front lines. For a brief time, it appears that these new technologies will prevail. This optimism lasts until Gorgon attacks again. This time, the Tyranids seed the skies above Sha'draig with clouds of choking spores. Hundreds of Fire Warriors collapse in frothing seizures as the spores clog their respirators. Mawlocs burst forth beneath the T'au defences, crushing the stricken defenders in avalanches of rubble. Those few T'au left alive rush to evacuate the planet. Sha'draig is devoured.

A Tentative Alliance

Finally grasping the scale of the Tyranid threat, the T'au forge a desperate alliance with the Imperium, smashing Hive Fleet Gorgon in a series of costly engagements. The remnant of Gorgon flees into deep space. Yet the truce between human and T'au quickly breaks down into open warfare, and neither pursues the Tyranids to deal the killing blow.

Plague Hulk

Decades after its apparent demise, Gorgon re-emerges. Its path converges with the plague hulk *Vomnivorax*. The hive fleet launches boarding tentacles, and swarms of gaunts pour into the corrupted vessel. Plague Marines of the Mouldering Claw obliterate the initial waves of invaders, their disease-ridden flesh immune to the toxins of the Gorgon. The swarm consumes those few who fall. During the next wave of the invasion, Toxicrenes lace the tunnels of the ship with a refined spore-agent which causes the Plague Marines' rancid flesh to slough from their bones.

A Tainted Bounty

Hive Fleet Gorgon enters the Imperial-held Pagrius System, known for its bountiful agri worlds. Several Astra Militarum regiments are rushed in to repel the Tyranids and ensure that the system's vital grain exports continue, unaware that Gorgon's bio-ships have already seeded each agri world with toxic spores. Millions give their lives to defend grano-plantations that are already hopelessly contaminated. The extent of the crisis is not discovered until several outlying planets report outbreaks of an unknown disease that drowns its victims in their own foaming blood.

A hive fleet that frequently clashes with Daemons and Chaos-corrupted prey, Kronos is well adapted to slaying its targets from afar. Its invasion swarms often include vast Termagant broods directed by Tyranid Warriors armed with long-range bio-cannons.

HIVE FLEET KRONOS

Where Hive Fleet Kronos travels, the Shadow in the Warp is at its most suffocatingly powerful. So strong is the psychic connection between Kronos and the Hive Mind, that a stifling aura of null power drifts ahead of its invasion swarms, agonising psychically active foes and draining their spirit energy to bolster its own hosts. Even as this phenomena throws the enemy into fearful confusion, thousands upon thousands of warrior-forms advance, unleashing a storm of organic missiles; Kronos avoids engaging its prey at close range when possible, for the prey it hunts revels in brutal close-quarters fighting, and thus a ranged kill is a more efficient method of extermination.

The raw matter of Chaos is anathema to the Tyranids, for it is inconstant and ethereal, possessing none of the nourishment that the hive fleets require to sate their endless hunger. Thus, the Tyranids – when possible – avoid areas plagued by warp storms and daemonic activity. As the impure essence of the immaterium pours into realspace across the galaxy, this is becoming increasingly difficult. Vital resources are being denied to the hive fleets as entire sectors are consumed by Chaos, and the Hive Mind has been forced to react to a looming catastrophe.

Hive Fleet Kronos appears to be the Hive Mind's first solution. This new terror is tracing a coreward path along the line of the Great Rift. Tendrils of Leviathan have diverted from their original course, leaving behind defenceless worlds for Kronos to consume. It uses such offerings well. The nascent hive fleet appears to be zeroing in on areas of intense psychic activity that threaten to tear the breach between realities wider. Scores of planets conquered by Chaos-worshipping cultists and warp-spawned abominations have fallen in its path, and Kronos has obliterated them all, like a maggot eating the corruption from an infected wound.

THE RAVENING SHADOW
Psykers, Chaos worshippers and creatures of the warp are the favoured quarry of Hive Fleet Kronos. The organisms spawned by its bio-ships are perfectly designed to eradicate the taint of the immaterium.

BATTLE OF THE WOLF'S HEAD

An Imperial fleet under the command of Admiral Groesson is engaging a massive Chaos fleet at the Wolf's Head Nebula when scores of bio-vessels enter the battle. Ignoring the Imperial ships, the Tyranids smash their way into the Chaos formation, swarming over the colossal Despoiler-class battleship at its centre. Not questioning his good fortune, Groesson unleashes a final salvo and orders the retreat.

SECOND BATTLE OF SHADOWBRINK

The world of Shadowbrink, where Hive Fleet Leviathan once defeated a vast daemonic force, erupts with Chaos energy as the Great Rift spreads its influence, and Daemons once again walk upon its surface. Drawn by Shadowbrink's malevolent aura, Hive Fleet Kronos arrives in orbit above the world. The Hive Mind deposits spores and swarms of organisms at eight points across the planet's surface, areas of heightened warp activity that are growing stronger with every passing moment. A neural node of Maleceptors and Zoanthropes leads each Tyranid host, and around these psychic organisms the Shadow in the Warp reaches such intensity that the wounds in reality begin to close. Khorne's legions storm towards the Tyranids, but Kronos refuses to answer the charge. Instead, the Daemons are met with a storm of fleshborer fire, and Tyranid artillery beasts blast apart thousands of warp-spawned horrors. Slowly but inevitably, the Daemons upon Shadowbrink are banished to the warp.

SPOILED FEAST

Kronos pauses its inexorable momentum to devour a chain of pre-digested worlds left behind by Hive Fleet Leviathan. The rancid gruel that remains has rotted and spoiled, but the capillary towers and ridged proboscises of Kronos' bio-ships devour it all the same.

CUTTING THE SIGNAL

A tendril of Kronos converges upon an intense astropathic beacon that a hunting pack of Night Lords have been using to bait lost ships. The Traitor Astartes scatter and launch harrying attacks against the Tyranids, hoping to redirect the larger hive fleet. In turn, Kronos disperses its bio-vessels, laying traps of its own. Unable to lure the Tyranids away from the tortured Astropaths that are broadcasting their siren signal, the Night Lords are forced to retreat.

A NIGHTMARE UNEARTHED

Far out on the northern edge of the galaxy lies the Tiamet System. This unremarkable region is home to one of the Hive Mind's most disturbing secrets, the truth of which is only now beginning to emerge…

CALL OF THE VOID

Upon the world of Heinrich's March, worshippers of the Dark Gods work their tortured slaves to death as they attempt to erect a monolithic ziggurat in honour of their foul patrons. A new and hidden cult propagates amidst the persecuted masses: the Choir of the Void. Its leader, the blind prophet known as the Conduit, preaches that a saviour race from beyond the stars awaits them in a far-off place, a paradise planet where they will find salvation. In a great uprising, millions of slaves overwhelm their masters and commandeer several dozen cargo hulks. This armada of the faithful makes for the nearby Tiamet System, guided by the visions of the Conduit.

OMINOUS REPORTS

More and more reports of missing ships and lost fleets drift in to Watch Fortress Haltmoat. The common denominator in each of these cases is that the vessels were last reported in the vicinity of the Tiamet System, far from safe haven. Watch Commander Vilnus orders an immediate survey of the area.

DREAD DISCOVERY

Kill Team Gjunheim departs from Haltmoat to investigate the reports of missing trade fleets near the Tiamet System. The Deathwatch drift in-system unnoticed, and land upon Ziaphoria. There, they discover the xenos super-structure that covers the planet's largest continent. When this vast device pulses, sending a tsunami of psychic energy rolling across the planet, the Kill Team's Librarian suffers a catastrophic cranial rupture. His screams alert nearby Tyranids, and soon the remaining battle-brothers are surrounded by swarming xenos. Before he and his remaining battle-brothers are torn apart, Watch Sergeant Gjunheim manages to send one final vox transmission to the team's orbiting Corvus Blackstar, warning of the nightmare his men have uncovered.

THE BUTCHER OF OCTARIUS

Haltmoat receives an unexpected guest – the exiled Inquisitor Kryptman. Watch Commander Vilnus agrees to an audience with the outcast, who has his own grim theories regarding the mysterious Hive Fleet Tiamet. Together, the two begin to formulate a plan that will see whatever the Tyranids are creating utterly obliterated.

Named after the system in which it was first encountered, Hive Fleet Tiamet is a unique phenomenon: a Tyranid incursion fleet which has claimed a cluster of planets without entirely stripping them of biomass, and continues to guard its conquered territory with single-minded ferocity. Built to protect as much as devour, Tiamet's hosts fight in dense clutches, grinding their way forward through hails of enemy fire, their diamond-hard exoskeletons forming a formidable living shield.

First discovered by an ill-fated Imperial exploration fleet in early M35, the Tiamet System went largely undisturbed for the next few thousand years. It was only when a small force of Aeldari Rangers from Craftworld Iyanden happened upon the isolated system that a troubling secret was discovered. Upon nearing the largest planet in the sector – the jungle world of Ziaphoria – the Rangers discovered a continent-spanning organic construct, a conical super-structure formed of chitin and soft, encephalic flesh that thrummed with immense psychic energy. The Shadow in the Warp was horrifically strong here, and several Aeldari went into convulsions upon nearing the super-structure, their minds sent into shock by the sheer force of Hive Fleet Tiamet's nullifying aura.

What purpose this bizarre device serves is yet unknown, but for the Hive Mind to devote an entire fleet to its protection is a worrying portent. Ordo Xenos Inquisitors have theorised it may be a powerful beacon, guiding yet more Tyranid hive fleets into the galaxy. In recent years, sightings of questing Tiamet tendrils have become worryingly common, as the hive fleet seeks fresh yields of biomass with which to finish its creation. These hosts have proven extremely difficult to kill, shrugging off volumes of fire that should have seen them utterly obliterated.

The carapace of every single organism spawned by Hive Fleet Tiamet is made of a unique chitin composite that provides excellent protection against extreme bursts of energy and kinetic force.

HIVE FLEET OUROBORIS

Hive Fleet Ouroboris is a nightmare from legend, a shadow from the stars that swoops from above on bat-like wings to devour its terrified prey. Death comes swiftly for those unfortunate enough to find themselves in the hive fleet's path, for Ouroboris strikes with blinding speed, cutting the heart from its victims before they even realise their doom.

There are some who believe that Hive Fleet Ouroboris was the very first Tyranid fleet to encounter Mankind. These theorists cite the ancient histories of Cardinal Miriamulus the Elder, who spoke of a nightmarish legion of 'winged entities, aflame with infernal ague', which savaged the Helican Sector sometime in early M36. Relics hailing from that distant time bear distinctive bio-plasma scarring consistent with Tyranid weaponry, and tales of flocks of winged horrors are certainly consistent with Ouroboris' typical predatory behaviour.

It is impossible to prove any connection, but recent encounters with Ouroboris have uncovered disturbing echoes of those old legends. Ouroboris favours massed aerial assaults, filling the air with so many Gargoyles and Harpies that those below must fight in near dark. It strikes swiftly, honing in upon areas of strategic value with unerring accuracy. By slaughtering officers and destroying communications outposts, Ouroboris tears the eyes from its prey, leaving them confused and vulnerable. Yet perhaps the most disturbing aspect of the hive fleet is its strange, primordial biology. Encounters with Ouroboris have revealed that the organisms spawned by this hive fleet contain cruder, primitive versions of common Tyranid bio-weapons and organs. Unfortunately, these strange mutations have rendered many weapons and tactics designed to counter the Tyranid menace largely ineffective against the sky-swarms of Ouroboris.

Bio-weapons spawned by Hive Fleet Ouroboris give off a soft, lambent glow. This unique phenomenon results in an unsettling haze of witch-light that surrounds its hosts in battle.

FROM ANCIENT LEGEND
Hive Fleet Ouroboris' primitive morphology bears an uncanny resemblance to the creatures recounted in a legend from the Imperium's dark past. Recent atrocities have only exacerbated its fell reputation.

MONSTERS FROM MYTH

In M36, Miriamulus the Elder of Thracian Primaris records the history of the 'Legion of Ouroboris', a vast host of winged xenos that descended upon the sector and stripped the life from dozens of planets. A grand crusade finally defeats these creatures in a twelve-day battle on the edge of the Eye of Terror.

SHADOW FROM THE STARS

Thousands of years after the death of Miriamulus, a chain of populated worlds bordering the Thracian Sector suddenly ceases communications. The Imperial fleets sent to investigate report back that every scrap of biomass on these planets has disappeared. Myths begin to spread on the remaining worlds, tales of a shadow from the stars that descends to devour the souls of the innocent.

OUROBORIS RISES

A previously unrecorded Tyranid hive fleet invades the Thracian Sector. The Imperium designates this new threat Hive Fleet Ouroboris, a name taken from the ancient records.

FATE OF THE SWARM CRUSHERS

A detachment of the Cadian 14th, known as the 'Swarm Crushers' due to their storied exploits during the Second Tyrannic War, is sent to wipe out a tendril of Ouroboris that threatens the desert world of Shukra. Drilled in the most efficient methods of slaying Tyranids, morale is high amongst the Cadians as they engage the first swarms. Confidence swiftly turns to panic as the Cadians' tactics have little or no impact upon the xenos. Pinpoint shots that should have ruptured vital organs have almost no effect, while salvoes of airburst shells filled with anti-Tyranid chemicals merely provide cover for the swarm. Stunned by the ineffectiveness of their defence, the Cadians nevertheless sell their lives dearly before they are devoured.

THE SKY HUNTERS

The Silver Drakes, a newly founded Primaris Chapter, are tasked with turning back Hive Fleet Ouroboris. Their Inceptor Squads cut a swathe through the hive fleet's sky-swarms, hunting the immense winged monsters at their heart. Though the Drakes' tactics are effective, their numbers are few. Isolated and outnumbered, the Chapter digs in for a bloody running war.

THE TYRANID INCURSIONS

SEGMENTUM OBSCURUS

M36/999.M41

HIVE FLEET OUROBORIS

DIMMAMAR

NAOGEDDON

HALO STARS

SCARUS SECTOR

FINIAL SECTOR

CYPRA MUNDI

MORDIAN

GOTHIC SECTOR

STORM OF THE EMPEROR'S WRATH

VALHALLA

CALIXIS SECTOR

THE EYE OF TERROR

BELIS CORONA

PISCINA

ALARIC

BAAL

CHINCHARE

CADIA

NECRON MEPHRIT DYNA

AGRIPINAA

FENRIS

MOLOV

HYDRAPHUR

ARMAGEDDON

ELYSIA

CICATRIX MALEDICTUM

LASTRATI

SEGMENTUM SOLAR

GOLGOTHA

VORDRAST

SEGMENTUM PACIFICUS

TERRA & MARS

RYZA

CATACHAN

THE MAELSTROM

GATHALAMOR

NECROMUNDA

OCTARIA

MACHARIA

VALEDOR

KRIEG

STORMVALD

GHEIST

NEW HOPE

TALLARN

UHULIS SECTOR

POSUL

SIREN'S STORM

SEGMENTUM TEMPESTUS

ALEUSIS

CARPATHIA

HIVE FLEET LEVIATHAN 997.M41

SOLSTICE

NEPHILIM SECTOR

FORGEFANE

RYNN'S WORLD

TARSI

REDUCTUS SECTOR

JORN V

ST. CASPALEN

GRYPHONNE IV

THE VEILED REGION

TIRATHAIN

RIGANT

HIVE FLEET 999.M41

SONDHEIM V

TESLA P

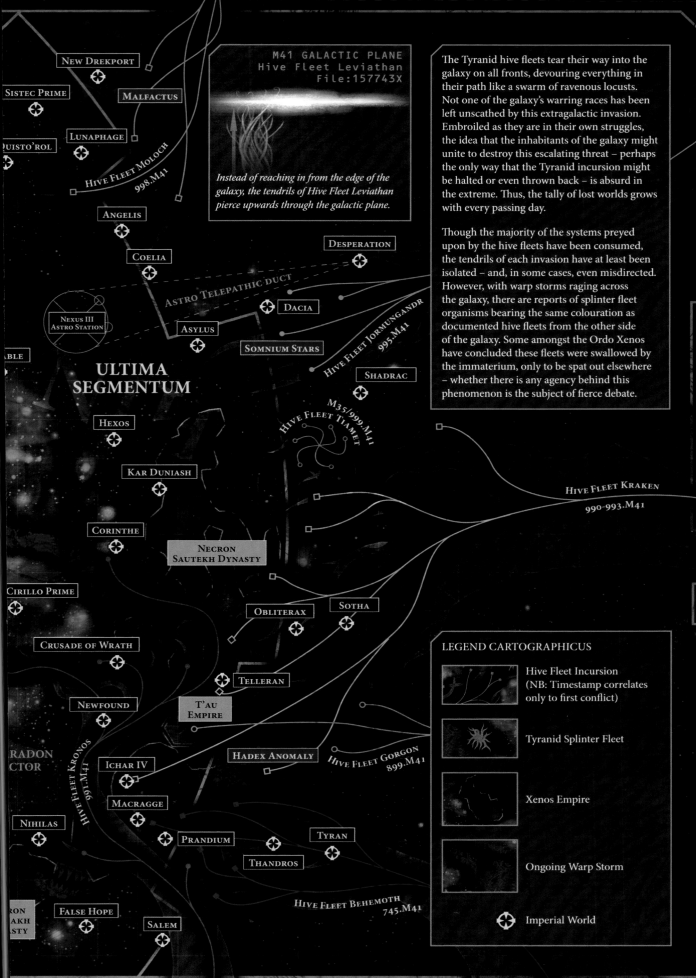

NEW DREKPORT

SISTEC PRIME

MALFACTUS

LUNAPHAGE

QUISTO'ROL

HIVE FLEET MOLOCH
998.M41

ANGELIS

COELIA

DESPERATION

NEXUS III
ASTRO STATION

ASTRO TELEPATHIC DUCT

DACIA

ASYLUS

SOMNIUM STARS

HIVE FLEET JORMUNGANDR
995.M41

SHADRAC

ULTIMA
SEGMENTUM

BLE

HEXOS

HIVE FLEET TIAMET
M35/999.M41

KAR DUNIASH

HIVE FLEET KRAKEN
990-993.M41

CORINTHE

NECRON
SAUTEKH DYNASTY

CIRILLO PRIME

OBLITERAX

SOTHA

CRUSADE OF WRATH

TELLERAN

NEWFOUND

T'AU
EMPIRE

RADON
CTOR

HIVE FLEET KRONOS
991.M41

HADEX ANOMALY

HIVE FLEET GORGON
899.M41

ICHAR IV

MACRAGGE

NIHILAS

PRANDIUM

TYRAN

THANDROS

RON
AKH
ASTY

FALSE HOPE

SALEM

HIVE FLEET BEHEMOTH
745.M41

M41 GALACTIC PLANE
Hive Fleet Leviathan
File:157743X

Instead of reaching in from the edge of the galaxy, the tendrils of Hive Fleet Leviathan pierce upwards through the galactic plane.

The Tyranid hive fleets tear their way into the galaxy on all fronts, devouring everything in their path like a swarm of ravenous locusts. Not one of the galaxy's warring races has been left unscathed by this extragalactic invasion. Embroiled as they are in their own struggles, the idea that the inhabitants of the galaxy might unite to destroy this escalating threat – perhaps the only way that the Tyranid incursion might be halted or even thrown back – is absurd in the extreme. Thus, the tally of lost worlds grows with every passing day.

Though the majority of the systems preyed upon by the hive fleets have been consumed, the tendrils of each invasion have at least been isolated – and, in some cases, even misdirected. However, with warp storms raging across the galaxy, there are reports of splinter fleet organisms bearing the same colouration as documented hive fleets from the other side of the galaxy. Some amongst the Ordo Xenos have concluded these fleets were swallowed by the immaterium, only to be spat out elsewhere – whether there is any agency behind this phenomenon is the subject of fierce debate.

LEGEND CARTOGRAPHICUS

Hive Fleet Incursion
(NB: Timestamp correlates
only to first conflict)

Tyranid Splinter Fleet

Xenos Empire

Ongoing Warp Storm

Imperial World

Baal will never be the same, for so much has been lost. A generation of battle-brothers laid low. Aspirants slaughtered alongside veterans of a hundred wars. Our buildings torn down around us, our proud history aflame. And all this from but a portion of the Leviathan's true might. By the Emperor, if this is victory against the Tyranids, what price defeat?

BIOMORPHS

The Tyranid race exists in a state of constant adaptation and evolution. With each victory and defeat the Hive Mind analyses previously encountered threats and enemy tactics, spawning fresh organic modifications, known as biomorphs, to counter its prey's advantages and exploit their weaknesses.

Biomorphs are rudimentary symbiotes, creatures that can be grafted to advanced Tyranids by a hive fleet's bio-ships, granting them new abilities or enhancing their existing powers. They come in many forms. Adrenal glands pump the host full of potent chemical stimulants, granting it a formidable turn of pace. Toxin sacs allow a bioform to secrete lethal venom from its claws and teeth, ensuring that even a minor graze will send their victims into agonised convulsions. Other biomorphs include thorax-embedded chitin barbs attached to lengths of tensile sinew, semi-sentient chitin plates that contract and harden upon being struck, and pitted cysts that spew clouds of spores to obscure the host creature from enemy fire. It is almost certain that the hive fleets are capable of creating a vast array other genetic mutations, should the need arise.

VANGUARD ORGANISMS

Crawling forth from the dark corners of the Imperium come lithe and powerful forms, razor-sharp claws gleaming in the twilight, predatory eyes filled with lethal cunning. These are the vanguard organisms of the Tyranids, sent ahead of the hive fleets to slaughter and subvert, paving the way for the devastation of entire sectors.

GENESTEALERS

There are many terrifying creatures in the Tyranid hive fleets, but one in particular has carved out a horrifying and bloody legend on more than a thousand worlds. It is a lurker in dark places, a clawed harbinger of sudden death. It is known as the Genestealer, and it is a plague upon the galaxy.

A Genestealer is a swift and powerful predator with lightning-fast reflexes and serrated claws that can tear through the thickest of armour. Genestealers also have large, highly adaptive brains and possess a form of brood telepathy that allows them to function independently from the Hive Mind. This autonomy allows them to destroy through stealth and guile that which cannot be defeated through numbers alone. The mightiest of these creatures are the Broodlords, hulking killers which lead the Genestealers in their bloody ambushes.

A strong survival instinct drives Genestealers outwards from the hive fleets, and they seek out space-bound vessels attempting to flee the surface of doomed prey worlds. It is simple for a Genestealer to stow away aboard such ships, nesting unseen amongst crawl spaces until it is brought to a new planet by the unsuspecting crew. If a single Genestealer reaches an inhabited world, it can spell disaster. Genestealers reproduce by implanting other life forms with their own genetic material. Once infected, a victim is enthralled by the Genestealers' nascent telepathy and Tyranid attributes are passed on to its offspring, creating monstrous hybrids completely under the alien's domination. These deformities eventually breed true, creating Purestrain Genestealers under the control of the progenitor of the cult, the Genestealer Patriarch – a formidably intelligent alpha beast possessing fearsome telepathic power. For years these creatures lurk in sewers and caves beneath cities, preying on the populace like folk-tale monsters. Within just a few years they will have assembled a vast network of mind-controlled operatives, embedded in every stratum of the local planetary government and military. Thus placed they wait, sometimes for many years, until the Hive Mind's will once again dominates their psyches.

No one knows how widespread the Genestealer infestation has become or how many worlds if affects. For every brood uncovered and purged, a dozen go unnoticed. When a Tyranid hive fleet enters an infested system, the Hive Mind asserts its synaptic dominion over the Broodlord and its clan. Planetary defenders are thrown into disarray as Genestealers suddenly burst from the shadows, overwhelming crucial systems and leaving the prey world vulnerable before the merciless Tyranid onslaught.

LICTORS

The Lictor is a highly specialised development of the Tyranid Warrior bioform, specifically adapted to fill a scout role in the vanguard of the Tyranid advance. Lictors rove ahead of the main body of a swarm, seeking out pockets of resistance to be eradicated and native life forms to be absorbed. Able to move swiftly and without sound through even the densest terrain, and concealed by a chameleonic carapace that renders it all but invisible to the naked eye, a Lictor can remain hidden until it chooses to strike. It can wait motionless for days, unnoticed by its victims, an unseen herald of approaching disaster.

Lictors are not instinctively aggressive, as they are created primarily to locate prey for the wider swarm. Lictors are opportunistic hunters and therefore tend to stalk their quarry from the shadows, avoiding confrontations where they would be vastly outmatched. A Lictor will often pick off its prey in ones and twos whilst they are separated from their comrades, sometimes retreating for days at a time before launching a further attack.

When the time comes to strike, Lictors are brutally efficient, with a whole arsenal of bio-weaponry that includes mantis-like claws, talons that can pierce steel, barbed flesh hooks and feeder tendrils. The feeder tendrils are tipped with sharpened bony plates that can pierce a victim's skull as easily as they poke through eyeballs and the sockets behind. They are used to lobotomise victims so that the Lictor can swiftly devour its brain and absorb its memories. Thus, in death, the enemy reveals more to a Lictor than it ever did in life, betraying the whereabouts of comrades and exposing any weaknesses that might be exploited.

Yet fearsome as the Lictor is as a physical foe, it has an altogether more deadly purpose than simple slaughter. Stalking Lictors exude a pheromone trail which draws other Tyranids; the larger the concentration of prey, the stronger the response and the more irresistible the lure. So it is that even killing a Lictor is no guarantee of survival, for the creature's mere presence ensures that the swarm already knows where its prey can be found. After that, it's only a matter of time…

DEATHLEAPER

Of all Mankind's phobias, it is the unknown and the unseen that commands the greatest fear. The pious people of St. Caspalen came to know such fear because of a single Tyranid organism, a solitary Lictor of such ruthless efficiency that many believed it was in fact a Daemon sent to punish them. So apt at avoiding detection was this predator that the first its victims knew of its presence was when clawed talons plunged into their back. All across the missionary world, watchguards and sentries mysteriously vanished, only to be found days later with their skulls pierced and their brains sucked out. Before long, the soldiers of the St. Caspalen defence force were jumping at every shadow, frightened by any mysterious sound and advancing only with wary trepidation on their patrols, their fears heightened by the unseen beast and the grisly death that awaited them. The scared soldiers of St. Caspalen named this predator in a vain attempt to salve their fears, a name uttered only in hushed whispers – they called it Deathleaper.

The rumours of Deathleaper spread like wildfire through the superstitious populace, and with each telling, the tales of carnage grew. That Deathleaper was created as Hive Fleet Leviathan's ultimate assassin seemed clear, but who the Lictor was seeking out remained elusive. This only increased people's anxiety; after all, it could be after them! However, Deathleaper was far more than just a mindless assassin; this is a task any Lictor can perform. Deathleaper was the perfect terror weapon, one crafted to destroy the enemy's morale and break their will to oppose the swarm.

On St. Caspalen, Deathleaper instinctively sensed that the execution of the planet's spiritual leader, Cardinal Salem, would have only accomplished the creation of a martyr, steeling the resolve of the St. Caspalen people in the face of the approaching hive fleet. Instead, Deathleaper infiltrated the Cardinal's cathedral-bunker and slaughtered his advisors, hacked through his bodyguard, and left only the prey-leader himself unharmed, covered in the blood and viscera of his closest aides. Like a monstrous predator toying with a mouse, Deathleaper repeated this gruesome carnage for ten days, bypassing the ever-increasing levels of security each time to come within a claw's grasp of the Cardinal before mysteriously fleeing from the bloody scene. The knowledge that the Tyranid assassin could eliminate him at any time was more than the Cardinal's sanity could take. His daily broadcasts became increasingly frantic, and his panic-stricken paranoia and broken mind did more to break the morale of the St. Caspalen defence forces than any mere execution could have.

Days later, St. Caspalen was devoured with barely a shot fired. This process has since played out on scores of worlds, with an organism matching Deathleaper's appearance and behaviour deployed by several different hive fleets to subdue and terrify their prey.

SKYSWARM BIOFORMS

Tyranid bioforms sweep across the sky in leather-winged clouds, casting flickering shadows across the terrified troops below. With a chorus of unnatural shrieks, they fold their wings and dive towards their prey, spitting caustic acid that scorches and blinds. Amidst the flock larger shapes can be seen, true monsters of the air with wings as vast as fighter craft.

GARGOYLES

Gargoyles are often the first wave of a Tyranid swarm to be seen in battle. They are agents of dismay whose prime purpose is to sow terror and confusion amongst the enemy, keeping their prey disordered and off-guard whilst the main body of the Tyranid assault arrives. Thus a Tyranid attack is preceded by the beating of thousands of membranous wings as Gargoyle broods descend upon the foe, blotting out the sun and spitting death from their fleshborers. The sheer psychological impact of such an overwhelming aerial assault is enough to break all but the most grizzled soldiers. In truth, turning to run is the worst thing a warrior can do when faced by a sky-swarm of Gargoyles. These predatory beasts excel in picking off isolated, panicked targets, either blasting them apart with torrents of bio-weapon fire, or snatching them into the air only to drop them to the hard ground with bone-shattering force.

Physically, Gargoyles strongly resemble the Termagants from which they are derived, with compact but lithe bodies encased in a lightly armoured exoskeleton. They also display the same animal cunning, and instinctively assail the foe from an unexpected quarter whenever the situation allows. Winged manoeuvrability gives the Gargoyles a distinct advantage over the majority of opponents, who for the most part rely on technological assistance to fly. As a result Gargoyles have earned a dread reputation, a legend that, in truth, far outstrips their physical threat. Wherever Gargoyles are abroad, the defenders look fearfully to the skies, for they know that every sky-borne shadow could be a flock of Gargoyles about to attack.

Those that face Gargoyles believe them to be skittish in nature, creatures that flee in the face of combat and instead prefer to fight at range. Indeed, a Gargoyle's leathery wings are easily damaged in close-quarter fighting, an unnecessary waste when the creatures are perfectly adapted at killing their prey from a distance whilst avoiding retaliation. On occasions when the Gargoyles' natural instincts are suppressed, they fight with all the desperate savagery of cornered beasts, entering a frenzied state that more than compensates for any perceived fragility. Gargoyles also spit a caustic venom that burns at skin. The Gargoyles instinctively aim for their prey's eyes, blinding their foe before tearing into them with barbed tails and talons until they either they or their prey are slain, or the Hive Mind relinquishes its control.

A deliberate quirk of the Gargoyles' physical structure means that they can squeeze through gaps seemingly far too small to permit passage. Enemy troops under Gargoyle attack have to be especially vigilant of any gap in the defences that the creatures could possibly exploit, be it an observation hatch, access portal, ventilation shaft or even an incinerator chute – given time, the Gargoyles will find their way in. Once inside, the Gargoyles lash out with every weapon at their disposal in a frenzied attempt to escape back into the open skies and unfurl their wings once more. Although Gargoyles may not display the same physical might as some of the larger Tyranid organisms, being trapped with one in a confined space is an invariably lethal experience.

HARRIDANS

Harridans are monstrous creatures, likened to the flying drakes and wyverns of legend. They are the largest of any Tyranid capable of flight, soaring through a prey world's skies on massive, leathery wings. Though they lack the sheer speed of attack aircraft, it is a brave fool indeed who thinks them an easy target. Harridans can slice an aircraft apart with a single swipe of their massive talons, or blast them into clouds of super-heated debris with precise volleys from their ventral bio-cannons. More impressive still is the Harridan's endurance, for it can remain aloft indefinitely and need never land.

Harridans act as brood mothers for the smaller Gargoyles, and their undersides writhe with the teeming flocks. When the Harridan has transported its broods to their destination, the Gargoyles unlatch their claws and open their own membranous wings, resembling a dark cloud that descends to swallow the prey below.

HARPIES

Harpies are monstrous bioforms that fly with a deftness and agility unattainable by even the most sophisticated fighter craft. As they soar overhead, they rain clusters of living bombs onto prey worlds whilst their forearms, which are melded with large bio-weapons, spit death as they fly.

Harpies appear in the early stages of a Tyranid attack, working in concert with Gargoyles to drive prey creatures out into the open. However, though the two species share a similar goal, they are physically very different. Where the Gargoyle is very much akin to a winged Termagant, the Harpy appears much closer in nature to a Trygon.

As with many of the larger Tyranid bioforms, the Harpy utilises a wide array of weaponry, according to the particular tactical needs of the hive fleet. In addition to the bloated Spore Mine cysts on their undersides and the bio-weapons fused to their forearms, the ribcages of many Harpies conceal rows of barbed spines. These are typically fired as the Harpy flies over the foe, ripping through infantry formations below.

However, the Harpy is most feared for the ear-splitting shriek that it makes as it dives for the kill. Such is the pitch and volume of this piercing noise that it is almost a weapon in itself. It is excruciatingly painful to lesser life forms, such as Orks and humans, and can even prove fatal to creatures with more highly developed senses, such as Aeldari or the genetically enhanced Space Marines. Those that survive this cacophonous assault are left dizzied and disoriented, easy prey for the Harpy's razor-sharp talons.

Perhaps due to its opportunistic nature, the Harpy tends to avoid protracted assaults, instead opting for strafing runs performed at the nadir of one of its swooping dives. This is not to say that the Harpy does not engage in bloody melee, but it rarely engages in such a contest unless the odds of victory are stacked in its favour. Accordingly, the Harpy's favoured quarry is something ill suited to fighting back – light enemy vehicles are a particular favourite, as they lack the speed to escape and the capacity to offer any real threat to the Harpy at short range.

HIVE CRONES

The Hive Crone is a flying monstrosity used by the Tyranids to establish air superiority over prey worlds. It is a creature perfectly adapted to aerial combat, able to wrestle enemy aircraft out of the skies as proficiently as any daredevil pilot at the controls of a sophisticated jet-fighter.

A clutch of parasitic tentaclids nestle underneath a Hive Crone's wings, latched on until they are launched at enemy aircraft. Upon leaving their host, these creatures speed through the air, homing in on their target with unerring accuracy. When these living missiles strike, they emit a massive bio-electric pulse that can cripple the target's electronics or stall their engines, leaving them without power or thrust and sending them into a fatal dive. But even without these impressive bio-missiles to shoot its prey, a Hive Crone is still deadly, flying close enough to its quarry to tear through them with the bladed spurs protruding from its underside. Once all of its aerial prey has been eliminated, a Hive Crone then softens up the planet's ground-bound defenders, swooping over the heads of the enemy soldiery and drizzling hyper-corrosive digestive fluids onto its victims.

Before reaching a target planet, Hive Crones also protect bio-ships in their journeys through extragalactic space against attacks from enemy assault shuttles and bomber craft; in silence, a hive fleet's Crones glide through the inky darkness, ripping enemy vessels open to the cold vacuum.

Perfectly designed for both atmospheric and zero-gravity flight, the agility of a Hive Crone can unsettle those fighter pilots more used to taking on conventional aircraft. Opponents must also beware the sheer quantity and variety of the creature's bio-weapons; more than one Imperial ace has been taken out of the sky by the swipe of a Hive Crone's bone-spur, having discounted the possibility of their target engaging with physical attacks.

Hive Crones often use flocks of Gargoyles to screen their attacks against enemy aircraft, dropping out of the swarm of leathery bodies at the last moment to fall upon their prey in one decisive strike. At the Battle of St. Mere-Salias, several wings of Valkyries were lost when the Hive Mind employed such tactics. The Hive Crone that came to be known as Bloodwing was responsible for no less than thirteen confirmed kills during this engagement, each marked by a precision thrust of its wing-tip through the cockpit of an Imperial fighter, impaling the pilot through his flight chair.

These distinctive tactics have led to several Aeronautica Imperialis training facilities seeking out veteran pilots of the Tyrannic Wars to better tutor their pilots in combating these biological horrors. Unfortunately for the Imperium, such surviving experts are few and far between.

GAUNTS

Termagants and Hormagaunts are simple bioforms created by the hive fleets in their billions. Onslaughts by these creatures often precede the main attack, wave after wave hurling themselves against enemy lines like an avalanche of teeth, claws and bio-weapons fire.

TERMAGANTS

Termagants are fast, agile and cunning creatures. They are amongst the smallest of the Hive Mind's warriors, little more than two metres from head to tail, having originally been created to roam the arterial passages of bio-ships in search of intruders. In planetary invasions, Termagants accompany Tyranid Warriors, scuttling forwards on four legs whilst unleashing torrents of fire from the anti-personnel bio-weaponry – commonly fleshborers – clutched in their clawed forelimbs.

There is a strange affinity between Termagants and Tyranid Warriors that goes beyond the usual unifying influence of the Hive Mind. The diminutive Termagants react instantly to any enemy that threatens their larger kin, drowning the foe in overwhelming numbers of squirming bodies before they have a chance to react. Whether this is an instinctive response or it speaks to something deeper is a mystery, but given the Tyranid Warriors' importance in maintaining the Hive Mind's control, its efficacy cannot be denied.

Bereft of a Hormagaunt's instinctive ferocity or wiry strength, a Termagant might be considered an unremarkable opponent by many of the galaxy's warring races, yet this would be a foolish assumption. Where the Hormagaunt is instinctively vicious and easily baited into a trap, a Termagant's cunning is honed by a desire for self-preservation, and it will commonly find a way to circumvent a potential ambush and assail the foe from an unexpected quarter. So it is that a combined assault of both Hormagaunts and Termagants is a deadly combination. The enemy can ill afford to ignore either group, but will be hard-pressed to prepare a defence that will thwart both. The Hormagaunts will overwhelm all but the strongest position, whilst the Termagants will uncannily seek out and exploit any trace of weakness.

Of course, there are times when a Tyranid assault requires that Termagants are thrown directly at the foe's lines, forcing the defenders to expend vast amounts of ammunition to hold back a tide of alien bodies. This is far from an exceptional tactic; it is simply part of the 'Termagants' role. On such occasions the Hive Mind simply suppresses the Termagants' survival instincts and sends them forward to die in droves until ammo stores are depleted and victory is assured.

A Termagant's mind is vicious but simplistic, and if separated from the Hive Mind's influence is apt to become confused. On such occasions the creature's self-preservation instincts take over, and it abandons the fight in search of shelter. So it is that an army that has driven off a Tyranid assault must proceed with great care. Every shadowed cave, tumbled ruin or patch of tangled undergrowth could conceal a nest of fugitive Termagants that will fight with incredible determination upon discovery.

HORMAGAUNTS

The Hormagaunt is a highly specialised iteration of the Termagant bioform and one that is utilised by the Tyranid hive fleets in its billions. Each Hormagaunt has four razor-sharp claws specially developed for ripping and piercing flesh and armour alike. The Hormagaunt also has powerful hind legs that drive it after its prey in a series of bounding leaps, giving the creature a skittering, insect-like gait.

The Hormagaunt is an extraordinarily single-minded creature and will pursue its victim without pause, ignoring injury and tiredness until it has run its quarry down

and torn it apart with frenzied strikes of its scythe-like forelimbs. Upon making a kill, a Hormagaunt will hungrily feed upon its prey's remains, tearing hunks of bloody flesh from the slaughtered corpse with razor-sharp teeth. Such a gruesome feast seldom lasts long, for the Hormagaunt's hyper-accelerated metabolism drives it to constantly seek out and gorge itself on fresh prey.

Onslaughts by Hormagaunt swarms often precede the main thrust of a Tyranid attack, for they have fearsome hunting instincts and require little direction from the Hive Mind. Once the assault begins, they are mostly left to their own devices. On occasion, the Hive Mind will make contact with the Hormagaunt's quicksilver consciousness, spurring it towards a more distant and more strategically important foe, but such situations are not commonplace. Hormagaunts are completely expendable, and the Hive Mind treats them as such.

Hormagaunts are often dropped onto a prey planet in Tyrannocyte spores. It matters not if most of these pods are destroyed by orbital defence emplacements before they even make planetfall, for if even a single spore's worth of Hormagaunts reaches the surface it can swiftly develop into a serious problem for the prey world's defenders. From the moment they have landed, the Hormagaunts rove the landscape in sweeping, nightmare flocks, constantly seeking out and attacking the native life forms.

Furthermore, unlike most other Tyranid bioforms, Hormagaunts are able to reproduce independently, and lay hundreds of eggs just below the surface of a planet before their short, hyperactive lifespan is over. No sooner has one wave of the creatures been exterminated than a fresh swarm has hatched and grown to maturity, ready to ravage the planet in the previous generation's stead. By the time the bulk of the hive fleet arrives, the defenders are already on the defensive, trapped behind fortress walls as a writhing sea of Hormagaunts rages back and forth across the planet.

FLESHBORER WEAPONS

The fleshborer is a compact brood nest for sharp-fanged borer beetles. When the weapon is fired, a frenzied borer beetle will hurtle itself forward with a single flick of its flea-like legs. The beetle then spends its remaining life energy in a few seconds, frantically boring through the armour, flesh and bone of the first thing in its path.

Not only does such a weapon inspire great fear and revulsion in the foe, but the nature of its biological ammunition means that the fleshborer can be easily adapted by the hive fleets to counter specific defences. Broad, arrow-shaped blade beetles are particularly effective at punching through armour, while the bulging thorax of the scorch bug is filled with a volatile blend of caustic chemicals that ignites upon impact, setting its target's armour and flesh ablaze.

The bizarre screamer beetle is designed purely to sow terror and confusion amongst the enemy's ranks, unleashing an ear-splitting shriek as it is propelled through the air at high speed. Massed salvoes of screamer beetles give rise to a nightmarish cacophony that is enough to shred the nerves of all but the most grizzled warriors, a phenomenon first recorded by the Aeldari of Craftworld Iyanden during the invasion of Hive Fleet Kraken.

SYNAPSE CREATURES

Stalking amidst the throng of xenos chattel come fearsome creatures, far more terrifying than their single-minded kin. Bipedal warrior-forms and towering abominations advance, a singular, hateful intellect burning behind their beady eyes. These are the agents of the Hive Mind, who direct the deadly flow of the invasion swarms with lethal cunning.

TYRANID WARRIORS

Tyranid Warriors are the most adaptable of all the Hive Mind's bioforms. They are creatures from the blackest of nightmares, unstoppable killing machines with pulsing ichor for blood, needle-sharp teeth and darkly gleaming eyes that reveal a terrible intelligence at work. A Tyranid Warrior stands twice the height of a man, its carapace protected by a thick chitin. One might expect such a creature to be slow in its actions, but a Tyranid Warrior is lithe, with reactions as swift as a whip.

Tyranid Warriors have the mental flexibility to employ a wide variety of bio-weapon symbiotes. As such, on the battlefield, they can be found leading all areas of a Tyranid swarm, fighting in close quarters with claws, boneswords and lash whips, or at longer ranges with devourers, deathspitters or even heavier bio-cannons. Whatever weaponry it wields, a Tyranid Warrior is a dangerous and unforgiving foe, able to identify and exploit the weaknesses of its targets with innate shrewdness. Worse, with its alien consciousness permanently bonded to the ageless Hive Mind, a Tyranid Warrior can instantly draw upon a reservoir of knowledge and experience that spans epochs, should its own prove insufficient to the task at hand.

Though they are formidable fighters in their own right, it is the Tyranid Warriors' role as the synaptic lynchpins of the swarm that makes them truly deadly. Tyranid Warriors are psychic resonators for the unwavering will of the Hive Mind and some of the more common conduits used to exert control over the less receptive creatures of the hive fleets. As such, Tyranid Warriors form a vital link in the Tyranid swarm, acting as relays and amplifiers through which Hive Tyrants issue their commands. So crucial is this role to a hive fleet's efforts to defeat a prey world's defenders that each Hive Tyrant is invariably accompanied by several broods of Tyranid Warriors cultured from its very own flesh – the better to enhance the psychic link throughout the swarm. This is not to imply that Tyranid Warriors are merely drones, for each is instinctively capable of assessing local battlefield situations. They can then, if the need arises, direct those Tyranid creatures near them, like an officer marshalling their forces, to exploit any tactical weakness that may appear in the enemy's defences.

TYRANID PRIMES

Tyranid Primes are the apex of the Tyranid Warrior strain – faster, stronger and smarter than the other Warriors they lead to battle, who instinctively emulate their deadly skill. In the absence of a Hive Tyrant or other advanced organism, these creatures will act as swarm leaders, a task at which they excel. Each Tyranid Prime has aided in the destruction of countless worlds, and slaughtered foes of all descriptions. They direct the bio-weapon fire of nearby Tyranid Warriors with unerring precision.

TERVIGONS

The Tervigon is a massive synapse creature whose towering carapace shields a swollen abdomen. Though possessed of a formidable array of bio-weapons, from monstrous claws that crush any prey that ventures too close, to banks of razor-tipped spines that can be fired a considerable distance, the Tervigon's true threat lies within.

Every Tervigon serves as a living incubator, within whose bloated form dozens upon dozens of Termagants slumber in a state of near-life. The Tervigon can spawn its dormant broods at will, jolting their minds into wakefulness. So it is that a foe engaging a Tervigon up close will find itself assailed by waves of skittering Termagants. Such a confrontation is terrible to behold, for a Tervigon's capacity to reinforce is vast, and its broods are driven into a near-frenzy by the need to protect their progenitor.

threat. Tervigons typically ensure that they retain a guard of recently birthed young to surround them during the battle, even as they spit more and more Termagants into the field to fulfil the Hive Mind's ravenous will.

While Tervigons typically remain positioned behind the main Tyranid swarm, bolstering its numbers and coordinating the attacks of its brood-spawn, there are times when the Hive Mind requires the creatures' full might to be unleashed. Their colossal forelimbs are perfectly capable of scything through heavy infantry and light vehicles, while some bear massive claws which can make a mockery of tank hulls and reinforced armour plating. Tervigons have even been

known to smash great breaches in fortress walls, before pressing their squirming birthing sacs to the gap and disgorging scores of hissing Termagants directly into the enemy's ranks.

When a hive fleet travels through space, Tervigons do not slumber in a dormant state like the majority of other Tyranids. Instead, they roam the ship's cavernous innards. Should a Tervigon detect intruders, it immediately spawns a veritable army of Termagants to repulse the foe whilst using its potent synaptic powers to hamper the enemy further or else awaken additional warriors. Unless the foe can act quickly, they will be engulfed and overwhelmed beneath a tide of drooling jaws and serrated claws.

The only way for a cool-headed enemy commander to end the horror is to have his troops concentrate all their firepower on the Tervigon. If the beast is slain, the resultant synaptic backlash may kill many of its young. This is easier said than done, for the weight of fire needed to fell a Tervigon is comparable to that needed to demolish a heavily armoured battle fortress. Even if such a tactic should prove successful, it will have drawn significant attention away from other sections of the Tyranids' advance.

The Termagants that are spewed forth from the Tervigon share a particularly strong bond with their progenitor, which in turn enhances the synaptic link between the gaunts and the Hive Mind. While they remain close to the Tervigon, the Termagants fight with a notable cohesion, as the brood parent directs their streams of fleshborer fire toward the most immediate

ZOANTHROPES

Zoanthropes are created solely to harness the psychic potential of the Hive Mind, and their entire bodies are perfected towards such a function. If necessary, a Zoanthrope can be used to extend the range of the Hive Mind's synaptic control, which utilises the beast's vast cerebral capacity to relay its instructions to lesser creatures. Under these circumstances, the Zoanthrope is little more than a highly sophisticated messenger, but this is only a fraction of what their alien minds are capable of. A Zoanthrope's link to the synaptic web is such that, by flexing the merest part of its mind, it can rain incandescent power on the enemy, projecting bolts of energy that boil through adamantium plate and disintegrate flesh with equal ease.

Despite their instinctive command over their otherworldly abilities, tapping into the Hive Mind's psychic potential is not without danger. It is not unknown for Zoanthropes to suffer massive cerebral trauma whilst attempting to harness the energies they wield. In such instances, a surge of psychic power courses through the Zoanthrope, overloading its synapses and burning out every neuron in its brain. The creature has just the time to emit a psychic howl of agony before falling limp to the ground, like a puppet whose strings have been severed.

Zoanthropes are vital nodes for harnessing the Hive Mind's psychic might and are created with a powerful sense of self-preservation. Therefore, they instinctively project a potent warp field to protect themselves in battle – a mental shield that is invisible but for a slight shimmer when small-arms and heavy-weapons fire alike patters harmlessly against it. However, Zoanthropes are still predators, capable of eliminating any perceived threat with bolts of flaming psychic energy.

NEUROTHROPES

Occasionally the Hive Mind will seed alpha beasts known as Neurothropes amidst clusters of Zoanthropes. These fell creatures possess the power to leech the very life force from their foes, mending their wounds even as the wizened cadaver of their victim topples to the floor. Neurothropes can also use their parasitic power to heal nearby Zoanthropes, which helps to safeguard against the overload of psychic energy that commonly overwhelms these creatures.

A combined host of these psychic bioforms is a formidable threat indeed. While the Zoanthropes blast the foe with waves of psychic energy, Neurothropes feast upon the souls of the fallen, bolstering the constitution of their kin, and adding their own prodigious might to the mental barrage. Few foes can stand in the face of such an onslaught, and those who manage to survive are left stunned – easy prey for gaunts or other warrior-forms.

Due to the relative scarcity of the Neurothropes, and the disturbingly familiar nature of their powers, it is thought by many of the Aeldari that these bioforms are in fact the offspring of the Doom of Malan'tai – the mysterious, mythical monster that once shattered an entire craftworld with its psychic might. That creature also feasted upon the souls of the slain, bolstering its powers with stolen life energy. The sentient races of the galaxy must hope there is no connection, for if the Neurothropes are indeed descended from that dread beast, they may yet grow to inherit its dark legacy.

THE DOOM OF MALAN'TAI

The Aeldari legend of the Doom of Malan'tai refers not only to the tale of an entire craftworld's death, but also to the abominable Tyranid creature that caused it – to the Aeldari, the two are indistinguishable. The lament speaks of a Tyranid creature unlike any other, a beast that gorged not upon flesh and blood, but upon the life-force of its victims, leaving only soulless oblivion in its wake. The Doom of Malan'tai was an adaptation of the Zoanthrope, and its weak physical appearance belied its true horror.

So it was that, when a lone, wounded bio-ship invaded Craftworld Malan'tai, the Aeldari did not at first realise that the true threat lay not with the gargantuan Tyranid monsters rampaging through their home, but with the unassuming creature left relatively unhindered to feed on Aeldari souls. As it fed, the Doom of Malan'tai's power grew, the absorbed life energy enhancing its fearsome psychic might. Once it had gorged on the spirits of the craftworld's infinity circuit, it was nigh invulnerable, possessing the power to pulp Aeldari warriors, snap titanic wraithbone war-constructs and shatter towering spires with cataclysmic bolts of psychic energy.

It was all that the few Aeldari survivors could do to escape Malan'tai. The craftworld was found adrift in space years later, reduced to naught but a cold, lifeless shell bearing the scars of psychic energy discharge on a cataclysmic scale. Of the loathsome creature that had brought about its destruction, there was no sign…

MALECEPTORS

The Maleceptor is the purest embodiment of the Hive Mind's psychic power, a living vessel for the gestalt consciousness that rules the Tyranid race. As it advances ominously into battle, warp energy spears from its eyeless cranium, vapourising all in its path. Those fortunate enough to survive the monster's keening psychic screams are spitted upon colossal talons, their torn bodies hurled aside. Bullets and energy bolts fired at the Maleceptor are consumed by a formidable psychic barrier, or deflect harmlessly from its thickly armoured hide. In response, ethereal pseudopods reach forth from the creature's glistening brain-arrays. The merest brush from one of these psychic tendrils overloads the victim's consciousness with a fraction of the Hive Mind's unimaginable energies, detonating their skull in an eruption of blood and cerebral matter.

Maleceptors are the response of the Hive Mind to some of the more psychically gifted races that populate the galaxy. At first they appear much like any other advanced Tyranid organism: hulking brutes armoured in thick chitin plate, towering over swarms of lesser bioforms. Those unlucky enough to encounter one up close witness the horrifying truth. Embedded in the beast's torso are glistening orbs of encephalic tissue, from which protrude twisting coils of shadowy energy. These tendrils are manifestations of the Tyranids' nullifying psychic presence – the Shadow in the Warp – and to touch one is to come into contact with the horrifying immensity of that psychic phenomenon. For nearly every living creature, this spells a spectacularly violent end.

It is fortunate that Maleceptors are such complex and valuable organisms that the Hive Mind rarely deploys more than a few such creatures to see its will done. A single Maleceptor is capable of obliterating the minds of several enemy psykers – gathered in sufficient numbers, they possess the power to tear entire cities to the ground, and slaughter battalions of foot soldiers and vehicles without laying a talon upon them. To enhance their already prodigious abilities, Maleceptors are often accompanied into battle by drifting hosts of Zoanthropes and Neurothropes. The resultant neural nodes not only bolster the resilience and ferocity of the swarms surrounding them, but also focus and direct the baleful effects of the Shadow in the Warp, unleashing roiling tides of psychic force.

Maleceptors are completely blind, and navigate via a combination of extra-sensory psychic perception, and by utilising their powerful synaptic link to the Hive Mind to sense the subtle psychic impulses of nearby Tyranids. Thus, while they lack the individualism and wealth of combat experience that a Hive Tyrant possesses, they are still able to react to emerging threats with startling speed. To these creatures the chaos of a battlefield is a phenomenally complex neural network, and they are able to instantly translate this maddening web of information, redirecting and redeploying lesser beasts in a fraction of a second.

When faced with heavy resistance, such as Imperial Knights and Aeldari wraith constructs, the hive fleets have deployed Maleceptors with notable success. The thick armour plating of those mighty war engines, so effective at repelling the massed attacks of a Tyranid swarm, is rendered almost useless in the face of a Maleceptor's psychic assault.

The Imperial Knights of House Raven grew to despise the Maleceptor they came to call the Vizier, which fought as part of the Behemoth splinter fleet known as the Court of the Nephilim King. The Vizier would prey upon single Knights who found themselves isolated from their comrades, peeling apart a machine's bulky carapace with waves of destructive energy, before rupturing the unfortunate pilot's brain with a caress of its psychic tendrils. Despite the best attempts of House Raven's hunting packs, the Vizier avoided every trap and ambush they laid for it, almost as if the beast could sense their every intent.

SPORES

The slow darkening of a prey world's skies is an omen of its impending doom, as unthinkable quantities of Tyranid spores are spewed into its atmosphere. Some of these are microscopic in size, and drift along in great clouds, wreaking disaster upon the planet's ecology. Others are bloated, chitin-plated things, their fleshy bulk packed with dormant organisms or explosive gases.

The bio-ships of each Tyranid hive fleet produce countless variations of simple spore organisms, each adapted to perform one of a number of different functions. These organisms may lack the adaptability and predatory intellect of more advanced bioforms, but can be no less deadly to the hive fleet's prey. At the most basic level there are microscopic pollutant spores, released into the atmosphere of a planet in order to denature its atmosphere until the air itself is ripe for consumption. At the most complex the spores are psychically resonant, capable of bolstering the synaptic links between the swarm.

Other, larger and more advanced spores are utilised during the invasion itself: giant, bulging sacks of flesh which bear clusters of Tyranid warrior-forms to the surface of a world, and bulky, armoured pods which embed themselves in the earth before spewing forth living mines and toxic pollutants. These are only the most commonly sighted spore organisms; for every battlefield challenge, the Hive Mind has fashioned a grisly solution.

SPOROCYSTS

Sporocysts are a vital element in the hive fleets' predatory cycle. These bloated, fleshy pods are released by bio-ships in low orbit. They float through a prey world's atmosphere until they make landfall, before spreading the segments of their chitinous shell for protection and burrowing into the earth like a tick digging into flesh. Once they are securely buried, with only the spore chimneys atop their structure showing, they begin to pump out billions of polluting microorganisms – these begin the process of violently altering the planet's atmosphere and ecology to better suit the Tyranids' needs.

When threatened, Sporocysts will squeeze out the flaccid spore-forms they carry. These simple bioforms quickly expand to become clusters of Spore Mines or larger, deadlier Mucolid Spores, before seeking out the nearest threat and detonating with catastrophic force. The Hive Mind occasionally deploys this ability for a more active purpose; there are records

of hundreds of Sporocysts creating vast fields of Spore Mines to halt the advance of armour and infantry, delaying reinforcements long enough for the Tyranids to pick apart the piecemeal forces of their prey.

There are also persistent theories that Sporocysts act as psychic resonators, boosting the abilities of synapse creatures nearby, so that they may better carry out the Hive Mind's ravenous imperative. Certainly, Tyranid bioforms appear to fight with increased cohesion and aggressiveness when defending these strange organisms. As well as rapidly advancing the deterioration of the local biosphere, the sheer number of Sporocysts scattered across a planet's surface may provide a series of synaptic staging posts: hotspots where Tyranid leader-beasts can better direct the flow of the invasion.

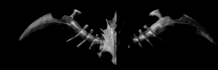

TYRANNOCYTES

These tentacled ovoids appear to be a variation on the Sporocyst bioform, but in fact they are adapted for an entirely different purpose. When a hive fleet launches a pre-digestive assault, many of its warrior-forms and battle organisms are transported to the surface of the prey world in Tyrannocytes. These pods are squeezed out from orifices upon circling bio-ships in great clusters, plummeting through the skies before slowing themselves with buoyant gases prior to impact. As a Tyrannocyte's tendrils brush the ground, the resulting stimulus causes it to disgorge its Tyranid passengers in a spray of grisly fluids.

This does not result in the organism's destruction, however. Though each spore seems to be nothing more than a giant, veiny sac, they are in fact sentient creatures possessed of a fierce hunger. Once their

living cargo has been deployed, the Tyrannocyte refills its body with gaseous emissions, before rising into the air and drifting eerily across the battlefield, searching for prey.

The outer hide of a Tyrannocyte bristles with bio-weaponry, from symbiotes that spit caustic acid, to cannons that hurl corrosive crystals which detonate in a storm of eviscerating shards. The barbed tendrils that dangle beneath the Tyrannocyte snatch enemy soldiers from the ground, slicing apart their flesh and choking the life from them.

MUCOLID SPORE CLUSTERS

The Mucolid Spore is a creature inimical to natural law, for its whole existence is geared towards spectacular self-sacrifice. Borne aloft by evil-smelling gases that roil inside the veined balloon of its body, this bioform can float either at ground level or thousands of feet above the earth, rising high enough to intercept enemy aircraft. As it floats, its dangling tentacles languidly taste the air for the scent of its prey.

When the proximity of a non-Tyranid life form is detected, the Mucolid Spore will drift close before detonating in a storm of bio-acid. Mucolid Spores are drawn towards anything moving swiftly in the air, exploding with lethal force the moment they close with their target. This makes them a particularly hazardous obstruction for enemy flyers. When confronted with a foe that dominates the skies, hive fleets will often seed the air with vast minefields of Mucolid Spores. Not only must pilots beware of crashing into these biological bombs, they must also account for the fact that the Mucolids will mindlessly make for their aircraft, drawn on by suicidal instincts.

SPORE MINE CLUSTERS

Clusters of Spore Mines are often seeded directly onto worlds from orbiting bio-ships. Spore Mines have been known to drift for days, just waiting for an unwary foe to come near, before detonating with brutal effect.

SPORECASTERS

As a Tyranid invasion progresses, the clouds of spores that choke the prey world's skies become thicker and thicker. These cloying particles are expelled in their billions by specialised bioforms – sporecaster organisms that ravage their foes with suffocating toxic miasmas, flesh-melting acids and predatory, semi-sentient viruses.

VENOMTHROPES

Venomthropes are gangrel creatures with scrawny bodies and whip-like tentacles that drip with alien poisons. Their carapaces house bulging, gas-filled bladders, allowing the Venomthropes to float ponderously across the battlefield, using their clusters of tendrils to steer themselves towards suitable prey.

In addition to providing the Venomthropes' mobility, the gas bladders also produce thick clouds of spores. Venomthropes are shrouded in a dense fog of these airborne spores that conceals not only them, but any other broods of Tyranid predators advancing in their wake. The spores are also the Venomthropes' most insidious form of attack, for they are extremely poisonous to non-Tyranid life forms. Brief exposure causes violent bouts of nausea and uncontrollable muscle spasms, leaving foes weakened and easy prey for the nearby Tyranids. If the enemy is unfortunate, or foolish enough to inhale the Venomthropes' emissions for any prolonged period, the alien spores will gain a foothold within the foe's body. Reproducing rapidly, they spread throughout the host's system, breaking down organic tissues at a horrifying rate. The victim ultimately drowns in its own frothing and infected bodily fluids, and as the diseased corpse collapses in on itself, the Venomthrope uses its feeder tendrils to suck up the bubbling remains.

The bodies of Venomthropes are coated in a variety of alien poisons, but it is their writhing tentacles that exude the most lethal of all Tyranid toxins. These venoms are so virulent that on contact, they cause the flesh of their prey to wither and slough from bone. Those victims that do not succumb immediately are entangled by the writhing limbs, bound in a poisonous embrace until the Venomthropes' toxic spores do their gruesome work.

Though Venomthropes are not the most physically imposing or aggressive Tyranid bioforms, they are, if anything, more dangerous to a prey world's continued survival than hordes of warrior-organisms. Left to their own devices, a single brood of Venomthropes will eventually poison not only the entire world's indigenous life, but also its soil and atmosphere, leaving the plague-shrouded planet fit only for consumption by the hive fleet.

TOXICRENES

The towering monstrosity known as the Toxicrene appears deadly enough as it lumbers across the battlefield, crushing the life from enemy warriors with its vicious tentacle-limbs. Yet it is not the Toxicrene's great strength that makes it such a feared aspect of the hive fleet's war machine, but the billowing clouds of poisonous spores that are spewed from its dorsal vents, seeping into the lungs of its victims and drowning them in their own frothing blood.

This reeking toxic emanation is in fact comprised of millions upon millions of nascent microscopic organisms, each possessing a fragment of predatory sentience. When the Toxicrene delivers its lethal payload, these spores hone in upon non-Tyranid lifeforms, breaking down even the most redoubtable immune systems and inflicting agonising, gruesome deaths.

So effective is the Toxicrene's poisonous emission that not even those wearing protective biohazard gear or clad in otherwise impenetrable power armour are safe. Millions of spores seep into respirator tubes and clog gas mask filters, feeding upon the moisture of their host and growing at an astonishing rate. Internal organs distend and rupture as the tiny life forms violently expand. Poisoned gore seeps into the victim's lungs even as it erupts from their every orifice. There is no cure once the spores take hold – only a horrific and painful end.

Toxicrenes are typically sent forth by the hive fleet after the initial swarms of gaunts and other basic warrior-forms have forced the prey world to expend the majority of its firepower. Accompanied by broods of Venomthropes, they begin the process of seeding the planet's atmosphere with spore clouds, altering its environment and ecosystems to ensure efficient breakdown of biomass, while simultaneously aiding in the slaughter of the remaining populace. Should the Hive Mind deem it necessary, however, they can be deployed at any stage of the invasion.

Hive Fleet Gorgon in particular is notable for its extensive use of Toxicrenes in the opening stages of battle, relying on the dense clouds pumped out by the creatures to mask its advancing swarms and wear down tightly packed ranks of enemy defenders. The damage they inflict lasts beyond these initial encounters. The Imperium has been forced to abandon scores of worlds, even when it has driven back the Tyranid swarm, simply because the sheer quantity of spores that have been pumped into the atmosphere by Toxicrenes has rendered the world uninhabitable. After losing several precious sept worlds in the same way, the T'au Empire began to assign entire sectors of Earth caste scientists to the task of developing technological counters to this monster's fell powers. Yet so adaptable are the microorganisms that the Toxicrene discharges, no anti-viral agents have proved successful on more than one or two occasions.

Should the enemy be foolish enough to engage a Toxicrene at close range, they will be torn apart or choked to death by whip-like, barbed tentacles. Even managing to pierce the beast's chitin armour may prove lethal, for a Toxicrene's blood is riddled with a noxious brew of venoms and corrosive acids that devour flesh and armour upon contact.

MALANTHROPES

Malanthropes are rarely seen Tyranid creatures. This is because they are not truly warrior-organisms, and so are not usually encountered by a prey world's defenders. Instead, these floating creatures follow behind the Tyranid attack; they are typically created only after a prey world's protectors have been defeated and the swarm is in the process of devouring the planet's biomass. On those few occasions that a survivor has seen a Malanthrope and somehow escaped, they have brought with them a tale of horror. They describe creatures superficially similar in appearance to Venomthropes, but far larger and more terrifying. They report seeing these giants drift across corpse-strewn battlefields, but unlike other Tyranids, which mindlessly devour everything in their way, Malanthropes seem to selectively search through the slain – as to what they are searching for, none can say. Once a morsel that suits their taste has been found, they grasp hold of the body with long groping tendrils before feeding the entire mass into their tentacled maw with small, dexterous arms. Those unfortunate enough to still be alive when caught by a Malanthrope are stung with a paralysing toxin and then swallowed whole. Living and awake, but trapped within the Malanthrope's bloated digestion sacs, the skin, flesh and bones of these victims is slowly absorbed over the following days – a terrible and excruciatingly painful death.

SUBTERRANEAN SWARMS

When faced with a fortified enemy position, the Hive Mind will deploy burrowing organisms – blade-limbed horrors that burst from the earth in the midst of the defenders and carve their terrified prey to bloody chunks. Some of these monsters stand as tall as buildings, and are able to peel the armour from a tank with sickening ease.

RAVENERS

Raveners are voracious predators, their clawed and snake-like bodies driven onwards by an all-consuming hunger that is remarkable even amongst their predatory race. Twisted musculature grants these beasts a terrifying turn of speed. Raveners can bound over small obstacles in an eye-blink, dart between larger obstructions and even slither through flooded marshland with bewildering swiftness. Yet such is not the Raveners' only form of approach and neither is it the most feared, for at least when these alien horrors are charging their prey down across the battlefield, the enemy has a chance to see their doom. The power housed within the Raveners' wiry forms allows them to burrow long distances beneath a world's surface, before emerging in a spray of earth right in front of an enemy position, claws eviscerating their ambushed prey whilst their thorax-mounted weapon symbiotes spit death.

THE RED TERROR

For twenty days, the so-called Red Terror preyed upon the defenders of the Imperial mining world of Devlan Primus. Entire excavation teams disappeared, scraps of torn flesh and pools of drying blood the only mark of their passing. Astra Militarum troops sent in to investigate the xenos menace fared little better, firing their lasguns blindly into the gloom even as a crimson blur snatched men and women away with terrifying speed. The few survivors spoke of a beast with a crimson-coloured carapace, talons that could tunnel through rockcrete, and a maw so wide it could swallow a man whole. With every retelling, the legends grew more fearsome and terrifying.

Since that first sighting, reports of a creature matching the same description have filtered in from battlefields across the galaxy. In every instance, a monster with an armoured hide the colour of spilt blood slaughtered scores of helpless soldiers before vanishing deep into the earth. Whether these reports concern the same creature – and, more worryingly, whether it is an advanced organism that the hive fleets can call upon at will – remains a mystery.

'EMPEROR KNOWS WHAT PIT SPAWNED THE HIDEOUS APPARITION WE CAME TO KNOW AS THE RED TERROR. IT FIRST ATTACKED THE OUTER BASTION AND TWENTY-FOUR MEN DIED BEFORE WE DROVE IT AWAY WITH FLAMERS. WE NEVER EVEN FOUND THE BODIES OF LIEUTENANT BORALES AND CAPTAIN LOWE, JUST A TRAIL OF SLIME THAT LED AWAY FROM THE COMMAND POST AND INTO THE TUNNELS. IT RETURNED THE FOLLOWING NIGHT, AND THE SLAUGHTER BEGAN ANEW, BUT THIS TIME WE WERE READY FOR IT... OR SO WE THOUGHT.'

- From 'Twenty Days in Hell: The Retreat from Devlan Primus'

MAWLOCS

Mawlocs are huge worm-like creatures with great distended jaws. They are the tunnelling outriders to the Tyranid swarm, and burrow deep beneath the ground to bypass a prey world's front-line defences. Once past the outer perimeter, a Mawloc bursts forth in a shower of dirt and stone, swallowing any foes unfortunate enough to be standing where it emerges. The Mawloc then runs rampant among the reeling enemy, wreaking as much havoc and carnage as it can with its overmuscled tail before vanishing back below ground once more. Severe tremors are the only warning of a Mawloc attack, making sentry duty on a seismically active world a particularly harrowing experience for the defenders should a hive fleet enter the system.

Physically, a Mawloc is an incredibly simple Tyranid bioform, with little concession given to other roles. Its six clawed limbs are comparatively small and whilst they lack the reach to be especially efficient in combat, they are nonetheless incredibly powerful, employed to gain extra traction whilst burrowing and haul the Mawloc through its tunnels. This should not be taken to mean a Mawloc is defenceless; nothing could be further from the truth. A Mawloc's massive, razor-toothed maw is the entryway to an equally cavernous gullet. Most of the creature's victims are swallowed whole, there to be painfully digested over the course of several days. Should an item of prey prove large enough to stick in the Mawloc's craw, they are first pounded flat by a battery of blows from the creature's muscular tail before being devoured.

A Mawloc is almost entirely blind, and relies on information provided by a series of pressure-sensitive organs that run the length of its flanks. These can absorb and decipher pressure waves, creating a many-layered picture of the world around the Mawloc. It is this ability that allows the creature to hunt its prey even whilst burrowing through the ground. Even the slightest tremor above ground grants a hunting Mawloc a wealth of information, enabling it to intercept a quarry with frightening speed and unerring accuracy. The more regular and rhythmic the sound, the more likely it is that a Mawloc will be able to home in on the source. The pounding thump of a terrified heartbeat is like a flaring beacon to a Mawloc. Thus it is a victim's own fear that betrays their whereabouts and brings about their destruction.

TRYGONS

The Trygon is a vast serpentine creature, so colossal that it towers over even the mighty Carnifex. It is a heavily armoured monster, covered from head to tail with a thick carapace of shifting plates. As the Trygon moves, these plates generate a potent bio-static charge that courses along the length of the beast's body and wreathes its bladed forelimbs with crackling power. The Trygon can direct this energy as a lethal high-voltage discharge – unleashing pulsing arcs of lightning that leave its prey as little more than a charred pile of scorched bones.

A Trygon's claws are not only fearsome in close combat, they also allow it to burrow through practically any material. When a Trygon detects an enemy above, it digs upwards, bursting through the ground with explosive force, its huge blade-limbs scything through warriors and tanks alike. Such subterranean attacks are hard to detect and harder to defend against, especially on worlds with background seismic activity. Once the beast emerges, only focused heavy-weapons fire can be relied upon to bring it down, for the Trygon's iron-hard carapace is proof against all else.

Trygons excavate a massive network of underground tunnels as they burrow beneath the surface of a prey world. Other Tyranid creatures use the passageways left in the Trygon's wake, scuttling unseen as battle rages overhead. The emergence of a tunnelling Trygon therefore often heralds a larger Tyranid attack, with hordes of creatures pouring out of the tunnel shortly after its emergence.

TRYGON PRIMES

As with many Tyranid organisms, different Trygons display substantial variety; one of the most distinct is the Trygon Prime. These beasts have elongated jaws and containment spines running the length of their sinuous bodies, to better harness and direct their bio-electric discharges. More dangerous still, these Trygons share a strong synaptic link with the Hive Mind and are able to dominate the will of lesser Tyranid creatures.

CARNIFEXES

Carnifexes are living engines of destruction, towering monsters of unyielding armoured chitin and knotted alien musculature. They are one of the toughest and deadliest of all a hive fleet's warrior creatures, created to spearhead assaults in massed battles. Though the Hive Mind has since created larger warrior-organisms, few are the Carnifex's equal in terms of size to strength, nor in terms of sheer destructive potential.

The Imperium's first recorded Carnifex encounters occurred in the battles leading to Hive Fleet Behemoth's invasion of Macragge. As the great star-vessels of Mankind strove with the unearthly living ships of the Tyranids, Carnifexes were to be found at the head of many boarding actions, tearing the defenders apart with scythe-shaped talons and immolating the survivors with incandescent bolts of bio-plasma. These creatures swiftly became known as 'Screamer Killers', named for the terrible ululating shriek that accompanied their bio-plasma discharges.

The Screamer-Killer was long thought by the Magos Biologis to be the only breed of Carnifex, but as the Tyrannic Wars grind on, many other iterations of this bioform have emerged to wreak horrific carnage upon Imperial forces. A particularly notorious example is the much-feared 'Thornback'. Created by the Hive Mind to excel as much at range as in the crush of melee, the Thornback can launch a volley of spines from its dorsal thorax plates with lethal force, and can wield an array of ranged bio-weapons. Doubtless there are many more Carnifex strains that have yet to be encountered by the Imperium, each with their own horrifying methods of slaughter.

Even as the Hive Mind creates increasingly complex organisms to enable it to hunt and kill its prey, the Carnifex has remained the combat standard, a reliable and relatively simple bioform that can perform well in any form of front-line conflict. Unlike specialised organisms such as Maleceptors and Toxicrenes, which require extensive time and resources for the hive fleets to spawn, the Carnifex can be generated swiftly and in great numbers; it is a rare Tyranid assault that does not include at least one brood of these mighty creatures. This allows the hive fleets to create a force perfectly suited to overcome and destroy a prey world's defenders. Worse still, Carnifexes are protected by a reinforced exoskeleton that is at least as dense as ceramite. Combined with their massive bulk and unnatural vitality, Carnifexes can shrug off an obscene amount of firepower and endure horrendous wounds before succumbing to death.

Though Carnifexes lack the swiftness of other creatures in the Tyranid swarm, they more than make up for it in sheer brute force. A Carnifex's thunderous charge starts slowly, steely sinews straining as the beast propels its improbable bulk to top speed, making the ground itself shake. Its heavy footfalls beat out a sonorous drum-beat of doom as it strides forth. As the beast reaches full speed, its prey scatters before it or is trampled to death. A charging Carnifex is likened to a living battering ram, for their immense bulk can crush any opponent that bars its way and smash through almost any obstacle. Indeed, only a hardened fortress wall or super-heavy tank has any hope of surviving the impact and stalling the Carnifex's stampede. Sometimes, not even this proves sufficient, as the few surviving records from Macragge's polar fortresses bear testament. The best way to survive a charging Carnifex is to be elsewhere when it arrives.

OLD ONE EYE
THE BEAST OF CALTH

The Carnifex known as Old One Eye is a monster of living legend. When Hive Fleet Behemoth descended upon the cavern world of Calth, Old One Eye spearheaded the Tyranid assault. Stampeding through the defenders, it swatted aside Imperial Guardsmen and Leman Russ Battle Tanks as if they were naught but bothersome insects. Only the most powerful of weaponry slowed the beast down and, to this day, its body bears the scars of the many blows that should by all rights have killed it. Foremost amongst these is a deep burn running across its armoured skull, a testament to the courage of a long-forgotten hero of the Imperium who fired a plasma pistol through one of the beast's eyes and into its brain. It was this very shot that brought the Carnifex's rampage to a dramatic halt, the first time such a feat had ever occurred.

The legend of Old One Eye might have ended there had it not been for a band of smugglers who stumbled across the monster's frozen body decades later. Hoping to reap a bounty for the corpse, they thawed the Carnifex out, but even as they did so, its grievous wounds began to heal. Isolated from the guiding presence of the Hive Mind, Old One Eye awoke with only the need to kill. Its one remaining eye gazed hungrily upon the unsuspecting smugglers who barely had time to register the beast was alive before they were slaughtered.

Released from its icy prison, Old One Eye roamed across the blizzard-swept landscape of Calth in search of more prey. Like much of the Ultramar System at this time, Termagants and Genestealers still lurked within caves there, despite Hive Fleet Behemoth's defeat. These creatures were drawn to Old One Eye, sensing in the Carnifex a powerful alpha leader. All over the planet, land convoys were destroyed, hab-domes smashed and entire populations massacred and devoured.

Calth's cries for help did not go unheeded; Sergeant Telion of the Ultramarines, a veteran of the First Tyrannic War, answered them. It did not take the Scout Sergeant long to track his quarry, but neither bolt shell nor knife-blade could pierce Old One Eye's armoured hide. As Telion's warriors were crushed to a pulp beneath the Carnifex's massive claws, the Sergeant somehow managed a one-in-a-million shot that found the pit of its ruined eye-socket. The mighty Carnifex howled in pain and, in its frenzied rage, stumbled into a cavernous ravine. Though Telion led a week-long search for the beast's body, it was never found.

Since that time, there have been scattered reports of Old One Eye re-emerging to wreak havoc, only to be felled through the actions of a bold hero. Indeed, if all the tales are true, Old One Eye has been slain more than a dozen times, but at great cost on each occasion. None know of Old One Eye's true fate; there are those that believe the creature is long dead and that the tales of its return are mere stories to frighten disobedient children. However, rumours persist that creatures matching Old One Eye's description have been seen plaguing planets across Ultramar and beyond.

The most recent sighting of a creature resembling the Beast of Calth was upon the world of Tartoros, during Hive Fleet Leviathan's assault on the Cryptus System. Ignoring the fire from Cadian heavy weapon teams that spattered off its scarred carapace, this alpha Carnifex smashed apart several of the void shield generators that kept Tartoros protected from devastating solar storms. Not a single Imperial soldier survived the resulting cataclysm.

If this is the same creature, it is unknown how it escaped the confines of Calth, but the fact remains that, wherever Old One Eye is sighted, carnage and slaughter follow in its wake.

HIVE TYRANTS

Hive Tyrants are the commanders of the Tyranid swarms and enact the Hive Mind's will on the field of battle. Though individuals display a wide variety of physical characteristics, all Hive Tyrants are fearsome hulking monsters that tower over even a Dreadnought. They are brutally strong, able to shatter ferrocrete with sickening ease. Every part of such a beast's body is perfectly created to kill, even the layers of chitinous plating that protect them. A Hive Tyrant is a formidable opponent at any distance, as deadly with ranged weapons as it is with bonesword or claw.

Hive Tyrants are highly psychic, and their relationship to the Hive Mind is amongst the closest of any known bioform. Indeed, the synaptic link is so strong that they are the primary conduits through which the Hive Mind enforces its dominance over a hive fleet's lesser creatures. The instinctive nature of a Tyranid swarm is smothered with implacable drive and purpose, and the need to hunt and devour is imbued with a cunning and tactical awareness that would put the galaxy's finest strategists to shame.

Hive Tyrants were created not only to overpower their prey, but also to out-think it. Unlike many Tyranid creatures, Hive Tyrants are incredibly intelligent and are even, to some extent, self-aware. Whilst they are still slaved to the gestalt consciousness of the Hive Mind, they are given wider latitude in achieving its goals. As such, they can respond to battlefield events far faster than the inscrutable Hive Mind and adapt the behaviour of the swarms they command accordingly.

As a result of their highly developed synaptic connection and greater levels of intelligence, Hive Tyrants are also able to manifest potent psychic powers. By harnessing tiny slivers of the Hive Mind's terrifying will, Hive Tyrants can invigorate the swarm, shatter their foe's morale or shred the minds of their prey.

Should the Hive Mind require it, Hive Tyrants can also be adapted to possess a pair of vast, leathery wings. Winged Hive Tyrants dominate the skies above a battlefield, swooping low to disembowel enemy commanders with a lash of their prehensile tails, or unleashing torrents of flesh-melting energy from monstrous bio-cannons. While such organisms may lack the speed of fighter aircraft, they are perfectly capable of smashing an unaware pilot out of the sky with their bladed hooves, sending burning fragments of his vessel raining onto the ground below.

Hive Tyrants embody the Tyranid Hive Mind completely, but their destruction does not in any way diminish it. Death is simply another learning experience that gives insight to the prey's strengths and weaknesses. This goes some way to explain why the Tyranids can rarely be defeated the same way twice. Should a Hive Tyrant be slain on the battlefield, the Hive Mind simply grows a replacement, imbuing it with the same knowledge as its predecessor. Fortunately for the rest of the galaxy, this does not lead to infallibility of purpose. Even the most fearsome Hive Tyrant cannot anticipate its prey's every ploy, nor can it oversee every quarter of the battlefield. However, the Hive Mind's capacity to regrow its fallen leaders does render each Hive Tyrant practically immortal. No matter how many times a Hive Tyrant is killed, sooner or later it will always come back to overcome and devour its prey.

The creature known as the Nephilim King is a particularly notorious Hive Tyrant specimen. This beast leads a splinter of Hive Fleet Behemoth, and fights at the head of a group of synapse creatures and gigantic bio-titans. This so-called Court of the Nephilim King relies not on sheer numbers, but on the ferocity and intelligence of the most advanced Tyranid bioforms, forming a twisted mirror of a knightly brotherhood. Countless foes have sought to slay the Nephilim King, but the monster has thus far turned the tables on all its would-be hunters, swiftly turning them from predator to prey.

THE SWARMLORD

HERALD OF THE HIVE MIND

Amongst the billions of creatures created by the Hive Mind, there exists one as old as the Tyranid race itself. This creature is the very pinnacle of the Hive Tyrant bioform, the ultimate conduit through which the Hive Mind's will is enforced. This creature is to a Hive Tyrant what a Hive Tyrant is to a Termagant. It is a monster of darkest nightmare that has preyed on empires and overseen the extinction of entire civilisations. It is a legendary destroyer of worlds and its names are legion. It is the Tyrantlord of the Hive Mind, the Herald of the Great Devourer and the Destroyer of the Kha'la Empire. To the Imperium of Man, the latest to face this ancient predator, it is the Swarmlord, and it represents the greatest Tyranid threat to the galaxy.

Since the First Tyrannic War, the Swarnlord has carved a path of carnage across the galaxy. It was responsible for the Scouring of the Megyre System, the destruction of the Brynarr race and the consumption of Waaagh! Gorgluk. Not only did these events span several centuries, but each was perpetrated by a different hive fleet. It would therefore appear that the Swarmlord's link with the Hive Mind transcends normal physical limitations. If the Swarmlord perishes on the battlefield, the Hive Mind reabsorbs its consciousness through the synaptic web. The Swarmlord is therefore deathless, and can be regrown to face the enemy again, returning stronger each time.

The reincarnation of the Swarmlord appears to be a stress-induced response by the hive fleets, one triggered when its prey cannot be defeated through biological adaptations alone. Indeed, each time it has been reborn, the Swarmlord has been created with the express purpose of out-thinking the enemy and developing new strategies to achieve the greatest results with the warrior-beasts fighting around it. To this end, the Swarmlord possesses more autonomy than any other Tyranid creature yet witnessed. The Swarmlord combines its own resourcefulness with experience accumulated through aeons of bloodshed. Such is the Swarmlord's alien cunning that, on several occasions during the Battle for Macragge, it was able to outmanoeuvre and outwit the Ultramarines, warriors whose own tactical acumen is legendary.

In the final days of the 41st Millenium, a colossal tendril of Hive Fleet Leviathan crashed down upon the Blood Angels' home world of Baal and its two moons, Baal Prime and Baal Secundus. Innumerable swarms of screeching bioforms fell upon the defending Blood Angels and their successor Chapters. At the heart of the Tyranid host that surrounded the great fortress monastery of Baal lurked a mighty Hive Tyrant wielding four vicious, serrated boneswords. This monster wreaked untold carnage during the assault, slaying scores of Space Marines and directing the flow of battle with lethal cunning.

As the battle approached its climax, Chapter Master Dante himself sallied forth to challenge the great beast. With a carving slice from the Axe Mortalis, Dante slew his foe, but he was gravely wounded in the act.

The Blood Angels were all but destroyed as a Chapter, and were saved only by the arrival of Primarch Guilliman and his Primaris Space Marine reinforcements.

None know the truth of what happened to the Swarmlord after the Cicatrix Maledictum tore reality open and devoured the tendril of Hive Fleet Leviathan surrounding Baal, yet only the foolishly hopeful believe the galaxy has seen the last of this dread creature. Should it return, the knowledge the Swarmlord will have absorbed from the war in the Baal System will only serve to make it a more dangerous foe than ever before.

TYRANID GUARDS

While many Tyranid creations are expendable, others are vital to a hive fleet's success. To this end, the Hive Mind has created a number of organisms whose sole role on the battlefield is the safeguarding and protection of other Tyranid bioforms. These creatures ignore even the most catastrophic wounds, single-mindedly defending their ward to the last.

TYRANT GUARD

Warriors who attempt to slay a Tyranid leader-beast are confronted with a wall of chitin-armoured bodies that bristles with huge, scything blades and crushing claws. There is no way past this deadly obstacle, and those who approach are clubbed to death or hacked apart, their ruptured bodies joining the moat of gore that surrounds the xenos shield wall. Not a single one of these organisms moves to chase a fleeing enemy; they stand immovable, ignoring the storms of fire that ricochet from their thick hides.

Tyrant Guard are colossal living shields. Their bulky bodies are protected by iron-hard exoskeletons covered by interlocking layers of impenetrable chitinous plates. As such they are all but impervious to small-arms fire. Tyrant Guard can wade through a torrent of rifle fire without breaking stride. Should heavy weaponry be brought to bear, several salvoes are required to fell even a single Tyrant Guard, for their bodies have developed an incredible resistance to injury. They are, at best, only dimly aware of pain and shrug off wounds that should, by rights, have blown them apart.

Tyrant Guard are the ultimate bodyguards; it is the entire purpose of their creation. They are driven by a bestial consciousness that knows little save for a ferocious loyalty to the Hive Tyrant they protect. Bodyguards from other races defend a charge out of a feeling of duty, suppressing their own survival instincts to do so – a fundamental conflict that slows reaction times. Tyrant Guard suffer no such limitations, for they are near mindless beasts engineered for but a single task. Their instincts tend not towards self-preservation, but to the defence of the Hive Tyrant to which they are bonded. Should the Hive Tyrant come under attack, its Tyrant Guard hurl themselves into the path of incoming fire without thought or concern, sheltering their master with their own bodies until the threat is ended or death takes them.

These organisms are blind, possessing no discernible means of seeing the enemy. However, eyes are not necessary for these bodyguards, for when they are guarding a Hive Tyrant they become extensions of their master's own body. The synaptic control of their ward provides the rudimentary direction these creatures need, alerting them to nearby threats and arranging them to best fend off any enemy assault. Furthermore, eyes would present a weak and vulnerable target for a canny foe to attack. Such a weakness would only expose a chink in the Tyrant Guard's otherwise impenetrable armour, compromising the role for which it was created.

Should their charge be slain, the Tyrant Guard go berserk, lashing out at the enemy with brutal ferocity and savage abandon. In such a state they slash and tear with their formidable bladed forelimbs, attacking with a ferocity that seems entirely at odds with their formerly stolid behaviour. In other races this might be seen as an emotional response driven by loss and failure, but such comparisons fare poorly when applied to Tyranids. A Tyrant Guard's rampage is not guided by grief, nor a sense of neglected duty, for such things are alien concepts to the Tyranids. Rather, the Tyrant Guards' reaction is part of the coldly calculated strategy of the Hive Mind. Hive Tyrants are vital to the Tyranid onslaught, and if the enemy finds a way to bring such a beast down, the Hive Mind does not want knowledge of how the feat was accomplished to survive the battle. The ensuing Tyrant Guard stampede is merely a conditioned response designed to slaughter the perpetrators so that the strategy cannot be passed on. Of course, this is of little consolation to anyone unfortunate enough to find themselves in the path of an enraged Tyrant Guard.

> 'We unleashed the fury of a Fenrisian blizzard upon those damned creatures, but no matter how true our axes struck, they would not fall. By the time Vjanr's plasma gun burned the last of them to slag there were but three of my pack still standing.'
>
> – Fynar Firepelt, Blood Claw

HIVE GUARD

Stocky, heavily armoured organisms lumber forward to form a phalanx in front of the advancing enemy, bracing their huge forms before unleashing a devastating volley from the massive bio-cannons fused to their flesh. Storms of vicious spines slice through the enemy ranks, punching through armour and bone, sending up a thick mist of blood. Even those warriors who dive for cover from this deadly barrage are not spared, for the hail of shards seems to veer unerringly past all obstacles, impaling them even as they look to return fire.

In the later stages of a Tyranid invasion, strange alien architecture blights a prey world. Towering spore chimneys burst from beneath the churned ground to belch their poisonous spores into the air, and capillary towers are grown to funnel the digested gruel of the planet's biomass to the hive ships in space. Such structures are vital to the Tyranids' attempt to consume a world, yet they have few defences of their own. Instead, the Hive Mind has created a specific beast for their protection – the Hive Guard.

Even amongst the Tyranid swarm, the Hive Guard stands out as being uniquely created to its role. It is essentially a gun-beast, with a heavily armoured centauroid form providing a durable and stable firing platform for the massive impaler cannon bonded to the beast's forelimbs. By bracing its powerful lower limbs, the Hive Guard is able to contain the impaler cannon's prodigious recoil, allowing a continuous and highly accurate stream of fire.

Though not as developed as that of the synapse creatures, Hive Guard possess a low-level telepathic ability that allows them to 'see' through the eyes of all other Tyranid organisms, giving them unconscious access to a wealth of tactical and targeting information that would overwhelm even the most sophisticated cogitators. Furthermore, a Hive Guard is even more closely bonded with the shard-beasts that comprise the ammunition of its impaler cannon. Through a complicated series of mental stimuli it can command the shard-beast to change vector whilst in flight, causing the projectile to veer and home in on the target with unerring accuracy. The combination of these two abilities means that a Hive Guard need not necessarily see a target itself to engage it.

A Hive Guard's nascent telepathic abilities do not come without a cost. The scant mental capacity apportioned to the Hive Guard for other tasks makes it an exclusively territorial beast. Without the direct goading of the Hive Mind, a Hive Guard is content to stand motionless, waiting for prey to come within range. Only when a Tyranid swarm encounters a heavily mechanised foe will the Hive Mind suppress the Hive Guard's natural imperatives and drive them forwards to the front lines. Whilst this might at first be thought of as an inherent flaw, it only furthers the Hive Guard's primary role. Indeed, what good is a stalwart defender if it aggressively pursues a target and leaves its charge unguarded?

Hive Guard have an incredibly short incubation cycle and can be maintained as end-stage larvae almost indefinitely. This means that rather than wasting precious biomass by creating and sustaining protectors that will stand idle, the Hive Mind can swiftly spawn Hive Guard wherever its advance is threatened, meeting an enemy counter-attack with salvo after salvo of intense firepower. Those few warriors who have launched a strike at the heart of a Tyranid bio-ship and returned alive report being suddenly surrounded by scores of these guardian organisms, spawned forth in haste by the vessel to defend its vital organs.

IMPALER CANNONS

Impaler cannons are huge assault weapons that propel osseous spines at a target with catastrophic force. These projectiles reach such a velocity that they can punch through reinforced plasteel.

At the base of each spine is a small creature known as a shard-beast that uses thin, membranous wings to steer the spine towards its target. Even enemy soldiers behind cover or moving at high speed must beware the fire of an impaler cannon, for shard-beasts home in on their quarry with unerring accuracy.

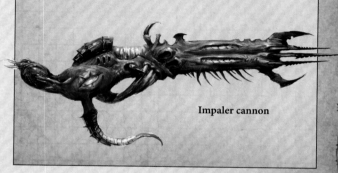

Impaler cannon

ARTILLERY ORGANISMS

Whilst many Tyranids organisms excel at tearing their prey apart at close quarters, the Hive Mind has created several with the express purpose of destroying its foes from a great distance. These 'living artillery' bioforms are not only powerful weapons in the Hive Mind's arsenal, but proof of the Tyranids' highly adaptive nature.

BIOVORES

A Biovore is a squat, bloated creature – yet no less deadly for all that. Deep within its lumpen form, the Biovore nurtures a clutch of Spore Mines – living bombs that blanket the enemy in acids, poisons and shrapnel-sized pieces of chitin. Biovores thump forward in battle, bony protrusions on their forelimbs anchoring themselves into the ground as they release their vile payload in a single shuddering spasm.

As the Spore Mine is flung through the air, its internal gas bladder inflates and it floats down towards ground level. Even if the shot misses its initial target, the danger it poses is far from over, for the Spore Mine is possessed of a rudimentary intelligence and detonates not on impact with the ground, but when it senses the proximity of a non-Tyranid life form.

When the Hive Mind wishes to deny the enemy access to a particular zone upon the battlefield, it will direct hosts of Biovores towards the area. There, they will unleash dozens of Spore Mines, creating a deadly and impassable hazard.

EXOCRINES

Exocrines are massive living weapon platforms that are rightly feared for their ability to deal death from afar. The most distinctive feature of an Exocrine is its dorsal bio-cannon, which emits a high-pitched hiss a second before firing, giving its prey just enough time to realise the danger they are in before searing plasma scours them into atoms. These artillery beasts are as lethal to heavy armour as they are to exposed troop formations. Exocrine plasma can eat its way through a tank's hull in moments, superheating the interior and incinerating the crew, or igniting munitions in a devastating fireball that tears the vehicle apart.

The Exocrine is purely a means of transportation for the weapon symbiote nested into its flesh. Whilst the Exocrine possesses considerable strength, it has a disproportionately small brain. Indeed, the dorsal bio-weapon has a larger mental capacity than its host and often diverts a portion of its own intelligence to subsume the Exocrine's will and guide it into a prime firing position. Only when the larger beast remains still can the symbiote focus all of its mental resources into targeting and destroying its prey.

Despite the Exocrine's relative simplicity, it is perfectly suited to its given task. Batteries of these lumbering beasts can wreak hideous damage upon armour columns or clustered groups of infantry. Though they are not amongst the fastest or most dexterous Tyranid bioforms, they are perfectly capable of tearing prey apart in close combat, smashing and crushing enemy soldiers with their powerful, bladed forelimbs.

TYRANNOFEXES

There can be little doubt that the massive Tyrannofex exists purely for destruction – it is a monster created for the most apocalyptic and gruelling of battlegrounds. Striding ominously towards their prey, these alien giants deal death from afar, shattering enemy battle lines with merciless salvos of bio-weapons fire. The only way to stop the unrelenting slaughter is to slay the beast, but a Tyrannofex has the fortitude of a living battle fortress and is heedless of all but the heaviest enemy ordnance. Clad in ablative layers of chitinous armour, a Tyrannofex is as unyielding as any war engine built of steel or born of conventional technology.

Given its enormous bulk, a Tyrannofex is ponderous and prone to being overwhelmed in a protracted melee. Therefore, the Hive Mind rarely unleashes such a creature without at least a brood or more of Termagants to act as close support and defence, allowing the Tyrannofex itself to concentrate on blasting the enemy asunder with its fearsome weapon symbiotes. Cluster spine launchers nestling within thick armour plates provide the Tyrannofex with a formidable anti-infantry arsenal, but it is for the giant bio-cannon cradled in its forelimbs that this hulking warrior-beast is most feared across the galaxy.

The Tyrannofex's primary bio-weapon is amongst the largest and most destructive to be carried by any Tyranid bioform smaller than a bio-titan. The precise nature of this weapon symbiote is different from creature to creature, ranging from acid sprays that can melt entire infantry formations to giant bio-cannons that can punch holes clean through Space Marine Land Raiders or Necron Monoliths.

TYRANID BIO-TITANS

Tyranid bio-titans are the most gigantic of all the monstrosities unleashed by the hive fleets, and are brought into action only against the most determined defences. They are immense creatures, towering over the battlefield and bristling with spines, claws, tendrils and apocalyptic bio-weapons. The most commonly encountered bio-titans unleashed by the hive fleets are the Hierodule and the even larger Hierophant. Though classified as Titans by the indigenous races of the galaxy, these monsters bear little resemblance to the noble war engines of the Adeptus Mechanicus, the graceful wraithbone constructs of the Aeldari, or even the idol-like Gargants of the Orks, except in terms of size and lethality.

As with all Tyranid organisms, rapid adaptation is common to bio-titans. Like the hive ships that created them, bio-titans appear to be composites of several different creatures so closely fused together that they have become an indistinguishable whole. Bio-titans are notoriously difficult to kill, even with super-heavy weaponry. They are protected by ridged plates of chitin that are angled to deflect incoming blasts. Even if this exterior is penetrated, the composite nature of these behemoths means that a fatal injury to one symbiote is unlikely to slay the bio-titan as a whole. Only the focused firepower of an enemy Titan, or the combined ordnance of an entire army, have a hope of destroying a bio-titan. Whether such arms can bring the beast down before it rips the enemy battle line to shreds is another question entirely…

'How ironic it is that, as fast as we spread progress and hope throughout the galaxy, the Tyranids spread death and despair.'

- Aun'Shi of Vior'la

FEEDER ORGANISMS

The hive fleets create many organisms whose sole role is the consumption of biomass. Whilst the Ripper is the simplest and most numerous of such creatures, the Hive Mind has also created several larger species of feeder-beast, hulking bioforms can speed up the digestion of a prey world tenfold, devouring and pre-digesting vast quantities of organic matter.

HARUSPEXES

The Tyranid Haruspex is a ferocious beast created to consume biomass at a sickening pace. It is possessed of a rapacious appetite, driven by the need to sate an infinite hunger. Few foes are foolish enough to stand before a feeding Haruspex, for it can devour an entire platoon of soldiers in a matter of moments, shovelling victim after victim into its craw without ever slowing down. Any morsel that proves too large to be swallowed in one gulp is seized with the Haruspex's gargantuan claws and ripped, crushed or battered apart with negligent ease. Buildings are smashed open, battle tanks torn asunder and the unfortunate prey sheltering inside hungrily devoured. Only those that turn and flee have any hope of survival, and only then if they can avoid the Haruspex's grasping tongue as it lashes out to grab hold of its prey and drag it, kicking and screaming, into its vast maw.

For the few who know the horror of the Tyranids, the appearance of a Haruspex upon the battlefield is a chilling omen of death, for the hive fleets send these creatures forth when the doom of a prey world is assured. It is the role of the Haruspexes to speed up the Tyranids' process of consumption and digestion, and they go about this task with a sickening fervour. Unleashed to carry out their ravenous imperative, a host of these creatures can devour every scrap of flesh upon a battlefield in a matter of hours, their dagger-like teeth crunching through armour and bone with ease. When a Haruspex has gorged itself to the point where it can consume no more, it will find the nearest Tyranid digestion pool and vomit forth the contents of its stomach. Then, it will begin the hunt once more.

PYROVORES

Pyrovores exist to pre-digest biomass; their maws drip with acids that reduce flesh, metal and even stone to a smouldering mucous for consumption by other Tyranids. A Pyrovore's primary threat is its dorsal bio-weapon, which can launch searing flames to reduce its foes to ash. Slaying a Pyrovore is not without risk either, for its deathblow can ignite volatile ichors within its stomachs in an explosion that leaves behind only charred scraps of flesh and a foul smell.

RIPPER SWARMS

From the moment a Tyranid hive fleet makes planetfall, countless voracious organisms are released. The most numerous amongst these feeder beasts are the Rippers. These diminutive creatures sweep across the world's surface, their numbers ever growing as they consume everything in their path. Rippers follow hard on the heels of the main Tyranid advance, hungrily devouring the dead and wounded.

A Ripper Swarm is a writhing mat of maggot-like Tyranid organisms driven by a single voracious appetite. Created in untold numbers by the hive fleets, each Ripper is little more than an armoured serpent, terminating in a broad maw crammed with needle-sharp teeth. They are persistent, and quite capable of pulling down creatures many times their size. Once a Ripper's jaws tighten around its prey, they stay clamped shut until a mouthful of flesh is torn away or the Ripper is slain. On the rare occasions when the Rippers discover an obstacle that cannot be chewed through, they burrow beneath the obstruction, guided towards the prey by ferocious feeding instincts.

Rippers are typically unleashed by the Hive Mind as the invasion cycle nears its end, as it is their task to devour every last trace of biomass upon the prey world. Nothing is left to waste. Every scrap of flesh, shred of vegetation and drop of water is consumed, until finally the world resembles little more than a rocky, airless tomb. Once a Ripper has devoured its fill, it will be instinctively drawn towards one of the gigantic digestion pools that the hive fleet has scattered across the planet. There, the Ripper does not waste valuable energy by depositing the contents of its stomach – rather, it hurls itself into the boiling gruel, its short, vicious life ending as it is reabsorbed into the Tyranid feeding cycle.

THE PARASITE OF MORTREX

The Imperial fortress world of Mortrex was one of the most heavily defended planets in Segmentum Ultima – a world where fortifications sprouted from every mountainside and bastions punctuated the landscape. For days, when Hive Fleet Kraken attacked, this formidable defence held back the vicious hordes. However, during the tenth day of the invasion, the Imperial Guard defending Mortrex encountered a winged bioform they had never seen before. Without warning, the monster dove towards the human entrenchments, stabbing at the Imperial Guardsmen with lightning-quick strikes of its tail. The creature's victims were thus injected with Ripper parasites, many of which grew to maturity within a few heartbeats, devouring their hosts from the inside out. Amidst agonised death screams, a swarm of Rippers ruptured through cracked bones and torn flesh as they emerged in a spray of blood. The few survivors told of the new Tyranid threat, a horrifying creature that implants organisms into its still-living prey.

They called this creature the Parasite, and all knew that to face it was to risk the most horrific death imaginable. Two weeks later, the planet of Mortrex was overrun by vast, ravenous tides of Ripper Swarms. All that remained was a single transmission that warned of the Parasite.

COLOURS OF THE HIVE FLEETS

A Tyranid swarm is a terrifying sight, a host of hungry-eyed xenos encased in chitin armour and wielding bizarre organic weaponry. No two forces will look entirely the same, for each hive fleet has adapted its own colouration and predatory behaviours.

Hive Fleet Leviathan Hive Tyrant with heavy venom cannon and monstrous bonesword

Hive Fleet Leviathan launches its invasion swarms across a fortress world garrisoned by the Ultramarines. Bolter rounds and missiles thunder into an ocean of surging, skittering bodies, but even the Space Marines' pinpoint fusillades cannot hold back the tide.

Tyrant Guard with scything talons and rending claws

Tyranid Warrior with devourer and scything talons

A Leviathan swarm falls upon a vectorium of Death Guard, encircling the Chaos Space Marines in a deadly trap.

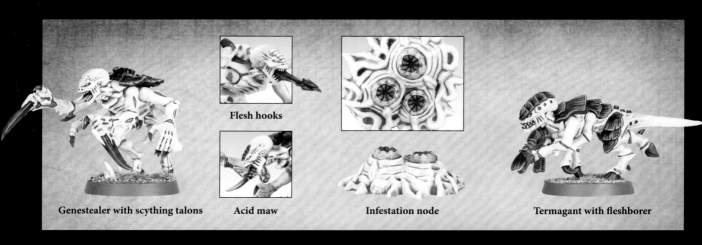

Genestealer with scything talons

Flesh hooks

Acid maw

Infestation node

Termagant with fleshborer

Hive Fleet Leviathan Tervigon with massive crushing claws

Hive Fleet Leviathan Haruspex

The T'au expend vital ammunition on surging gaunts and Genestealers, while hulking, blade-limbed monsters draw ever closer.

Gargoyle

Genestealer with scything talons

Termagant

Hive Fleet Kraken Hive Guard
with shockcannon

Carnifexes are brutal killing machines used as linebreakers and siege beasts. The spined Thornback and plasma-spitting Screamer-Killer are rightly feared by those few that know of their existence.

Bone mace

Adrenal glands

Stranglethorn cannon

Carnifex with stranglethorn cannon and adrenal glands

Spine banks

Thresher scythe

Chitin thorns

Thornback with thresher scythe and two deathspitters with slimer maggots

Spore cysts

Enhanced senses

Monstrous acid maw

Bio-plasma

Tusks

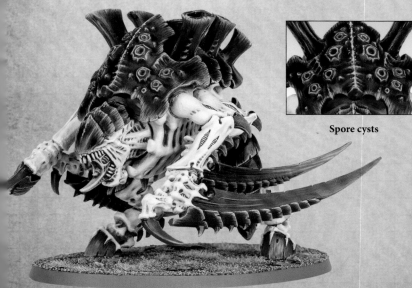

Screamer-Killer with spore cysts and monstrous scything talons

Hive Fleet Leviathan Exocrine

Hive Fleet Leviathan Tyrannofex with rupture cannon

Tyranid Warrior with venom cannon and boneswords

Hive Fleet Behemoth Lictor

Gargoyle

Genestealer

Hormagaunt

The ground shakes as the hyper-aggressive organisms of Hive Fleet Behemoth charge towards their prey in a roaring stampede.

The Tyranids are an utterly alien race for whom biological adaptation is rapid and instinctive. There is no limit to the colours and markings borne by the different hive fleets.

Hive Fleet Tiamet

Hive Fleet Gorgon

Hive Fleet Hydra

Hive Fleet Jormungandr

Hive Fleet Kronos

Hive Fleet Ouroboris

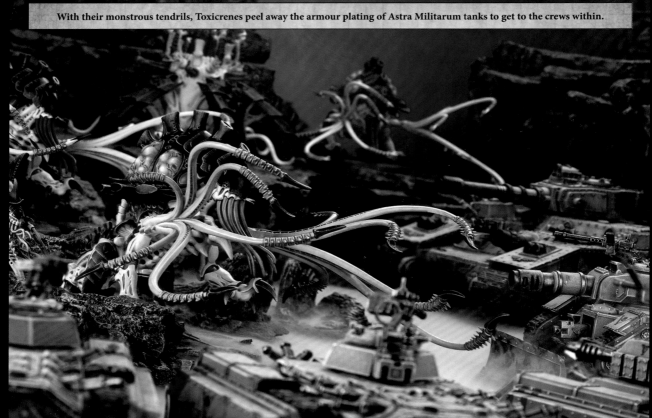

With their monstrous tendrils, Toxicrenes peel away the armour plating of Astra Militarum tanks to get to the crews within.

COLLECTING A TYRANID SWARM

A Tyranid swarm is an adaptable and deadly force upon the battlefield, capable of obliterating foes from afar or closing in to tear them to shreds. The sample force below is designed to dominate its prey in close combat.

When collecting a Tyranid army, think about the way you want it to fight on the tabletop – would you prefer to overwhelm your opponent with massed firepower or rip their forces apart in close combat with blade-talons and slavering jaws? You can have the best of both worlds, of course – most Tyranids with long-range weapons are more than capable of holding their own in an assault. On the other hand, a pure close-combat army can easily swamp enemy formations with huge broods of creatures.

The force shown below focuses on getting up close and personal with the enemy. It is led by a Broodlord, a hulking monster rippling with muscle and boasting monstrous rending claws that can tear through power armour as if it were kindling.

A pack of Genestealers is the Troops choice, another potent melee unit that directly benefits from the Broodlord's support abilities. Finally, a Trygon adds significant muscle; its own scything talons are perfect for shredding any vehicles foolish enough to stray close.

This collection of gorgeously detailed models provides an impressive core to build upon. With one HQ choice, a Troops unit and a single Heavy Support, it also fulfills the requirements for a Patrol Detachment, as described in the *Warhammer 40,000* rulebook. As a Battle-forged army, this means you can make use of three Command Points to spend on Statagems during a game.

This Broodlord and its Genestealers utilise the subterranean channels clawed out by a Trygon to launch their deadly ambushes.

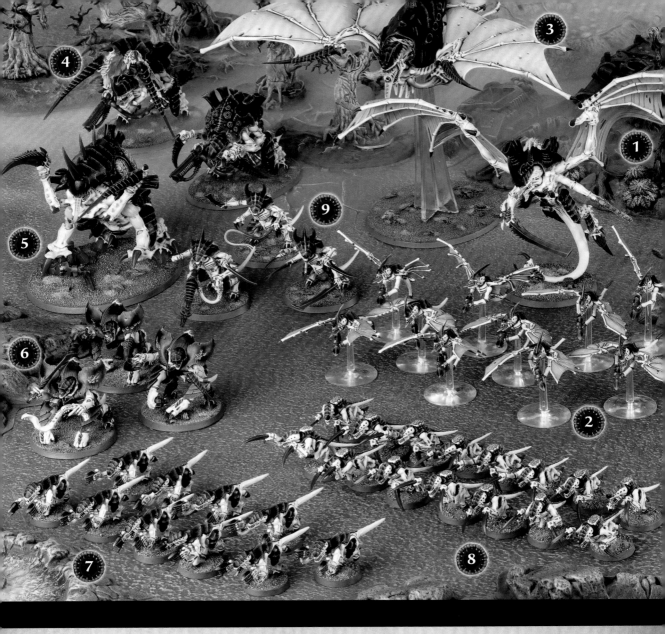

CLAWS OF THE GREAT DEVOURER

The army pictured above represents the overwhelming force of Hive Fleet Leviathan, and shows just how versatile and visually satisfying the Tyranid range can be. Based around the models from the previous page, it has been expanded to add a formidable core of infantry, flying troops and psychic bioforms, as well as a number of super-heavy organisms who will wreak utter destruction upon your enemies in any game of Warhammer 40,000!

A Tyranid ground swarm forms the backbone of this force. Dozens of Termagants and Hormagaunts – as well as voracious Ripper Swarms – will bound towards the enemy lines, a skittering horde of blade-limbed killers that will soak up enemy fire and provide cover for more advanced organisms, even as they rip and tear at the foe. Meanwhile, the Broodlord and its Genestealers can provide a nasty surprise for unsuspecting foes, appearing from

their hidden lairs in the heat of battle and falling upon their stunned prey with slashing claws. Deathleaper provides another stealth option, and is equally capable of ripping infantry and isolated enemy leaders to shreds.

At the heart of the swarm is the Winged Hive Tyrant, which acts as both leader and spear-tip; its potent psychic powers, considerable combat prowess and xenos cunning making it a formidable foe. Soaring over the battlefield on leathery, bat-like wings, this devastatingly powerful creature can quickly respond to any danger, rallying nearby Termagants and Hormagaunts with the power of its synaptic domination. A unit of Tyrant Guard will ensure the enemy does not stray too close to this vital leader-beast. Also supporting the Hive Tyrant is a gathering of some of the deadliest creations in the Hive Mind's arsenal. A Tervigon matches the Hive

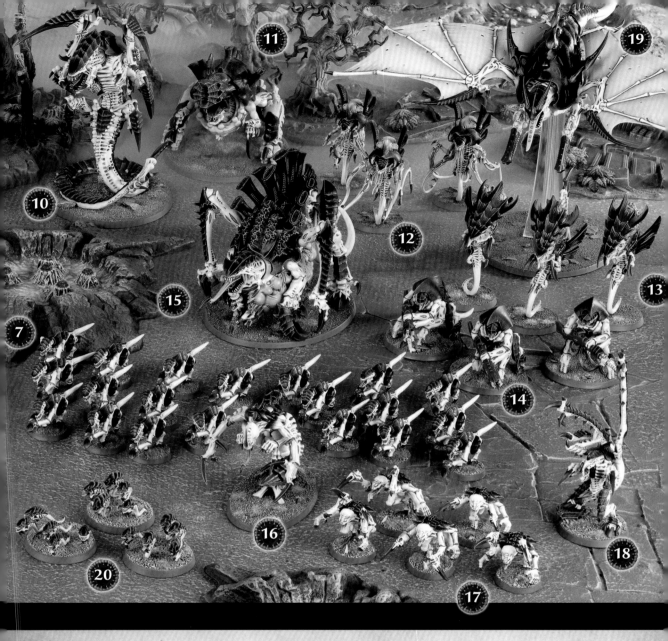

Tyrant for psychic power and can spew Termagant reinforcements into the fray. The Maleceptor is a potent psyker that can ravage nearby foes with the full power of the Shadow in the Warp, while an Exocrine provides long-range blasts of searing bio-plasma. An elite unit of Tyranid Warriors and two Carnifexes will exploit any weaknesses in the enemy line with brutal force, while Venomthropes, Zoanthropes and a unit of Hive Guard provide formidable and adaptable firepower. A Harpy and Hive Crone will dominate the skies, using their high manoeuvrability to pose a significant threat to enemies both on the ground and in the air. They are accompanied by a flock of Gargoyles, who are excellent at harrying and tying up enemy infantry units.

Though this army operates as a formidable Battalion Detachment, its owner could easily opt for a smaller, more specialised force by selecting a number of units from the larger swarm to form a separate Detachment, with its own complement of Command Points.

1. **Winged Hive Tyrant**

2. **Gargoyles**

3. **Hive Crone**

4. **Carnifexes**

5. **Maleceptor**

6. **Tyrant Guard**

7. **Termagants**

8. **Hormagaunts**

9. **Tyranid Warriors**

10. **Trygon**

11. **Exocrine**

12. **Venomthropes**

13. **Zoanthropes**

14. **Hive Guard**

15. **Tervigon**

16. **Broodlord**

17. **Genestealers**

18. **Deathleaper**

19. **Harpy**

20. **Ripper Swarms**

THE TYRANID SWARM

This section contains all of the datasheets that you will need in order to fight battles with your Tyranids miniatures. Each datasheet includes the characteristics profiles of the unit it describes, as well as any wargear and abilities it may have. Some rules are common to several Tyranids units – these are described below and are referenced on the datasheets.

KEYWORDS

Throughout this section you will come across a keyword that is within angular brackets, specifically <HIVE FLEET>. This is shorthand for a keyword of your own choosing, as described below.

<HIVE FLEET>

All Tyranids belong to a hive fleet. When you include a Tyranids unit in your army, you must nominate which hive fleet that unit is from. There are many different hive fleets to choose from; you can use any of the hive fleets described in this book, or make up your own if you prefer. You then simply replace the <HIVE FLEET> keyword in every instance on that unit's datasheet, and in any psychic powers they know, with the name of your chosen hive fleet.

For example, if you were to include a Tervigon in your army, and you decided it was from Hive Fleet Kraken, then its <HIVE FLEET> keyword is changed to KRAKEN, and its 'Brood Progenitor' ability would say 'You can re-roll hit rolls of 1 in the Shooting phase for friendly KRAKEN Termagant units within 6" of this model.'

ABILITIES

The following abilities are common to several Tyranids units:

SYNAPSE

Some Tyranids serve as synaptic conduits or nodal relays through which a portion of the Hive Mind's iron will flows, overriding the natural instincts of the swarm.

<HIVE FLEET> units automatically pass Morale tests if they are within 12" of any friendly <HIVE FLEET> units with this ability.

INSTINCTIVE BEHAVIOUR

Unless controlled or coordinated by the domineering will of the Hive Mind, many Tyranid organisms will revert to their baser instincts.

Unless a <HIVE FLEET> unit with this ability is within 24" of any friendly <HIVE FLEET> SYNAPSE unit, you must subtract 1 from any hit rolls made for it when shooting any target other than the nearest visible enemy unit, and you must subtract 2 from its charge roll if it declares a charge against any unit other than the nearest enemy unit.

SHADOW IN THE WARP

The unfathomable presence of the Hive Mind radiates out from its synapse creatures, smothering the ability of the psykers who stand before them to draw upon their mystic powers.

Enemy PSYKERS must subtract 1 from any Psychic tests they make if they are within 18" of any units with this ability. TYRANID PSYKERS are not affected.

> 'By the Dark Prince, how I despise these dull creatures. No matter the mutilations I work upon the canvas of their bodies, I gain no satisfaction. Denied the exquisite sensations of mortal horror, my art becomes meaningless. Prosaic.'
>
> - Lord Gadrovian, the Flesh Sculptor

TYRANIDS WARGEAR LISTS

Many of the units you will find on the following pages reference one or more of the following wargear lists (e.g. Basic Bio-cannons). When this is the case, the unit may take any item from the appropriate list below. The profiles for the weapons in these lists can be found in the Weapons of the Hive Fleets section (pg 111-113).

BASIC BIO-WEAPONS
- Scything talons
- Spinefists
- Deathspitter

BASIC BIO-CANNONS
- Barbed strangler
- Venom cannon

MELEE BIO-WEAPONS
- Rending claws
- Boneswords
- Lash whip and bonesword

MONSTROUS BIO-WEAPONS
- Monstrous rending claws
- Monstrous boneswords
- Lash whip and monstrous bonesword

MONSTROUS BIO-CANNONS
- Two deathspitters with slimer maggots
- Two devourers with brainleech worms
- Stranglethorn cannon*
- Heavy venom cannon*

*A model cannot be armed with more than one of these weapons.

BROODLORD

NAME	M	WS	BS	S	T	W	A	Ld	Sv
Broodlord	8"	2+	-	5	5	6	6	10	4+

A Broodlord is a single model armed with monstrous rending claws.

WEAPON	RANGE	TYPE	S	AP	D	ABILITIES
Monstrous rending claws	Melee	Melee	User	-3	D3	You can re-roll failed wound rolls for this weapon. In addition, each time you make a wound roll of 6+, that hit is resolved with an AP of -6 and Damage of 3.

ABILITIES	Synapse, Shadow in the Warp (pg 82)
	Lightning Reflexes: This model has a 5+ invulnerable save.
	Swift and Deadly: This model can charge even if it Advanced during its turn.
	Brood Telepathy: You can add 1 to hit rolls in the Fight phase for <Hive Fleet> Genestealer units within 6" of any friendly <Hive Fleet> Broodlords.
PSYKER	A Broodlord can attempt to manifest one psychic power in each friendly Psychic phase, and attempt to deny one psychic power in each enemy Psychic phase. It knows the *Smite* psychic power and one psychic power from the Hive Mind discipline (pg 121).
FACTION KEYWORDS	TYRANIDS, <Hive Fleet>
KEYWORDS	CHARACTER, INFANTRY, GENESTEALER, PSYKER, SYNAPSE, BROODLORD

Guided by the synaptic impulses of a Broodlord, Genestealers attack with increased ferocity and coordination.

HIVE TYRANT

DAMAGE			
Some of this model's characteristics change as it suffers damage, as shown below:			
REMAINING W	M	WS	BS
7-12+	9"/16"	2+	3+
4-6	7"/12"	3+	3+
1-3	5"/8"	4+	4+

NAME	M	WS	BS	S	T	W	A	Ld	Sv
Hive Tyrant	*	*	*	6	7	12	4	10	3+

A Hive Tyrant is a single model armed with two pairs of monstrous scything talons and a prehensile pincer tail.

WEAPON	RANGE	TYPE	S	AP	D	ABILITIES
Monstrous scything talons	Melee	Melee	User	-3	3	You can re-roll hit rolls of 1 for this weapon. If the bearer has more than one pair of monstrous scything talons, it can make 1 additional attack with this weapon each time it fights.
Prehensile pincer tail	Melee	Melee	User	0	D3	Each time the bearer fights, it can make one (and only one) attack with this weapon. This is in addition to the bearer's attacks.

WARGEAR OPTIONS	
	• A Hive Tyrant may replace one pair of monstrous scything talons with one item from the *Monstrous Bio-cannons* or *Monstrous Bio-weapons* list. • A Hive Tyrant may replace both pairs of monstrous scything talons with two items from the *Monstrous Bio-cannons* or two items from the *Monstrous Bio-weapons* list, or with one item from each list. • This model may have wings (**Power Rating +2**). If it does, it uses the second set of Move characteristics in the damage table above, and it gains the **FLY** keyword. • This model may have toxin sacs and/or adrenal glands (pg 113).

ABILITIES		
	Shadow in the Warp, **Synapse** (pg 82) **The Will of the Hive Mind:** The range of a Hive Tyrant's Synapse ability is 18" rather than 12". **Swooping Assault:** During deployment, you can set up a Hive Tyrant with wings circling high above instead of placing it on the battlefield. At the end of any of your Movement phases it can swoop down – set it up anywhere on the battlefield that is more than 9" from any enemy models.	**Death Throes:** If this model is reduced to 0 wounds, roll a dice before removing the model from the battlefield; on a 6, it lashes out in its death throes, and each unit within 3" suffers D3 mortal wounds. **Psychic Barrier:** A Hive Tyrant has a 4+ invulnerable save.

PSYKER	
	A Hive Tyrant can attempt to manifest two psychic powers in each friendly Psychic phase, and attempt to deny one psychic power in each enemy Psychic phase. It knows the *Smite* power and two psychic powers from the Hive Mind discipline (pg 121).

FACTION KEYWORDS	**TYRANIDS, <HIVE FLEET>**
KEYWORDS	**CHARACTER, MONSTER, PSYKER, SYNAPSE, HIVE TYRANT**

'A new Tyrant joined the fray, and in an eye-blink the whole character of the swarm changed. The ravening berserker-spirit that had driven the Tyranids onto the ridge was gone, as if it had never existed. Left in its place was something cannier, and infinitely more worrisome. It was then that I knew the battle to be lost.'

- Sergeant Telion, Ultramarines 10th Company

THE SWARMLORD

15 POWER

NAME	M	WS	BS	S	T	W	A	Ld	Sv
The Swarmlord	*	2+	3+	*	7	12	*	10	3+

DAMAGE
Some of this model's characteristics change as it suffers damage, as shown below:

REMAINING W	M	S	A
7-12+	9"	8	6
4-6	7"	7	5
1-3	5"	6	4

The Swarmlord is a single model armed with bone sabres and a prehensile pincer tail. Only one of this model may be included in your army.

WEAPON	RANGE	TYPE	S	AP	D	ABILITIES
Bone sabres	Melee	Melee	User	-3	3	Each time you make a wound roll of 6+ for this weapon, the target unit suffers a mortal wound in addition to any other damage.
Prehensile pincer tail	Melee	Melee	User	0	D3	Each time the bearer fights, it can make one (and only one) attack with this weapon. This is in addition to the bearer's attacks.

| ABILITIES | Shadow in the Warp, Synapse (pg 82)

Psychic Barrier: The Swarmlord has a 4+ invulnerable save.

Blade Parry: Add 1 to the Swarmlord's invulnerable saves against wounds caused by Melee weapons.

Hive Commander: In each of your Shooting phases, you can pick one friendly <Hive Fleet> unit within 6" of the Swarmlord. That unit can move (and Advance, if you wish) as if it were the Movement phase instead of shooting. | The Will of the Hive Mind: The range of the Swarmlord's Synapse ability is 18" rather than 12".

Death Throes: If this model is reduced to 0 wounds, roll a dice before removing the model from the battlefield; on a 6, it lashes out in its death throes, and each unit within 3" suffers D3 mortal wounds. |
|-----------|---|

PSYKER	The Swarmlord can attempt to manifest two psychic powers in each friendly Psychic phase, and attempt to deny two psychic powers in each enemy Psychic phase. It knows the *Smite* power and two psychic powers from the Hive Mind discipline (pg 121).
FACTION KEYWORDS	TYRANIDS, <HIVE FLEET>
KEYWORDS	CHARACTER, MONSTER, HIVE TYRANT, PSYKER, SYNAPSE, THE SWARMLORD

TYRANID PRIME

6 POWER

NAME	M	WS	BS	S	T	W	A	Ld	Sv
Tyranid Prime	6"	2+	3+	5	5	6	4	10	3+

A Tyranid Prime is a single model armed with scything talons and a devourer.

WEAPON	RANGE	TYPE	S	AP	D	ABILITIES
Devourer	18"	Assault 3	4	0	1	-
Flesh hooks	6"	Assault 2	User	0	1	This weapon can be fired within 1" of an enemy unit, and can target enemy units within 1" of friendly units.
Scything talons	Melee	Melee	User	0	1	You can re-roll hit rolls of 1 for this weapon. If the bearer has more than one pair of scything talons, it can make 1 additional attack with this weapon each time it fights.

| WARGEAR OPTIONS | • This model may replace its devourer with one weapon from the *Basic Bio-weapons* or *Melee Bio-weapons* list.
• This model may replace its scything talons with one weapon from the *Melee Bio-weapons* list.
• This model may have flesh hooks.
• This model may have toxin sacs and/or adrenal glands (pg 113). |
|-----------------|---|
| ABILITIES | Shadow in the Warp, Synapse (pg 82)

Alpha Warrior: You can add 1 to hit rolls for all <Hive Fleet> Tyranid Warrior units that are within 6" of any friendly <Hive Fleet> Tyranid Primes. |
| FACTION KEYWORDS | TYRANIDS, <HIVE FLEET> |
| KEYWORDS | CHARACTER, INFANTRY, SYNAPSE, TYRANID PRIME |

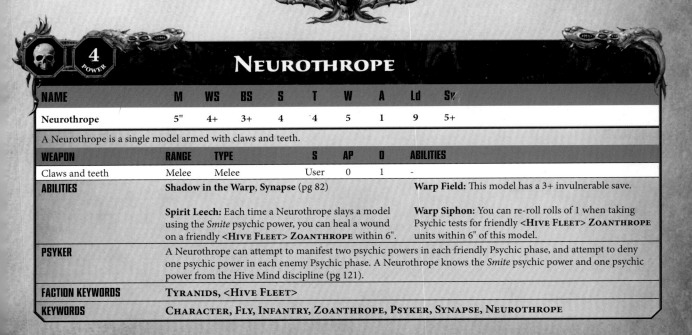

TERVIGON

POWER 13

NAME	M	WS	BS	S	T	W	A	Ld	Sv
Tervigon	*	*	*	7	8	14	3	9	3+

A Tervigon is a single model armed with massive scything talons. It can also fire stinger salvoes.

DAMAGE

Some of this model's characteristics change as it suffers damage, as shown below:

REMAINING W	M	WS	BS
8-14+	8"	4+	4+
4-7	6"	5+	5+
1-3	4"	5+	6+

WEAPON	RANGE	TYPE	S	AP	D	ABILITIES
Stinger salvo	24"	Assault 4	5	-1	1	-
Massive crushing claws	Melee	Melee	x2	-3	D6	When attacking with this weapon, you must subtract 1 from the hit roll.
Massive scything talons	Melee	Melee	User	-3	D6	You can re-roll hit rolls of 1 for this weapon. If the bearer has more than one pair of massive scything talons, it can make 1 additional attack with this weapon each time it fights.

WARGEAR OPTIONS	• This model may replace its massive scything talons with massive crushing claws. • This model may have toxin sacs and/or adrenal glands (pg 113).

ABILITIES	Shadow in the Warp, Synapse (pg 82) **Brood Progenitor:** You can re-roll hit rolls of 1 in the Shooting phase for friendly <Hive Fleet> Termagant units within 6" of this model. **Synaptic Backlash:** If a Tervigon is reduced to 0 wounds, roll a D6 before removing the model from the battlefield. Each friendly <Hive Fleet> Termagant unit within 6" of the Tervigon immediately suffers a number of mortal wounds equal to the result.	**Spawn Termagants:** At the start of your Movement phase, a Tervigon can spawn Termagants. If it does so, add a new unit of 10 Termagants to your army and set it up on the battlefield so that it is wholly within 6" of the Tervigon and more than 1" from the enemy. All of these models are armed with fleshborers. Alternatively, you can replace up to 10 models lost earlier in the battle in an existing unit of Termagants from your army that is within 6" of the Tervigon. Models placed in this way must be within 6" of the Tervigon and more than 1" from the enemy. You can only replace models armed with fleshborers. If you cannot place some of the models the excess is discarded.

PSYKER	A Tervigon can attempt to manifest one psychic power in each friendly Psychic phase, and attempt to deny one psychic power in each enemy Psychic phase. It knows the *Smite* power and one psychic power from the Hive Mind discipline (pg 121).

FACTION KEYWORDS	TYRANIDS, <Hive Fleet>
KEYWORDS	CHARACTER, MONSTER, PSYKER, SYNAPSE, TERVIGON

NEUROTHROPE

POWER 4

NAME	M	WS	BS	S	T	W	A	Ld	Sv
Neurothrope	5"	4+	3+	4	4	5	1	9	5+

A Neurothrope is a single model armed with claws and teeth.

WEAPON	RANGE	TYPE	S	AP	D	ABILITIES
Claws and teeth	Melee	Melee	User	0	1	-

ABILITIES	Shadow in the Warp, Synapse (pg 82) **Spirit Leech:** Each time a Neurothrope slays a model using the *Smite* psychic power, you can heal a wound on a friendly <Hive Fleet> Zoanthrope within 6".	**Warp Field:** This model has a 3+ invulnerable save. **Warp Siphon:** You can re-roll rolls of 1 when taking Psychic tests for friendly <Hive Fleet> Zoanthrope units within 6" of this model.

PSYKER	A Neurothrope can attempt to manifest two psychic powers in each friendly Psychic phase, and attempt to deny one psychic power in each enemy Psychic phase. A Neurothrope knows the *Smite* psychic power and one psychic power from the Hive Mind discipline (pg 121).

FACTION KEYWORDS	TYRANIDS, <Hive Fleet>
KEYWORDS	CHARACTER, FLY, INFANTRY, ZOANTHROPE, PSYKER, SYNAPSE, NEUROTHROPE

OLD ONE EYE

10 POWER

NAME	M	WS	BS	S	T	W	A	Ld	Sv
Old One Eye	7"	3+	-	7	7	9	5	7	3+

Old One Eye is a single model armed with monstrous crushing claws, monstrous scything talons and a thresher scythe. Only one of this model may be included in your army.

WEAPON	RANGE	TYPE	S	AP	D	ABILITIES
Monstrous crushing claws	Melee	Melee	x2	-3	3	When attacking with this weapon, you must subtract 1 from the hit roll.
Monstrous scything talons	Melee	Melee	User	-3	3	You can re-roll hit rolls of 1 for this weapon.
Thresher scythe	Melee	Melee	4	-1	1	Each time the bearer fights, it can make one (and only one) attack with this weapon. Make D3 hit rolls for this attack instead of one. This is in addition to the bearer's attacks.

ABILITIES	**Instinctive Behaviour** (pg 82) **Immortal Battering Ram:** When Old One Eye finishes a charge move, roll a dice; on a 4+ one enemy unit within 1" suffers D3 mortal wounds. In addition, add 1 to all hit rolls for Old One Eye in the Fight phase if it charged in the same turn. **Alpha Leader:** You can add 1 to hit rolls in the Fight phase for friendly <Hive Fleet> Carnifex units that are within 6" of this model.	**Berserk Rampage:** Each time you make a hit roll of 6+ for Old One Eye (except for thresher scythe attacks), you may immediately make 1 additional attack with the same weapon against the same unit. These additional attacks do not confer extra attacks. **Regeneration:** At the beginning of each of your turns, this model heals one wound.
FACTION KEYWORDS	**TYRANIDS, <HIVE FLEET>**	
KEYWORDS	**CHARACTER, MONSTER, CARNIFEX, OLD ONE EYE**	

Old One Eye is an unstoppable force of destruction that has plagued the Imperium for centuries.

5 POWER
TYRANID WARRIORS

NAME	M	WS	BS	S	T	W	A	Ld	Sv
Tyranid Warrior	6"	3+	4+	4	4	3	3	9	4+

This unit contains 3 Tyranid Warriors. It can include up to 3 additional Tyranid Warriors (**Power Rating +4**) or up to 6 additional Tyranid Warriors (**Power Rating +8**). Each model is armed with a pair of scything talons and a devourer.

WEAPON	RANGE	TYPE	S	AP	D	ABILITIES
Devourer	18"	Assault 3	4	0	1	-
Flesh hooks	6"	Assault 2	User	0	1	This weapon can be fired within 1" of an enemy unit, and can target enemy units within 1" of friendly units.
Scything talons	Melee	Melee	User	0	1	You can re-roll hit rolls of 1 for this weapon. If the bearer has more than one pair of scything talons, it can make 1 additional attack with this weapon each time it fights.

WARGEAR OPTIONS	
	• Any model may replace its devourer with one weapon from the *Basic Bio-weapons* or *Melee Bio-weapons* list. • Any model may replace its scything talons with one weapon from the *Melee Bio-weapons* list. • For every three models in the unit, one model may replace its devourer with one weapon from the *Basic Bio-cannons* list. • All models in the unit may have flesh hooks. • All models in the unit may have toxin sacs and/or adrenal glands (pg 113).

ABILITIES	**Synapse**, **Shadow in the Warp** (pg 82)
FACTION KEYWORDS	**TYRANIDS, <HIVE FLEET>**
KEYWORDS	**INFANTRY, SYNAPSE, TYRANID WARRIORS**

4 POWER
GENESTEALERS

NAME	M	WS	BS	S	T	W	A	Ld	Sv
Genestealer	8"	3+	4+	4	4	1	3	9	5+

This unit contains 5 Genestealers. It can include up to 5 additional Genestealers (**Power Rating +4**), up to 10 additional Genestealers (**Power Rating +8**), or up to 15 additional Genestealers (**Power Rating +12**). Each model is armed with rending claws.

WEAPON	RANGE	TYPE	S	AP	D	ABILITIES
Flesh hooks	6"	Assault 2	User	0	1	This weapon can be fired within 1" of an enemy unit, and can target enemy units within 1" of friendly units.
Acid maw	Melee	Melee	User	-3	1	-
Rending claws	Melee	Melee	User	-1	1	Each time you make a wound roll of 6+ for this weapon, that hit is resolved with an AP of -4.
Scything talons	Melee	Melee	User	0	1	You can re-roll hit rolls of 1 for this weapon.

WARGEAR OPTIONS	
	• Any model may also have a pair of scything talons. • For every four models in the unit, one model may have flesh hooks and/or one model may have an acid maw. • All models in the unit may have toxin sacs (pg 113) and/or extended carapaces.

ABILITIES	
	Flurry of Claws: Genestealers have 4 Attacks instead of 3 whilst their unit has 10 or more models. **Lightning Reflexes:** Genestealers have a 5+ invulnerable save. **Swift and Deadly:** Genestealers can charge even if they Advanced during their turn. **Extended Carapaces:** Genestealers with extended carapaces have a Save characteristic of 4+ but lose the Swift and Deadly ability.	**Infestation:** If your army includes any units of Genestealers, you can place up to four infestation nodes anywhere in your deployment zone when your army deploys. You can then set up any units of Genestealers lurking, instead of setting them up on the battlefield. If an enemy model is ever within 9" of an infestation node, the node is destroyed and removed from the battlefield. Whilst there are any friendly infestation nodes on the battlefield, this unit can stop lurking: at the end of your Movement phase, set it up wholly within 6" of a friendly infestation node. That infestation node is then removed from the battlefield. If this unit is still lurking when the last friendly infestation node is removed, this unit is destroyed.

FACTION KEYWORDS	**TYRANIDS, <HIVE FLEET>**
KEYWORDS	**INFANTRY, GENESTEALERS**

TERMAGANTS

NAME	M	WS	BS	S	T	W	A	Ld	Sv
Termagant	6"	4+	4+	3	3	1	1	5	6+

This unit contains 10 Termagants. It can include up to 10 additional Termagants (**Power Rating +3**) or up to 20 additional Termagants (**Power Rating +6**). Each model is armed with a fleshborer.

WEAPON	RANGE	TYPE	S	AP	D	ABILITIES
Devourer	18"	Assault 3	4	0	1	-
Fleshborer	12"	Assault 1	4	0	1	-
Spinefists	12"	Pistol *	3	0	1	When a model fires this weapon, it makes a number of shots equal to its Attacks characteristic.

WARGEAR OPTIONS	• Any model may replace its fleshborer with a devourer or spinefists. • All models in the unit may have toxin sacs and/or adrenal glands (pg 113).
ABILITIES	**Instinctive Behaviour** (pg 82) **Hail of Living Ammunition:** If this unit contains 20 or more models, you can re-roll wound rolls of 1 when it shoots.
FACTION KEYWORDS	**TYRANIDS, <HIVE FLEET>**
KEYWORDS	**INFANTRY, TERMAGANTS**

'The torchlight showed up a trail of blood leading to the back room, so like a fool I followed it. Lying in the darkness was one of the smaller ones, its jaws distended around the torso of what I assume used to be the father. He was still convulsing. In my horror, I shot the victim first. Big mistake.'

- Enforcer Maitland, Epsilon Hive

HORMAGAUNTS

NAME	M	WS	BS	S	T	W	A	Ld	Sv
Hormagaunt	8"	4+	4+	3	3	1	2	5	6+

This unit contains 10 Hormagaunts. It can include up to 10 additional Hormagaunts (**Power Rating +3**) or up to 20 additional Hormagaunts (**Power Rating +6**). Each model is armed with a pair of scything talons.

WEAPON	RANGE	TYPE	S	AP	D	ABILITIES
Scything talons	Melee	Melee	User	0	1	You can re-roll hit rolls of 1 for this weapon.

WARGEAR OPTIONS	• All models in the unit may take toxin sacs and/or adrenal glands (pg 113).
ABILITIES	**Instinctive Behaviour** (pg 82) **Bounding Leap:** Whenever this unit piles in and consolidates, it can move up to 6". **Hungering Swarm:** If this unit contains 20 or more models, you can re-roll wound rolls of 1 when it fights.
FACTION KEYWORDS	**TYRANIDS, <HIVE FLEET>**
KEYWORDS	**INFANTRY, HORMAGAUNTS**

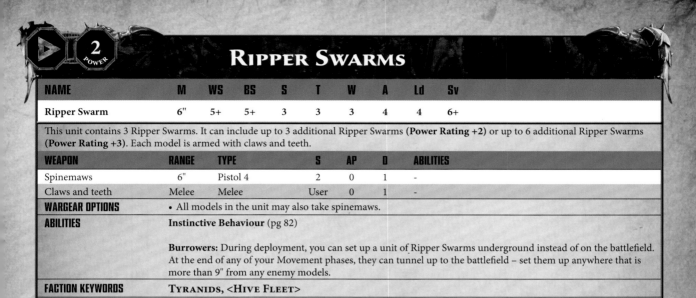

RIPPER SWARMS

NAME	M	WS	BS	S	T	W	A	Ld	Sv
Ripper Swarm	6"	5+	5+	3	3	3	4	4	6+

This unit contains 3 Ripper Swarms. It can include up to 3 additional Ripper Swarms (**Power Rating +2**) or up to 6 additional Ripper Swarms (**Power Rating +3**). Each model is armed with claws and teeth.

WEAPON	RANGE	TYPE	S	AP	D	ABILITIES
Spinemaws	6"	Pistol 4	2	0	1	-
Claws and teeth	Melee	Melee	User	0	1	-

WARGEAR OPTIONS	• All models in the unit may also take spinemaws.

ABILITIES	**Instinctive Behaviour** (pg 82)

Burrowers: During deployment, you can set up a unit of Ripper Swarms underground instead of on the battlefield. At the end of any of your Movement phases, they can tunnel up to the battlefield – set them up anywhere that is more than 9" from any enemy models.

FACTION KEYWORDS	TYRANIDS, <HIVE FLEET>

KEYWORDS:	SWARM, RIPPERS

Hormagaunts soak up desperate volleys of lasgun fire, masking the advance of larger Tyranid organisms.

TYRANT GUARD

NAME	M	WS	BS	S	T	W	A	Ld	Sv
Tyrant Guard	7"	3+	4+	5	5	3	3	6	3+

This unit contains 3 Tyrant Guard. It can include up to 3 additional Tyrant Guard (**Power Rating +6**). Each model is armed with rending claws and scything talons.

WEAPON	RANGE	TYPE	S	AP	D	ABILITIES
Crushing claws	Melee	Melee	x2	-3	D3	When attacking with this weapon, you must subtract 1 from the hit roll.
Lash whip and bonesword	Melee	Melee	User	-2	1	If the bearer is slain in the Fight phase before it has made its attacks, leave it where it is. When its unit is chosen to fight in that phase, the bearer can do so as normal before being removed from the battlefield.
Rending claws	Melee	Melee	User	-1	1	Each time you make a wound roll of 6+ for this weapon, that hit is resolved with an AP of -4.
Scything talons	Melee	Melee	User	0	1	You can re-roll hit rolls of 1 for this weapon.

WARGEAR OPTIONS	• Any model may replace its scything talons with crushing claws or a lash whip and bonesword. • All models in the unit may have toxin sacs and/or adrenal glands (pg 113).

ABILITIES	**Instinctive Behaviour** (pg 82) **Blind Rampage:** If a friendly <**Hive Fleet**> **Hive Tyrant** is killed within 6" of this unit, from the end of that turn increase the Attacks characteristic of each model in this unit by 1 for the rest of the battle.	**Shieldwall:** Roll a dice each time a friendly <**Hive Fleet**> **Hive Tyrant** loses a wound whilst they are within 3" of this unit; on a 2+ a model from this unit can intercept that hit – the Hive Tyrant does not lose a wound but this unit suffers a mortal wound.

FACTION KEYWORDS	**TYRANIDS, <HIVE FLEET>**

KEYWORDS	**INFANTRY, TYRANT GUARD**

'The blasphemy of the Tyranids is such that only one solution is acceptable. Extermination.'

- Chaplain Ortan Cassius, Ultramarines

HIVE GUARD

NAME	M	WS	BS	S	T	W	A	Ld	Sv
Hive Guard	5"	4+	3+	4	5	3	2	7	4+

This unit contains 3 Hive Guard. It can include up to 3 additional Hive Guard (**Power Rating +6**). Each model is armed with an impaler cannon.

WEAPON	RANGE	TYPE	S	AP	D	ABILITIES
Impaler cannon	36"	Heavy 2	8	-2	D3	This weapon can target units that are not visible to the bearer. In addition, units attacked by this weapon do not gain any bonus to their saving throws for being in cover.
Shockcannon	24"	Assault D3	7	-1	D3	If the target is a **VEHICLE** and you make a wound roll of 4+, the target suffers 1 mortal wound in addition to any other damage. If you make a wound roll of 6+, inflict D3 mortal wounds instead.

WARGEAR OPTIONS	• Any model may replace its impaler cannon with a shockcannon. • All models in the unit may have toxin sacs and/or adrenal glands (pg 113).

ABILITIES	**Instinctive Behaviour** (pg 82)

FACTION KEYWORDS	**TYRANIDS, <HIVE FLEET>**

KEYWORDS	**INFANTRY, HIVE GUARD**

LICTOR

2 POWER

NAME	M	WS	BS	S	T	W	A	Ld	Sv
Lictor	9"	2+	4+	6	4	4	3	9	5+

A Lictor is a single model armed with flesh hooks, grasping talons and rending claws.

WEAPON	RANGE	TYPE	S	AP	D	ABILITIES
Flesh hooks	6"	Assault 2	User	0	1	This weapon can be fired within 1" of an enemy unit, and can target enemy units within 1" of friendly units.
Grasping talons	Melee	Melee	User	-1	2	-
Rending claws	Melee	Melee	User	-1	1	Each time you make a wound roll of 6+ for this weapon, that hit is resolved with an AP of -4.

ABILITIES	**Chameleonic Skin:** Your opponent must subtract 1 from their hit rolls for attacks that target this model. In addition, add 2 instead of 1 to saving throws for this model when it is in cover.	**Hidden Hunter:** During deployment, you can set up a Lictor in hiding instead of placing it on the battlefield. At the end of any of your Movement phases, the Lictor can spring from its hiding place – set it up anywhere on the battlefield that is more than 9" away from any enemy models. You can re-roll the Lictor's charge distance in the turn in which it uses this ability to arrive on the battlefield.

FACTION KEYWORDS	TYRANIDS, <HIVE FLEET>
KEYWORDS	INFANTRY, LICTOR

DEATHLEAPER

5 POWER

NAME	M	WS	BS	S	T	W	A	Ld	Sv
Deathleaper	9"	2+	4+	6	4	6	4	10	5+

Deathleaper is a single model armed with flesh hooks, grasping talons and rending claws. Only one of this model can be included in your army.

WEAPON	RANGE	TYPE	S	AP	D	ABILITIES
Flesh hooks	6"	Assault 2	User	0	1	This weapon can be fired within 1" of an enemy unit, and can target enemy units within 1" of friendly units.
Grasping talons	Melee	Melee	User	-1	2	-
Rending claws	Melee	Melee	User	-1	1	Each time you make a wound roll of 6+ for this weapon, that hit is resolved with an AP of -4.

ABILITIES	**Superior Chameleonic Skin:** Your opponent must subtract 2 from their hit rolls for attacks that target Deathleaper. In addition, add 2 instead of 1 to saving throws for Deathleaper when it is in cover. **It's After Me!:** At the start of the first battle round but before the first turn begins, pick a **CHARACTER** from the opposing army. You can re-roll hit and wound rolls in the Fight phase for any of Deathleaper's attacks that target that **CHARACTER**.	**Hidden Hunter:** During deployment, you can set up Deathleaper in hiding instead of placing it on the battlefield. At the end of any of your Movement phases, Deathleaper can spring from its hiding place – set it up anywhere on the battlefield that is more than 9" away from any enemy models. You can re-roll Deathleaper's charge distance in the turn in which it uses this ability to arrive on the battlefield.

FACTION KEYWORDS	TYRANIDS, <HIVE FLEET>
KEYWORDS	CHARACTER, INFANTRY, LICTOR, DEATHLEAPER

ZOANTHROPES

NAME	M	WS	BS	S	T	W	A	Ld	Sv
Zoanthrope	5"	4+	3+	4	4	3	1	9	5+

This unit contains 3 Zoanthropes. It can include up to 3 additional Zoanthropes (**Power Rating +2 per model**). Each model is armed with claws and teeth.

WEAPON	RANGE	TYPE	S	AP	D	ABILITIES
Claws and teeth	Melee	Melee	User	0	1	-

ABILITIES	**Shadow in the Warp, Synapse** (pg 82)	**Warp Blast:** When this unit manifests the *Smite* psychic power, it affects the closest visible enemy unit within 24", instead of within 18". In addition, it inflicts an additional D3 mortal wounds on that enemy unit if this unit contains 4 or 5 Zoanthropes, or an additional 3 mortal wounds if it contains 6 Zoanthropes.
	Warp Field: Models in this unit have a 3+ invulnerable save.	

PSYKER	A unit of Zoanthropes can attempt to manifest one psychic power in each friendly Psychic phase, and attempt to deny one psychic power in each enemy Psychic phase. A Zoanthrope unit of 4 or more models can instead attempt to manifest two psychic powers in each friendly Psychic phase, and attempt to deny one psychic power in each enemy Psychic phase. A Zoanthrope unit knows the *Smite* psychic power and one psychic power from the Hive Mind discipline (pg 121).
	When manifesting or denying a psychic power with a Zoanthrope unit, first select a model in the unit – measure range, visibility etc. from this model. If this unit suffers Perils of the Warp, it suffers D3 mortal wounds as described in the core rules, but units within 6" will only suffer damage if the Perils of the Warp causes the last model in the Zoanthrope unit to be slain.

FACTION KEYWORDS	**TYRANIDS, <HIVE FLEET>**
KEYWORDS	**INFANTRY, FLY, PSYKER, SYNAPSE, ZOANTHROPES**

MALECEPTOR

DAMAGE
Some of this model's characteristics change as it suffers damage, as shown below:

REMAINING W	WS	S	PSYCHIC OVERLOAD
7-12+	4+	7	6 units
4-6	5+	6	3 units
1-3	6+	5	D3 units

NAME	M	WS	BS	S	T	W	A	Ld	Sv
Maleceptor	7"	★	4+	★	7	12	3	9	3+

A Maleceptor is a single model armed with massive scything talons.

WEAPON	RANGE	TYPE	S	AP	D	ABILITIES
Massive scything talons	Melee	Melee	User	-3	D6	You can re-roll hit rolls of 1 for this weapon. If the bearer has more than one pair of massive scything talons, it can make 1 additional attack with this weapon each time it fights.

ABILITIES	**Shadow in the Warp, Synapse** (pg 82)
	Psychic Overload: Instead of manifesting any psychic powers in your Psychic phase, a Maleceptor can unleash brain-bursting psychic tendrils. If it does so, roll a dice for each enemy unit within 6", to a maximum number of units shown in the damage table above. On a 2+ the Maleceptor deals 1 mortal wound to that unit, but on a 6 it deals 3 mortal wounds to that unit instead.
	Psychic Barrier: A Maleceptor has a 4+ invulnerable save.

PSYKER	A Maleceptor can attempt to manifest two psychic powers in each friendly Psychic phase, and attempt to deny two psychic powers in each enemy Psychic phase. It knows the *Smite* psychic power and one psychic power from the Hive Mind discipline (pg 121). Whenever a Maleceptor attempts to manifest a psychic power, add 1 to its Psychic test.

FACTION KEYWORDS	**TYRANIDS, <HIVE FLEET>**
KEYWORDS	**MONSTER, PSYKER, SYNAPSE, MALECEPTOR**

VENOMTHROPES

5 POWER

NAME	M	WS	BS	S	T	W	A	Ld	Sv
Venomthrope	5"	4+	4+	4	4	3	2	5	5+

This unit contains 3 Venomthropes. It can include up to 3 additional Venomthropes (**Power Rating +4**). Each model is armed with toxic lashes.

WEAPON	RANGE	TYPE	S	AP	D	ABILITIES
Toxic lashes (shooting)	6"	Assault 2	User	0	D3	This weapon can be fired within 1" of an enemy unit, and can target enemy units within 1" of friendly units. In addition, you can re-roll failed wound rolls for this weapon.
Toxic lashes (melee)	Melee	Melee	User	0	D3	You can re-roll failed wound rolls for this weapon. A model armed with this weapon always fights first in the Fight phase, even if it didn't charge. If the enemy has units that have charged, or that have a similar ability, then alternate choosing units to fight with, starting with the player whose turn is taking place.

ABILITIES	**Instinctive Behaviour** (pg 82)	**Shrouding Spores:** Your opponent must subtract 1 from hit rolls made for ranged weapons that target <Hive Fleet> units (excluding **Monsters**) whilst they are within 6" of any <Hive Fleet> Venomthropes. In addition, your opponent must subtract 1 from hit rolls made for ranged weapons that target <Hive Fleet> **Monsters** whilst they are within 6" of any <Hive Fleet> Venomthrope units that contain 3 or more models. Increase the range of both these effects to 9" whilst this unit contains 6 models.
	Toxic Miasma: At the end of the Fight phase, roll a D6 for each enemy unit within 1" of any Venomthropes. On a 5+, that unit suffers a mortal wound.	

FACTION KEYWORDS	TYRANIDS, <HIVE FLEET>
KEYWORDS	INFANTRY, FLY, VENOMTHROPES

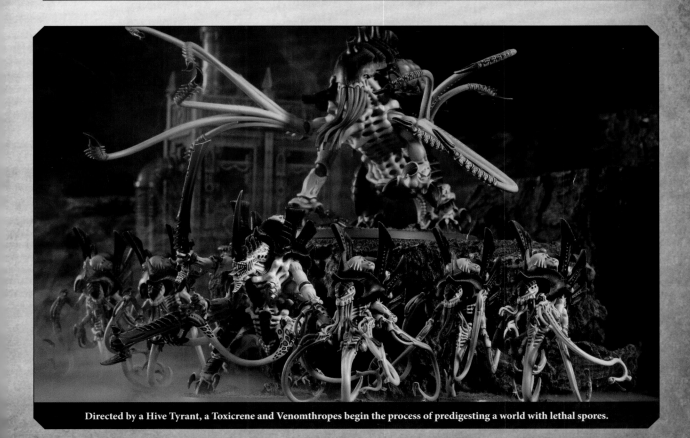

Directed by a Hive Tyrant, a Toxicrene and Venomthropes begin the process of predigesting a world with lethal spores.

PYROVORES

NAME	M	WS	BS	S	T	W	A	Ld	Sv
Pyrovore	5"	4+	4+	5	4	4	2	5	4+

This unit contains 1 Pyrovore. It can include 1 additional Pyrovore (**Power Rating +2**) or 2 additional Pyrovores (**Power Rating +4**). Each model is armed with a flamespurt and acid maw.

WEAPON	RANGE	TYPE	S	AP	D	ABILITIES
Flamespurt	10"	Assault D6	5	-1	1	This weapon automatically hits its target.
Acid maw	Melee	Melee	User	-3	1	-

ABILITIES	**Instinctive Behaviour** (pg 82)
	Acid Blood: Each time this model loses a wound in the Fight phase, roll a dice; on a 6, the unit that inflicted the damage suffers a mortal wound after all of their attacks have been resolved.
	Volatile: When a Pyrovore is slain, roll a dice. On a 4+ it bursts in a shower of acid – the nearest enemy unit within 3" (if any) suffers a mortal wound.

FACTION KEYWORDS	TYRANIDS, <HIVE FLEET>
KEYWORDS	INFANTRY, PYROVORES

HARUSPEX

DAMAGE
Some of this model's characteristics change as it suffers damage, as shown below:

REMAINING W	WS	BS	S
7-13+	4+	4+	7
4-6	4+	5+	6
1-3	5+	5+	5

NAME	M	WS	BS	S	T	W	A	Ld	Sv
Haruspex	7"	✶	✶	✶	8	13	4	6	3+

A Haruspex is a single model armed with a grasping tongue, a ravenous maw and shovelling claws.

WEAPON	RANGE	TYPE	S	AP	D	ABILITIES
Grasping tongue	12"	Assault 1	6	-3	D3	This weapon can be fired within 1" of an enemy unit, and can target enemy units within 1" of friendly units. In addition, when a model is slain by this weapon, the Haruspex regains 1 lost wound.
Ravenous maw	Melee	Melee	User	-1	D3	Make D3 hit rolls for each attack made with this weapon, instead of 1.
Shovelling claws	Melee	Melee	x2	-3	D6	-

ABILITIES	**Instinctive Behaviour** (pg 82)	**Rapacious Hunger:** Each time a Haruspex slays an enemy model with its ravenous maw, it can immediately make one extra attack with its shovelling claws. In addition, at the end of a Fight phase in which a Haruspex slew any models with its ravenous maw, it regains 1 wound lost earlier in the battle.
	Acid Blood: Each time this model loses a wound in the Fight phase, roll a dice; on a 6, the unit that inflicted the damage suffers a mortal wound after all of their attacks have been resolved.	
	Frenzied Death Throes: If a Haruspex is reduced to 0 wounds, roll a dice before removing the model from the battlefield; on a 6, it lashes out in its death throes, and each unit within 3" suffers 3 mortal wounds.	

FACTION KEYWORDS	TYRANIDS, <HIVE FLEET>
KEYWORDS	MONSTER, HARUSPEX

GARGOYLES

3 POWER

NAME	M	WS	BS	S	T	W	A	Ld	Sv
Gargoyle	12"	4+	4+	3	3	1	1	5	6+

This unit contains 10 Gargoyles. It can include up to 10 additional Gargoyles (**Power Rating + 3**) or up to 20 additional Gargoyles (**Power Rating +6**). Each model is armed with a fleshborer and blinding venom.

WEAPON	RANGE	TYPE	S	AP	D	ABILITIES
Fleshborer	12"	Assault 1	4	0	1	-
Blinding venom	Melee	Melee	3	0	1	If a unit suffers any unsaved wounds from this weapon, your opponent must subtract 1 from hit rolls for that unit until the end of the turn.

ABILITIES		
Instinctive Behaviour (pg 82) **Hail of Living Ammunition:** If this unit contains 20 or more models, you can re-roll wound rolls of 1 when it shoots.		**Swooping Assault:** During deployment you can set this unit up clinging to an airborne Harridan instead of placing them on the battlefield. At the end of any of your Movement phases this unit can swoop down from above – set them up anywhere on the battlefield that is more than 9" away from any enemy models.

FACTION KEYWORDS	TYRANIDS, <HIVE FLEET>
KEYWORDS	INFANTRY, FLY, GARGOYLES

A winged Hive Tyrant and its Gargoyle brood descend from the skies like figures from some primordial nightmare.

RAVENERS

4 POWER

NAME	M	WS	BS	S	T	W	A	Ld	Sv
Ravener	12"	3+	4+	4	4	3	4	5	5+

This unit contains 3 Raveners. It can include up to 3 additional Raveners (**Power Rating +4**) or up to 6 additional Raveners (**Power Rating +8**). Each model is armed with two pairs of scything talons.

WEAPON	RANGE	TYPE	S	AP	D	ABILITIES
Deathspitter	24"	Assault 3	5	-1	1	-
Devourer	18"	Assault 3	4	0	1	-
Spinefists	12"	Pistol *	3	0	1	When a model fires this weapon, it makes a number of shots equal to its Attacks characteristic.
Rending claws	Melee	Melee	User	-1	1	Each time you make a wound roll of 6+ for this weapon, that hit is resolved with an AP of -4.
Scything talons	Melee	Melee	User	0	1	You can re-roll hit rolls of 1 for this weapon. If the bearer has more than one pair of scything talons, it can make 1 additional attack with this weapon each time it fights.

WARGEAR OPTIONS	• Any model may replace one of its pairs of scything talons with rending claws. • Any model may have spinefists, a devourer or a deathspitter.
ABILITIES	**Instinctive Behaviour** (pg 82) **Death From Below:** During deployment, you can set up a Ravener unit underground instead of placing it on the battlefield. At the end of any of your Movement phases, the Raveners can burrow to the surface – set them up anywhere on the battlefield that is more than 9" away from any enemy models.
FACTION KEYWORDS	**TYRANIDS, <HIVE FLEET>**
KEYWORDS	**INFANTRY, RAVENERS**

THE RED TERROR

4 POWER

NAME	M	WS	BS	S	T	W	A	Ld	Sv
The Red Terror	12"	3+	4+	5	5	6	4	7	4+

The Red Terror is a single model armed with a prehensile pincer tail and two pairs of scything talons. Only one of this model can be included in your army.

WEAPON	RANGE	TYPE	S	AP	D	ABILITIES
Prehensile pincer tail	Melee	Melee	User	0	D3	Each time the bearer fights, it can make one (and only one) attack with this weapon. This is in addition to the bearer's attacks.
Scything talons	Melee	Melee	User	0	1	You can re-roll hit rolls of 1 for this weapon. If the bearer has more than one pair of scything talons, it can make 1 additional attack with this weapon each time it fights.

ABILITIES	**Instinctive Behaviour** (pg 82) **Death From Below:** During deployment, you can set up the Red Terror underground instead of placing it on the battlefield. At the end of any of your Movement phases, the Red Terror can burrow to the surface – set it up anywhere on the battlefield that is more than 9" away from any enemy models.	**Swallow Whole:** If 4 or more of the Red Terror's scything talons attacks hit the same unit, instead of causing damage normally it can attempt to swallow a victim whole. Roll a D6, and if the result is equal to or higher than the highest Wounds characteristic of the unit, one model from that unit is slain. **Feeding Frenzy:** You can add 1 to hit rolls in the Fight phase for friendly **<HIVE FLEET> RAVENER** units that are within 6" of this model.
FACTION KEYWORDS	**TYRANIDS, <HIVE FLEET>**	
KEYWORDS	**CHARACTER, INFANTRY, RAVENER, THE RED TERROR**	

MUCOLID SPORES

1 POWER

NAME	M	WS	BS	S	T	W	A	Ld	Sv
Mucolid Spore	3"	-	-	1	3	3	1	10	6+

This unit contains 1 Mucolid Spore. It can include 1 additional Mucolid Spore (**Power Rating +1**) or 2 additional Mucolid Spores (**Power Rating +2**).

ABILITIES	**Instinctive Behaviour** (pg 82)	**Living Bombs:** Mucolid Spores automatically pass Morale tests. Furthermore, Mucolid Spores are discounted for the purposes of any victory conditions – their destruction never awards victory points, they do not count towards the number of models controlling an objective, and they do not count when determining if a player has any models left on the battlefield. If you are playing a matched play game, the creation of new Mucolid Spores by another unit (e.g. from a Sporocyst's Spore Node ability) is free, and the Mucolid Spores' points cost does not come out of your pool of reinforcement points.
	Float Down: During deployment, you can set up a Mucolid Spore unit in the upper atmosphere instead of on the battlefield. At the end of any of your Movement phases, it can float down to the battlefield – set it up anywhere that is more than 12" from any enemy models.	
	Floating Death: A Mucolid Spore explodes if it is within 3" of any enemy units at the end of any Charge phase. Each time a Mucolid Spore explodes, roll a D6; on a 1 it fails to inflict any harm, on a 2-5 it inflicts D3 mortal wounds on the nearest enemy unit, and on a 6 it inflicts D6 mortal wounds on that unit. The Mucolid Spore is then destroyed.	
FACTION KEYWORDS	TYRANIDS, \<HIVE FLEET\>	
KEYWORDS	FLY, MUCOLID SPORES	

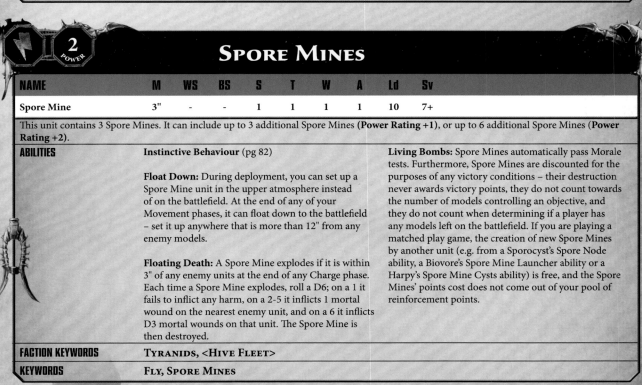

SPORE MINES

2 POWER

NAME	M	WS	BS	S	T	W	A	Ld	Sv
Spore Mine	3"	-	-	1	1	1	1	10	7+

This unit contains 3 Spore Mines. It can include up to 3 additional Spore Mines (**Power Rating +1**), or up to 6 additional Spore Mines (**Power Rating +2**).

ABILITIES	**Instinctive Behaviour** (pg 82)	**Living Bombs:** Spore Mines automatically pass Morale tests. Furthermore, Spore Mines are discounted for the purposes of any victory conditions – their destruction never awards victory points, they do not count towards the number of models controlling an objective, and they do not count when determining if a player has any models left on the battlefield. If you are playing a matched play game, the creation of new Spore Mines by another unit (e.g. from a Sporocyst's Spore Node ability, a Biovore's Spore Mine Launcher ability or a Harpy's Spore Mine Cysts ability) is free, and the Spore Mines' points cost does not come out of your pool of reinforcement points.
	Float Down: During deployment, you can set up a Spore Mine unit in the upper atmosphere instead of on the battlefield. At the end of any of your Movement phases, it can float down to the battlefield – set it up anywhere that is more than 12" from any enemy models.	
	Floating Death: A Spore Mine explodes if it is within 3" of any enemy units at the end of any Charge phase. Each time a Spore Mine explodes, roll a D6; on a 1 it fails to inflict any harm, on a 2-5 it inflicts 1 mortal wound on the nearest enemy unit, and on a 6 it inflicts D3 mortal wounds on that unit. The Spore Mine is then destroyed.	
FACTION KEYWORDS	TYRANIDS, \<HIVE FLEET\>	
KEYWORDS	FLY, SPORE MINES	

EXOCRINE

DAMAGE
Some of this model's characteristics change as it suffers damage, as shown below:

REMAINING W	WS	BS	A
7-12+	4+	4+	3
4-6	4+	5+	D3
1-3	5+	5+	1

NAME	M	WS	BS	S	T	W	A	Ld	Sv
Exocrine	6"	*	*	7	8	12	*	6	3+

An Exocrine is a single model armed with a bio-plasmic cannon and powerful limbs.

WEAPON	RANGE	TYPE	S	AP	D	ABILITIES
Bio-plasmic cannon	36"	Heavy 6	7	-3	2	-
Powerful limbs	Melee	Melee	User	-1	2	-

ABILITIES	Instinctive Behaviour (pg 82)

Symbiotic Targeting: If this model does not move in its Movement phase, you can add 1 to its hit rolls in the following Shooting phase. If you do so, it cannot charge in the same turn.

Weapon Beast: If this model does not move in your Movement phase, it can shoot all of its weapons twice in your Shooting phase.

Death Throes: If this model is reduced to 0 wounds, roll a dice before removing the model from the battlefield; on a 6, it lashes out in its death throes, and each unit within 3" suffers D3 mortal wounds.

FACTION KEYWORDS	TYRANIDS, <HIVE FLEET>
KEYWORDS	MONSTER, EXOCRINE

'You fight the Tyranids, you better have eyes in the back of your head. Won't be the one you're blasting away at with your lasgun that gets you. No, no, no. It'll be the skulker that sneaks up close enough to suck your brains right out of your skull. Or the ground-drake that bursts out from under your bivouac and drags you screaming into the dark. Welcome to hell, new blood.'

- *Trooper Mern 'Sunshine' Golbech, 67th Cadian Mechanised Infantry*

TYRANNOFEX

DAMAGE
Some of this model's characteristics change as it suffers damage, as shown below:

REMAINING W	BS	S	A
8-14+	4+	7	4
4-7	5+	6	3
1-3	5+	5	2

NAME	M	WS	BS	S	T	W	A	Ld	Sv
Tyrannofex	6"	4+	*	*	8	14	*	7	3+

A Tyrannofex is a single model armed with acid spray and powerful limbs. It can also fire stinger salvoes.

WEAPON	RANGE	TYPE	S	AP	D	ABILITIES
Acid spray	18"	Heavy 2D6	User	-1	D3	This weapon automatically hits its target.
Fleshborer hive	18"	Heavy 20	5	0	1	-
Rupture cannon	48"	Heavy 3	10	-3	D6	-
Stinger salvo	24"	Assault 4	5	-1	1	-
Powerful limbs	Melee	Melee	User	-1	2	-

WARGEAR OPTIONS	• This model may replace its acid spray with a fleshborer hive or rupture cannon. • This model may have toxin sacs and/or adrenal glands (pg 113).

ABILITIES	Instinctive Behaviour (pg 82)

Bio-tank: This model does not suffer the penalty to its hit rolls for moving and firing Heavy weapons.

Weapon Beast: If this model does not move in your Movement phase, it can shoot all of its weapons twice in your Shooting phase.

Death Throes: If a Tyrannofex is reduced to 0 wounds, roll a dice before removing the model from the battlefield; on a 6 it lashes out in its death throes, and each unit within 3" suffers D3 mortal wounds.

FACTION KEYWORDS	TYRANIDS, <HIVE FLEET>
KEYWORDS	MONSTER, TYRANNOFEX

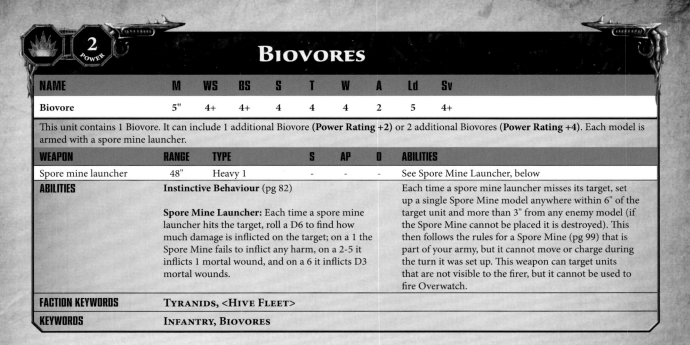

BIOVORES

2 POWER

NAME	M	WS	BS	S	T	W	A	Ld	Sv
Biovore	5"	4+	4+	4	4	4	2	5	4+

This unit contains 1 Biovore. It can include 1 additional Biovore (**Power Rating +2**) or 2 additional Biovores (**Power Rating +4**). Each model is armed with a spore mine launcher.

WEAPON	RANGE	TYPE	S	AP	D	ABILITIES
Spore mine launcher	48"	Heavy 1	-	-	-	See Spore Mine Launcher, below

ABILITIES		
	Instinctive Behaviour (pg 82) **Spore Mine Launcher:** Each time a spore mine launcher hits the target, roll a D6 to find how much damage is inflicted on the target; on a 1 the Spore Mine fails to inflict any harm, on a 2-5 it inflicts 1 mortal wound, and on a 6 it inflicts D3 mortal wounds.	Each time a spore mine launcher misses its target, set up a single Spore Mine model anywhere within 6" of the target unit and more than 3" from any enemy model (if the Spore Mine cannot be placed it is destroyed). This then follows the rules for a Spore Mine (pg 99) that is part of your army, but it cannot move or charge during the turn it was set up. This weapon can target units that are not visible to the firer, but it cannot be used to fire Overwatch.
FACTION KEYWORDS	**TYRANIDS, <HIVE FLEET>**	
KEYWORDS	**INFANTRY, BIOVORES**	

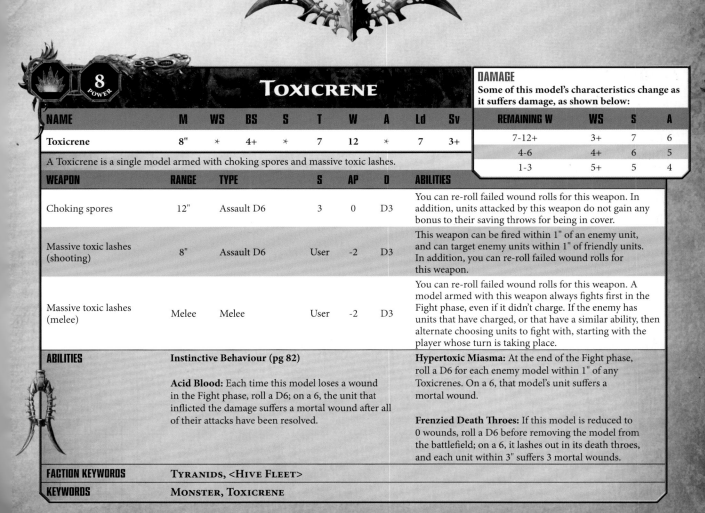

TOXICRENE

8 POWER

NAME	M	WS	BS	S	T	W	A	Ld	Sv
Toxicrene	8"	*	4+	*	7	12	*	7	3+

A Toxicrene is a single model armed with choking spores and massive toxic lashes.

DAMAGE
Some of this model's characteristics change as it suffers damage, as shown below:

REMAINING W	WS	S	A
7-12+	3+	7	6
4-6	4+	6	5
1-3	5+	5	4

WEAPON	RANGE	TYPE	S	AP	D	ABILITIES
Choking spores	12"	Assault D6	3	0	D3	You can re-roll failed wound rolls for this weapon. In addition, units attacked by this weapon do not gain any bonus to their saving throws for being in cover.
Massive toxic lashes (shooting)	8"	Assault D6	User	-2	D3	This weapon can be fired within 1" of an enemy unit, and can target enemy units within 1" of friendly units. In addition, you can re-roll failed wound rolls for this weapon.
Massive toxic lashes (melee)	Melee	Melee	User	-2	D3	You can re-roll failed wound rolls for this weapon. A model armed with this weapon always fights first in the Fight phase, even if it didn't charge. If the enemy has units that have charged, or that have a similar ability, then alternate choosing units to fight with, starting with the player whose turn is taking place.

ABILITIES		
	Instinctive Behaviour (pg 82) **Acid Blood:** Each time this model loses a wound in the Fight phase, roll a D6; on a 6, the unit that inflicted the damage suffers a mortal wound after all of their attacks have been resolved.	**Hypertoxic Miasma:** At the end of the Fight phase, roll a D6 for each enemy model within 1" of any Toxicrenes. On a 6, that model's unit suffers a mortal wound. **Frenzied Death Throes:** If this model is reduced to 0 wounds, roll a D6 before removing the model from the battlefield; on a 6, it lashes out in its death throes, and each unit within 3" suffers 3 mortal wounds.
FACTION KEYWORDS	**TYRANIDS, <HIVE FLEET>**	
KEYWORDS	**MONSTER, TOXICRENE**	

CARNIFEXES

NAME	M	WS	BS	S	T	W	A	Ld	Sv
Carnifex	7"	4+	4+	6	7	8	4	6	3+

This unit contains 1 Carnifex. It can include 1 additional Carnifex (**Power Rating +6**) or 2 additional Carnifexes (**Power Rating +12**). Each model is armed with two pairs of monstrous scything talons.

WEAPON	RANGE	TYPE	S	AP	D	ABILITIES
Bio-plasma	12"	Assault D3	7	-3	1	-
Spine banks	6"	Assault 4	5	0	1	This weapon can be fired within 1" of an enemy unit, and can target enemy units within 1" of friendly units.
Bone mace	Melee	Melee	8	-1	D3	Each time the bearer fights, it can make one (and only one) attack with this weapon. This is in addition to the bearer's attacks.
Monstrous acid maw	Melee	Melee	User	-5	D3	-
Monstrous crushing claws	Melee	Melee	x2	-3	3	When attacking with this weapon, you must subtract 1 from the hit roll.
Monstrous scything talons	Melee	Melee	User	-3	3	You can re-roll hit rolls of 1 for this weapon. If the bearer has more than one pair of monstrous scything talons, it can make 1 additional attack with this weapon each time it fights.
Thresher scythe	Melee	Melee	4	-1	1	Each time the bearer fights, it can make one (and only one) attack with this weapon. Make D3 hit rolls for this attack instead of one. This is in addition to the bearer's attacks.

WARGEAR OPTIONS	
	• Any model may replace one of its pairs of monstrous scything talons with an item from the *Monstrous Bio-cannons* list.
	• Any model may replace both of its pairs of monstrous scything talons with two items from the *Monstrous Bio-cannons* list.
	• Any model may replace one of its pairs of monstrous scything talons with monstrous crushing claws.
	• Any model may have toxin sacs and/or adrenal glands (pg 113).
	• Any model may have one of the following: bio-plasma, enhanced senses, a monstrous acid maw or tusks.
	• Any model may have a thresher scythe or a bone mace.
	• Any model may have spine banks or spore cysts.
	• Any model may have chitin thorns.

ABILITIES

Instinctive Behaviour (pg 82)

Living Battering Ram: When a Carnifex finishes a charge move, roll a dice; on a 4+ one enemy unit within 1" suffers a mortal wound. In addition, add 1 to all hit rolls in the Fight phase for a Carnifex that charged in the same turn.

Monstrous Brood: The first time this unit is set up on the battlefield, all of its models must be placed within 6" of at least one other model in their unit. From that point onwards, each operates independently and is treated as a separate unit.

Chitin Thorns: At the end of the Fight phase, roll a D6 for each enemy unit within 1" of any models with chitin thorns. On a 6, that unit suffers a mortal wound.

Enhanced Senses: A Carnifex with enhanced senses has a Ballistic Skill characteristic of 3+.

Spore Cysts: Your opponent must subtract 1 from their hit rolls for ranged attacks that target a Carnifex with spore cysts. This is not cumulative with the penalties to hit rolls incurred from the Shrouding Spores ability (pg 95).

Tusks: You can add 1 to the Attacks characteristic of a Carnifex with tusks in the Fight phase if it charged in the preceding Charge phase.

FACTION KEYWORDS	TYRANIDS, <HIVE FLEET>
KEYWORDS	MONSTER, CARNIFEXES

SCREAMER-KILLERS

NAME	M	WS	BS	S	T	W	A	Ld	Sv
Screamer-Killer	7"	4+	4+	6	7	8	4	6	3+

This unit contains 1 Screamer-Killer. It can include 1 additional Screamer-Killer (**Power Rating +6**) or 2 additional Screamer-Killers (**Power Rating +12**). Each model is armed with a bio-plasmic scream and two pairs of monstrous scything talons.

WEAPON	RANGE	TYPE	S	AP	D	ABILITIES
Bio-plasmic scream	18"	Assault D6	7	-4	1	-
Monstrous scything talons	Melee	Melee	User	-3	3	You can re-roll hit rolls of 1 for this weapon. If the bearer has more than one pair of monstrous scything talons, it can make 1 additional attack with this weapon each time it fights.

WARGEAR OPTIONS	• Any model may have toxin sacs and/or adrenal glands (pg 113). • Any model may have spore cysts.

ABILITIES	**Instinctive Behaviour** (pg 82) **Living Battering Ram:** When a Screamer-Killer finishes a charge move, roll a dice; on a 4+ one enemy unit within 1" suffers a mortal wound. In addition, add 1 to all hit rolls in the Fight phase for a Screamer-Killer that charged in the same turn. **Monstrous Brood:** The first time this unit is set up on the battlefield, all of its models must be placed within 6" of at least one other model in their unit. From that point onwards, each operates independently and is treated as a separate unit.	**Spore Cysts:** Your opponent must subtract 1 from their hit rolls for ranged attacks that target a Screamer-Killer with spore cysts. This is not cumulative with the penalties to hit rolls incurred from the Shrouding Spores ability (pg 95). **Terrifying:** Your opponent must add 1 to any Morale tests for enemy units within 8" of one or more Screamer-Killers.

FACTION KEYWORDS	TYRANIDS, <HIVE FLEET>

KEYWORDS	MONSTER, CARNIFEX, SCREAMER-KILLERS

An ear-splitting shriek fills the air as super-hot bio-plasma builds up within a Screamer-Killer's maw.

THORNBACKS

NAME	M	WS	BS	S	T	W	A	Ld	Sv
Thornback	7"	4+	4+	6	7	8	4	6	3+

This unit contains 1 Thornback. It can include 1 additional Thornback (**Power Rating +6**) or 2 additional Thornbacks (**Power Rating +12**). Each model is armed with a pair of monstrous scything talons, two devourers with brainleech worms and chitin thorns.

WEAPON	RANGE	TYPE	S	AP	D	ABILITIES
Deathspitter with slimer maggots	24"	Assault 3	7	-1	1	-
Devourer with brainleech worms	18"	Assault 6	6	0	1	-
Spine banks	6"	Assault 4	5	0	1	This weapon can be fired within 1" of an enemy unit, and can target enemy units within 1" of friendly units.
Stranglethorn cannon	36"	Assault D6	7	-1	2	You can add 1 to hit rolls for this weapon when attacking a unit with 10 or more models.
Monstrous scything talons	Melee	Melee	User	-3	3	You can re-roll hit rolls of 1 for this weapon. If the bearer has more than one pair of monstrous scything talons, it can make 1 additional attack with this weapon each time it fights.
Thresher scythe	Melee	Melee	4	-1	1	Each time the bearer fights, it can make one (and only one) attack with this weapon. Make D3 hit rolls for this attack instead of one. This is in addition to the bearer's attacks.

WARGEAR OPTIONS
- Any model may replace its monstrous scything talons with a stranglethorn cannon.
- Any model may replace both of its devourers with two deathspitters with slimer maggots.
- Any model may have toxin sacs and/or adrenal glands (pg 113).
- Any model may have enhanced senses, spine banks and/or a thresher scythe.

ABILITIES

Instinctive Behaviour (pg 82)

Thorned Battering Ram: When a Thornback finishes a charge move, roll a dice; on a 4+ one enemy unit within 1" suffers a mortal wound. **INFANTRY** units instead suffer D3 mortal wounds. In addition, add 1 to all hit rolls in the Fight phase for a Thornback that charged in the same turn.

Monstrous Brood: The first time this unit is set up on the battlefield, all of its models must be placed within 6" of at least one other model in their unit. From that point onwards, each operates independently and is treated as a separate unit.

Chitin Thorns: At the end of the Fight phase, roll a D6 for each enemy unit within 1" of any models with chitin thorns. On a 6, that unit suffers a mortal wound.

Enhanced Senses: A Thornback with enhanced senses has a Ballistic Skill characteristic of 3+.

Vicious Hunter: Enemy **INFANTRY** units never gain any bonus to their saving throws for being in cover against attacks made by a Thornback.

FACTION KEYWORDS | **TYRANIDS, <HIVE FLEET>**

KEYWORDS | **MONSTER, CARNIFEX, THORNBACKS**

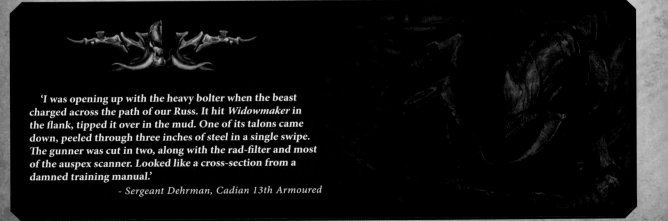

'I was opening up with the heavy bolter when the beast charged across the path of our Russ. It hit *Widowmaker* in the flank, tipped it over in the mud. One of its talons came down, peeled through three inches of steel in a single swipe. The gunner was cut in two, along with the rad-filter and most of the auspex scanner. Looked like a cross-section from a damned training manual.'

- Sergeant Dehrman, Cadian 13th Armoured

MAWLOC

DAMAGE

Some of this model's characteristics change as it suffers damage, as shown below:

REMAINING W	M	WS	S
7-12+	9"	4+	6
4-6	7"	5+	5
1-3	5"	6+	4

NAME	M	WS	BS	S	T	W	A	Ld	Sv
Mawloc	*	*	-	*	6	12	7	7	3+

A Mawloc is a single model armed with distensible jaws, a prehensile pincer tail and three pairs of scything talons.

WEAPON	RANGE	TYPE	S	AP	D	ABILITIES
Biostatic rattle	Melee	Melee	User	-1	1	Each time the bearer fights, it can make one (and only one) attack with this weapon. This is in addition to the bearer's attacks. If a unit suffers any unsaved wounds from this weapon, add 1 to any Morale tests they take until the end of the turn.
Distensible jaws	Melee	Melee	User	-3	D6	Each time the bearer fights, one (and only one) of its attacks must be made with this weapon.
Prehensile pincer tail	Melee	Melee	User	0	D3	Each time the bearer fights, it can make one (and only one) attack with this weapon. This is in addition to the bearer's attacks.
Scything talons	Melee	Melee	User	0	1	You can re-roll hit rolls of 1 for this weapon. If the bearer has more than one pair of scything talons, it can make 1 additional attack with this weapon each time it fights.
Toxinspike	Melee	Melee	1	0	D3	Each time the bearer fights, it can make one (and only one) attack with this weapon. This is in addition to the bearer's attacks. This weapon always wounds targets (other than VEHICLES) on a 2+.

WARGEAR OPTIONS	• This model may replace its prehensile pincer tail with a biostatic rattle or a toxinspike. • This model may have toxin sacs and/or adrenal glands (pg 113).

ABILITIES

Instinctive Behaviour (pg 82)

Terror from the Deep: During deployment, you can set up a Mawloc underground instead of placing it on the battlefield. At the end of any of your Movement phases, set up the Mawloc anywhere on the battlefield that is more than 1" away from any enemy models and more than 6" from any other Mawlocs set up this way this turn, then roll a D6 for each enemy unit within 2" of it; on a 1 the unit escapes unharmed, on a 2-3 it suffers 1 mortal wound, on a 4-5 it suffers D3 mortal wounds and on a 6 it suffers 3 mortal wounds. The Mawloc cannot charge in the same turn.

Burrow: At the beginning of any of your Movement phases, any Mawloc that is not within 1" of an enemy unit can burrow. Remove it from the battlefield – it can return as described in the Terror from the Deep ability. A Mawloc may not burrow and return to the battlefield in the same turn. If the battle ends while the Mawloc is underground, it is considered to be slain.

Death Throes: If this model is reduced to 0 wounds, roll a D6 before removing the model from the battlefield; on a 6, it lashes out in its death throes, and each unit within 3" suffers D3 mortal wounds.

FACTION KEYWORDS	TYRANIDS, <HIVE FLEET>
KEYWORDS	MONSTER, MAWLOC

A Mawloc and Ravener brood burst forth from their subterranean lair, ready to fall upon the foe in an eruption of gore.

TRYGON

DAMAGE

Some of this model's characteristics change as it suffers damage, as shown below:

REMAINING W	M	WS	BS
7-12+	9"	3+	4+
4-6	7"	4+	5+
1-3	5"	5+	6+

NAME	M	WS	BS	S	T	W	A	Ld	Sv
Trygon	*	*	*	7	6	12	6	7	3+

A Trygon is a single model armed with a bio-electric pulse, three pairs of massive scything talons and a toxinspike.

WEAPON	RANGE	TYPE	S	AP	D	ABILITIES
Bio-electric pulse	12"	Assault 6	5	0	1	-
Biostatic rattle	Melee	Melee	User	-1	1	Each time the bearer fights, it can make one (and only one) attack with this weapon. This is in addition to the bearer's attacks. If a unit suffers any unsaved wounds from this weapon, add 1 to any Morale tests they take until the end of the turn.
Massive scything talons	Melee	Melee	User	-3	D6	You can re-roll hit rolls of 1 for this weapon. If the bearer has more than one pair of massive scything talons, it can make 1 additional attack with this weapon each time it fights.
Prehensile pincer tail	Melee	Melee	User	0	D3	Each time the bearer fights, it can make one (and only one) attack with this weapon. This is in addition to the bearer's attacks.
Toxinspike	Melee	Melee	1	0	D3	Each time the bearer fights, it can make one (and only one) attack with this weapon. This is in addition to the bearer's attacks. This weapon always wounds targets (other than **VEHICLES**) on a 2+.

WARGEAR OPTIONS	• This model may replace its toxinspike with a biostatic rattle or a prehensile pincer tail. • This model may have toxin sacs and/or adrenal glands (pg 113).

ABILITIES	**Instinctive Behaviour** (pg 82) **Death Throes:** If this model is reduced to 0 wounds, roll a D6 before removing the model from the battlefield; on a 6, it lashes out in its death throes, and each unit within 3" suffers D3 mortal wounds.	**Subterranean Assault:** During deployment, you can set up a Trygon underground instead of placing it on the battlefield. At the same time, you can set up a <**HIVE FLEET**> Troops unit in the Trygon's tunnel. At the end of any of your Movement phases, set up the Trygon anywhere on the battlefield that is more than 9" away from any enemy models. If there is another unit in the Trygon's tunnel, set it up at the same time wholly within 3" of the Trygon and more than 9" away from any enemy models. Any models that you cannot place in this way are destroyed.

FACTION KEYWORDS	**TYRANIDS, <HIVE FLEET>**

KEYWORDS	**MONSTER, TRYGON**

The Trygon is a burrowing horror capable of tearing a battle tank in half with its mighty talons.

TRYGON PRIME

NAME	M	WS	BS	S	T	W	A	Ld	Sv
Trygon Prime	*	*	*	7	6	12	6	9	3+

A Trygon Prime is a single model armed with a bio-electric pulse with containment spines, a biostatic rattle and three pairs of massive scything talons.

DAMAGE

Some of this model's characteristics change as it suffers damage, as shown below:

REMAINING W	M	WS	BS
7-12+	9"	3+	4+
4-6	7"	4+	5+
1-3	5"	5+	6+

WEAPON	RANGE	TYPE	S	AP	D	ABILITIES
Bio-electric pulse with containment spines	12"	Assault 12	5	0	1	-
Biostatic rattle	Melee	Melee	User	-1	1	Each time the bearer fights, it can make one (and only one) attack with this weapon. This is in addition to the bearer's attacks. If a unit suffers any unsaved wounds from this weapon, add 1 to any Morale tests they take until the end of the turn.
Massive scything talons	Melee	Melee	User	-3	D6	You can re-roll hit rolls of 1 for this weapon. If the bearer has more than one pair of massive scything talons, it can make 1 additional attack with this weapon each time it fights.
Prehensile pincer tail	Melee	Melee	User	0	D3	Each time the bearer fights, it can make one (and only one) attack with this weapon. This is in addition to the bearer's attacks.
Toxinspike	Melee	Melee	1	0	D3	Each time the bearer fights, it can make one (and only one) attack with this weapon. This is in addition to the bearer's attacks. This weapon always wounds targets (other than **Vehicles**) on a 2+.

WARGEAR OPTIONS
- This model may replace its biostatic rattle with a prehensile pincer tail or toxinspike.
- This model may have toxin sacs and/or adrenal glands (pg 113).

ABILITIES

Shadow in the Warp, **Synapse** (pg 82)

Death Throes: If this model is reduced to 0 wounds, roll a D6 before removing the model from the battlefield; on a 6, it lashes out in its death throes, and each unit within 3" suffers D3 mortal wounds.

Subterranean Assault: During deployment, you can set up a Trygon Prime underground instead of placing it on the battlefield. At the same time, you can set up a <**Hive Fleet**> Troops unit in the Trygon Prime's tunnel. At the end of any of your Movement phases, set up the Trygon Prime anywhere on the battlefield that is more than 9" away from any enemy models. If there is another unit in the Trygon Prime's tunnel, set it up at the same time wholly within 3" of the Trygon Prime and more than 9" away from any enemy models. Any models that you cannot place in this way are destroyed.

FACTION KEYWORDS **Tyranids**, <**Hive Fleet**>

KEYWORDS **Monster**, **Character**, **Synapse**, **Trygon Prime**

Sergeant Vhorle emptied his lasgun into the surging tide of xenos sweeping towards the Catachans' firing holes and ducked back behind the parapet, reaching for another power cell. It was then that he became aware of a tremor, deeper and more insistent than the staccato grind of stubber fire and the periodic thud of high explosives. Vhorle felt a shiver of dread trickle down his spine.

'Get clear!' he screamed, spinning around to face the rest of his platoon, 'Get cl–'

The ground beneath them erupted as if struck by an artillery round. Vhorle was thrown backwards, and crashed into the corrugated steel of the trench wall. An enormous serpentine form rose from the breach, taller than a super-heavy tank, its mouth crammed with jagged fangs. Two colossal talons swept down, and Troopers Lale and Torrin came apart in a shower of gore. Vhorle's trembling hand reached for his lasgun, and closed around the grip. The creature turned, and its dead eyes met his own.

'Come on then,' Vhorle growled, bringing his weapon to bear. 'Finish it, you piece of filth.'

He managed one shot before the beast's jaws snapped out with lightning speed, and everything went dark.

8 POWER

TYRANNOCYTE

NAME	M	WS	BS	S	T	W	A	Ld	Sv
Tyrannocyte	*	5+	5+	*	6	12	*	7	4+

A Tyrannocyte is a single model armed with five deathspitters.

WEAPON	RANGE	TYPE	S	AP	D	ABILITIES
Barbed strangler	36"	Assault D6	5	-1	1	You can add 1 to hit rolls for this weapon when attacking a unit with 10 or more models.
Deathspitter	24"	Assault 3	5	-1	1	-
Venom cannon	36"	Assault D3	8	-2	D3	-

WARGEAR OPTIONS	• This model may replace all of its deathspitters with either five barbed stranglers or five venom cannons.

ABILITIES

Instinctive Behaviour (pg 82)

Invasion Organism: During deployment, you can set up a Tyrannocyte in its hive ship instead of placing it on the battlefield. If you do so, the hive ship can launch the Tyrannocyte at the end of any of your Movement phases – set it up anywhere on the battlefield that is more than 9" away from any enemy models.

Any models that are inside the Tyrannocyte (see right) must immediately disembark in the same manner as a unit disembarking from a transport, except that they must be set up more than 9" away from any enemy models. Any models that cannot be set up in this way are destroyed.

Transport Spore: When you set up a Tyrannocyte in its hive ship, you can also set up a <Hive Fleet> Infantry unit of up to 20 models or a <Hive Fleet> Monster with a Wounds characteristic of 14 or less inside it (this cannot be another Tyrannocyte or a Sporocyst).

Death Throes: If this model is reduced to 0 wounds, roll a dice before removing the model from the battlefield; on a 6, it lashes out in its death throes, and each unit within 3" suffers D3 mortal wounds.

FACTION KEYWORDS	TYRANIDS, <Hive Fleet>
KEYWORDS	MONSTER, FLY, TYRANNOCYTE

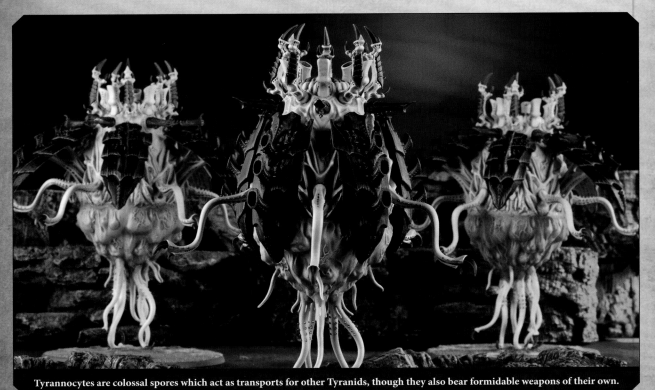

Tyrannocytes are colossal spores which act as transports for other Tyranids, though they also bear formidable weapons of their own.

HARPY

9 POWER

NAME	M	WS	BS	S	T	W	A	Ld	Sv
Harpy	*	*	*	6	6	12	3	9	4+

DAMAGE
Some of this model's characteristics change as it suffers damage, as shown below:

REMAINING W	M	WS	BS
7-12+	30"	4+	4+
4-6	20"	4+	5+
1-3	10"	5+	5+

A Harpy is a single model armed with two stranglethorn cannons and scything wings. It can also fire stinger salvoes.

WEAPON	RANGE	TYPE	S	AP	D	ABILITIES
Heavy venom cannon	36"	Assault D3	9	-2	3	-
Stinger salvo	24"	Assault 4	5	-1	1	-
Stranglethorn cannon	36"	Assault D6	7	-1	2	You can add 1 to hit rolls for this weapon when attacking a unit with 10 or more models.
Scything wings	Melee	Melee	User	-2	D3	You can re-roll hit rolls of 1 for this weapon.

WARGEAR OPTIONS	• This model may replace both its stranglethorn cannons with two heavy venom cannons.

ABILITIES	**Instinctive Behaviour** (pg 82) **Death Throes:** If this model is reduced to 0 wounds, roll a D6 before removing the model from the battlefield; on a 6, it lashes out in its death throes, and each unit within 3" suffers D3 mortal wounds. **Sonic Screech:** When a Harpy successfully charges, until the end of the turn enemy units within 1" cannot be chosen to Fight until all other eligible units have done so.	**Spore Mine Cysts:** A Harpy can drop Spore Mines as it flies over enemy units in its Movement phase. To do so, after the Harpy has moved, pick one enemy unit that it flew over and roll a D6 for each model in that unit, up to a maximum of 3 dice. Each time you roll a 4+ a Spore Mine has hit the target and explodes. Roll a D6 to find out how much damage is inflicted on the unit; on a 1 the Spore Mine fails to inflict any harm, on a 2-5 it inflicts 1 mortal wound, and on a 6 it inflicts D3 mortal wounds. Each time a Spore Mine misses its target, set up a single Spore Mine anywhere within 6" of the target unit and more than 3" from any enemy model (if the Spore Mine cannot be placed it is destroyed). This then follows the rules for Spore Mines (pg 99) that are part of your army, but it cannot move or charge during the turn it was set up.

FACTION KEYWORDS	TYRANIDS, <HIVE FLEET>
KEYWORDS	MONSTER, FLY, HARPY

HIVE CRONE

8 POWER

NAME	M	WS	BS	S	T	W	A	Ld	Sv
Hive Crone	*	*	*	6	6	12	3	9	4+

DAMAGE
Some of this model's characteristics change as it suffers damage, as shown below:

REMAINING W	M	WS	BS
7-12+	30"	4+	4+
4-6	20"	4+	5+
1-3	10"	5+	5+

A Hive Crone is a single model armed with a drool cannon, tentaclids, scything wings and a wicked spur. It can also fire stinger salvoes.

WEAPON	RANGE	TYPE	S	AP	D	ABILITIES
Drool cannon	8"	Assault D6	6	-1	1	This weapon automatically hits its target.
Stinger salvo	24"	Assault 4	5	-1	1	-
Tentaclids	36"	Assault 4	5	0	1	You may re-roll failed hit rolls for this weapon against units that can FLY. In addition, if the target is a VEHICLE and you make a wound roll of 4+, it suffers 1 mortal wound in addition to any other damage. If you make a wound roll of 6+, inflict D3 mortal wounds instead.
Scything wings	Melee	Melee	User	-2	D3	You can re-roll hit rolls of 1 for this weapon.
Wicked spur	Melee	Melee	8	-3	D3	Each time the bearer fights, it can make one (and only one) attack with this weapon. This is in addition to the bearer's attacks.

ABILITIES	**Instinctive Behaviour** (pg 82) **Death Throes:** If this model is reduced to 0 wounds, roll a D6 before removing the model from the battlefield; on a 6, it lashes out in its death throes, and each unit within 3" suffers D3 mortal wounds.

FACTION KEYWORDS	TYRANIDS, <HIVE FLEET>
KEYWORDS	MONSTER, FLY, HIVE CRONE

SPOROCYST

DAMAGE
Some of this model's characteristics change as it suffers damage, as shown below:

REMAINING W	S	A
7-12+	5	D6
4-6	4	D3
1-3	3	1

NAME	M	WS	BS	S	T	W	A	Ld	Sv
Sporocyst	-	5+	5+	*	6	12	*	7	4+

A Sporocyst is a single model armed with a spore node and five deathspitters.

WEAPON	RANGE	TYPE	S	AP	D	ABILITIES
Barbed strangler	36"	Assault D6	5	-1	1	You can add 1 to hit rolls for this weapon when attacking a unit with 10 or more models.
Deathspitter	24"	Assault 3	5	-1	1	-
Spore node	9"	Heavy 1	-	-	-	See Spore Node, below
Venom cannon	36"	Assault D3	8	-2	D3	-

WARGEAR OPTIONS	• This model may replace all of its deathspitters with either five barbed stranglers or five venom cannons.

ABILITIES	**Instinctive Behaviour** (pg 82)

Bombardment Organism: During deployment, you can set up a Sporocyst in its hive ship instead of placing it on the battlefield. If you do so, at the beginning of the first battle round but before the first turn begins, the hive ship can launch the Sporocyst – set it up anywhere on the battlefield that is more than 9" away from any enemy models.

Bio-fortress: A Sporocyst can shoot with its weapons even if there are enemies within 1" of it.

Psychic Resonator: Whilst a Sporocyst is within 12" of a friendly <HIVE FLEET> SYNAPSE unit, it has the SYNAPSE keyword and the Synapse ability (pg 82).

Spawn Spore Mines: At the end of your Movement phase, a Sporocyst can spawn spore mines. If it does so, add a new unit of 3 Spore Mines or 1 Mucolid Spore to your army and set it up on the battlefield so that it is wholly within 6" of the Sporocyst and more than 1" from the enemy.

Spore Node: Each time a spore node attack hits its target, roll a D6 to find out how much damage is inflicted on the unit; on a 1 the mines fail to inflict any harm, on a 2-5 they inflict D3 mortal wounds, and on a 6 they inflict D6 mortal wounds.

Each time a spore node attack misses its target, set up a single Mucolid Spore or a unit of up to 3 Spore Mines, anywhere within 6" of the target unit and more than 3" from any enemy model (any models that cannot be placed are destroyed). These then follow the rules for Mucolid Spores or Spore Mines (pg 99) that are part of your army, but they cannot move or charge during the turn they were set up. This weapon cannot be used to fire Overwatch.

Death Throes: If this model is reduced to 0 wounds, roll a D6 before removing the model from the battlefield; on a 6, it lashes out in its death throes, and each unit within 3" suffers D3 mortal wounds.

Immobile: A Sporocyst cannot move for any reason.

FACTION KEYWORDS	TYRANIDS, <HIVE FLEET>
KEYWORDS	MONSTER, SPOROCYST

WEAPONS OF THE HIVE FLEETS

The spawn of the hive fleets bear all manner of biological weaponry to war, killing their prey with chitinous blade-limbs or symbiotic gun-beasts grafted inextricably to the host creature's nervous system. Even the ammunition used by many of the Tyranids' weapons takes the form of a living organism, from the voracious fleshborer beetle to the repulsive brainleech worm.

MELEE WEAPONS

WEAPON	RANGE	TYPE	S	AP	D	ABILITIES
Acid maw	Melee	Melee	User	-3	1	-
Biostatic rattle	Melee	Melee	User	-1	1	Each time the bearer fights, it can make one (and only one) attack with this weapon. This is in addition to the bearer's attacks. If a unit suffers any unsaved wounds from this weapon, add 1 to any Morale tests they take until the end of the turn.
Blinding venom	Melee	Melee	3	0	1	If a unit suffers any unsaved wounds from this weapon, your opponent must subtract 1 from hit rolls for that unit until the end of the turn.
Bone mace	Melee	Melee	8	-1	D3	Each time the bearer fights, it can make one (and only one) attack with this weapon. This is in addition to the bearer's attacks.
Bone sabres	Melee	Melee	User	-3	3	Each time you make a wound roll of 6+ for this weapon, the target unit suffers a mortal wound in addition to any other damage.
Boneswords	Melee	Melee	User	-2	1	A model armed with boneswords can make 1 additional attack with them in the Fight phase.
Claws and teeth	Melee	Melee	User	0	1	-
Crushing claws	Melee	Melee	x2	-3	D3	When attacking with this weapon, you must subtract 1 from the hit roll.
Distensible jaws	Melee	Melee	User	-3	D6	Each time the bearer fights, one (and only one) of its attacks must be made with this weapon.
Grasping talons	Melee	Melee	User	-1	2	-
Lash whip and bonesword	Melee	Melee	User	-2	1	If the bearer is slain in the Fight phase before it has made its attacks, leave it where it is. When its unit is chosen to fight in that phase, the bearer can do so as normal before being removed from the battlefield.
Lash whip and monstrous bonesword	Melee	Melee	User	-2	3	
Monstrous acid maw	Melee	Melee	User	-5	D3	-
Monstrous boneswords	Melee	Melee	User	-2	3	A model armed with monstrous boneswords can make 1 additional attack with them in the Fight phase.
Massive crushing claws	Melee	Melee	x2	-3	D6	When attacking with this weapon, you must subtract 1 from the hit roll.
Monstrous crushing claws	Melee	Melee	x2	-3	3	
Monstrous rending claws	Melee	Melee	User	-3	D3	You can re-roll failed wound rolls for this weapon. In addition, each time you make a wound roll of 6+, that hit is resolved with an AP of -6 and Damage of 3.
Massive scything talons	Melee	Melee	User	-3	D6	You can re-roll hit rolls of 1 for this weapon. If the bearer has more than one pair of monstrous/massive scything talons, it can make 1 additional attack with this weapon each time it fights.
Monstrous scything talons	Melee	Melee	User	-3	3	
Massive toxic lashes (melee)	Melee	Melee	User	-2	D3	You can re-roll failed wound rolls for this weapon. A model armed with this weapon always fights first in the Fight phase, even if it didn't charge. If the enemy has units that have charged, or that have a similar ability, then alternate choosing units to fight with, starting with the player whose turn is taking place.
Powerful limbs	Melee	Melee	User	-1	2	-
Prehensile pincer tail	Melee	Melee	User	0	D3	Each time the bearer fights, it can make one (and only one) attack with this weapon. This is in addition to the bearer's attacks.
Ravenous maw	Melee	Melee	User	-1	D3	Make D3 hit rolls for each attack made with this weapon, instead of 1.
Rending claws	Melee	Melee	User	-1	1	Each time you make a wound roll of 6+ for this weapon, that hit is resolved with an AP of -4.
Shovelling claws	Melee	Melee	x2	-3	D6	-
Scything talons	Melee	Melee	User	0	1	You can re-roll hit rolls of 1 for this weapon. If the bearer has more than one pair of scything talons, it can make 1 additional attack with this weapon each time it fights.
Scything wings	Melee	Melee	User	-2	D3	You can re-roll hit rolls of 1 for this weapon.
Thresher scythe	Melee	Melee	4	-1	1	Each time the bearer fights, it can make one (and only one) attack with this weapon. Make D3 hit rolls for this attack instead of one. This is in addition to the bearer's attacks.
Toxic lashes (melee)	Melee	Melee	User	0	D3	You can re-roll failed wound rolls for this weapon. A model armed with this weapon always fights first in the Fight phase, even if it didn't charge. If the enemy has units that have charged, or that have a similar ability, then alternate choosing units to fight with, starting with the player whose turn is taking place.
Toxinspike	Melee	Melee	1	0	D3	Each time the bearer fights, it can make one (and only one) attack with this weapon. This is in addition to the bearer's attacks. This weapon always wounds targets (other than **Vehicles**) on a 2+.
Wicked spur	Melee	Melee	8	-3	D3	Each time the bearer fights, it can make one (and only one) attack with this weapon. This is in addition to the bearer's attacks.

RANGED WEAPONS

WEAPON	RANGE	TYPE	S	AP	D	ABILITIES
Acid spray	18"	Heavy 2D6	User	-1	D3	This weapon automatically hits its target.
Barbed strangler	36"	Assault D6	5	-1	1	You can add 1 to hit rolls for this weapon when attacking a unit with 10 or more models.
Bio-electric pulse	12"	Assault 6	5	0	1	-
Bio-electric pulse with containment spines	12"	Assault 12	5	0	1	-
Bio-plasma	12"	Assault D3	7	-3	1	-
Bio-plasmic cannon	36"	Heavy 6	7	-3	2	-
Bio-plasmic scream	18"	Assault D6	7	-4	1	-
Choking spores	12"	Assault D6	3	0	D3	You can re-roll failed wound rolls for this weapon. In addition, units attacked by this weapon do not gain any bonus to their saving throws for being in cover.
Deathspitter	24"	Assault 3	5	-1	1	-
Deathspitter with slimer maggots	24"	Assault 3	7	-1	1	-
Devourer	18"	Assault 3	4	0	1	-
Devourer with brainleech worms	18"	Assault 6	6	0	1	-
Drool cannon	8"	Assault D6	6	-1	1	This weapon automatically hits its target.
Flamespurt	10"	Assault D6	5	-1	1	This weapon automatically hits its target.
Flesh hooks	6"	Assault 2	User	0	1	This weapon can be fired within 1" of an enemy unit, and can target enemy units within 1" of friendly units.
Fleshborer	12"	Assault 1	4	0	1	-
Fleshborer hive	18"	Heavy 20	5	0	1	-
Grasping tongue	12"	Assault 1	6	-3	D3	This weapon can be fired within 1" of an enemy unit, and can target enemy units within 1" of friendly units. In addition, when a model is slain by this weapon, the bearer regains 1 lost wound.
Heavy venom cannon	36"	Assault D3	9	-2	3	-
Impaler cannon	36"	Heavy 2	8	-2	D3	This weapon can target units that are not visible to the bearer. In addition, units attacked by this weapon do not gain any bonus to their saving throws for being in cover.

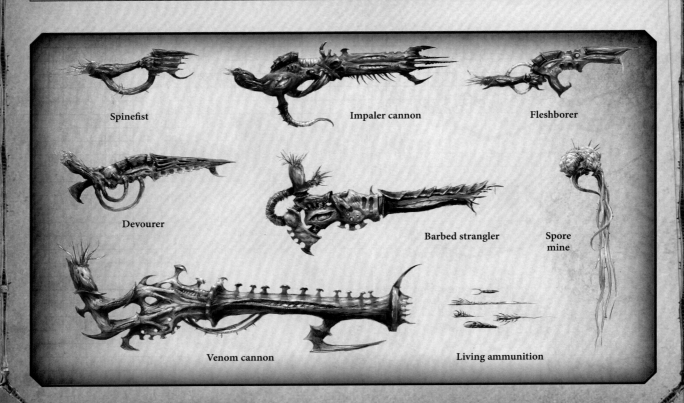

Spinefist

Impaler cannon

Fleshborer

Devourer

Barbed strangler

Spore mine

Venom cannon

Living ammunition

RANGED WEAPONS CONT.

WEAPON	RANGE	TYPE	S	AP	D	ABILITIES
Massive toxic lashes (shooting)	8"	Assault D6	User	-2	D3	This weapon can be fired within 1" of an enemy unit, and can target enemy units within 1" of friendly units. You can re-roll all failed wound rolls for this weapon.
Rupture cannon	48"	Heavy 3	10	-3	D6	-
Shockcannon	24"	Assault D3	7	-1	D3	If the target is a VEHICLE and you make a wound roll of 4+, the target suffers 1 mortal wound in addition to any other damage. If you make a wound roll of 6+, inflict D3 mortal wounds instead.
Spine banks	6"	Assault 4	5	0	1	This weapon can be fired within 1" of an enemy unit, and can target enemy units within 1" of friendly units.
Spinefists	12"	Pistol *	3	0	1	When a model fires this weapon, it makes a number of shots equal to its Attacks characteristic.
Spinemaws	6"	Pistol 4	2	0	1	-
Spore mine launcher	48"	Heavy 1				*See Biovore datasheet (pg 101)*
Stinger salvo	24"	Assault 4	5	-1	1	
Stranglethorn cannon	36"	Assault D6	7	-1	2	You can add 1 to hit rolls for this weapon when attacking a unit with 10 or more models.
Tentaclids	36"	Assault 4	5	0	1	You may re-roll failed hit rolls for this weapon against units that can FLY. In addition, if the target is a VEHICLE and you make a wound roll of 4+, it suffers 1 mortal wound in addition to any other damage. If you make a wound roll of 6+, inflict D3 mortal wounds instead.
Toxic lashes (shooting)	6"	Assault 2	User	0	D3	This weapon can be fired within 1" of an enemy unit, and can target enemy units within 1" of friendly units. In addition, you can re-roll failed wound rolls for this weapon.
Venom cannon	36"	Assault D3	8	-2	D3	-

BIOMORPHS

BIOMORPH	EFFECT
Adrenal glands	If a unit has adrenal glands, add 1" to the distance it can move when it Advances or charges.
Toxin sacs	Any wound rolls of 6+ in the Fight phase for a model with toxin sacs cause 1 additional damage.

Attacking from the skies and from beneath the earth, the Tyranids tear apart their prey in a frenzy of slashing claws.

THE SHADOW IN THE WARP

In this section you'll find rules for Battle-forged armies that include Tyranids Detachments – that is, any Detachment which only includes units with the TYRANIDS keyword. These rules include the abilities below and a series of Stratagems. This section also includes the Tyranids' unique Warlord Traits, Psychic Discipline, Bio-artefacts and Tactical Objectives. Together, these rules reflect the character and fighting style of the Tyranids in your games of Warhammer 40,000.

ABILITIES

Tyranids Detachments gain the following abilities:

EXTENSIONS OF THE HIVE MIND

The organisms that make up a Tyranid army are all extensions of the psychic gestalt known as the Hive Mind – its tendrils and its jaws, all working with a single purpose.

If your army is Battle-forged, all Troops units in Tyranids Detachments gain this ability. Such a unit that is within range of an objective marker (as specified in the mission) controls the objective marker even if there are more enemy models within range of that objective marker. If an enemy unit within range of the same objective marker has a similar ability, then the objective marker is controlled by the player who has the most models within range of it as normal.

HIVE FLEET ADAPTATIONS

Each of the hive fleets has its own distinct methods of predation, from the movement patterns of entire swarms to the behaviours and morphology of individual organisms.

If your army is Battle-forged, all units in Tyranids Detachments gain a Hive Fleet Adaptation, so long as every unit in that Detachment is from the same hive fleet. The Hive Fleet Adaptation gained depends upon the hive fleet they are from, as shown in the table opposite. For example, a **BEHEMOTH** unit with the Hive Fleet Adaptation ability gains the Hyper-aggression adaptation.

If you are using a splinter fleet rather than a hive fleet, use the Hive Fleet Adaptation of its parent hive fleet. For example, the Court of the Nephilim King is a splinter fleet of Hive Fleet Behemoth, so should use the Behemoth Hive Fleet Adaptation. If you are unsure of a splinter fleet's parent hive fleet, either consult the background sections of our books or choose an adaptation from the table that best describes its character and fighting style.

> 'Perhaps the Tyranids are a punishment for all the galaxy's warring races, we who could not see beyond our reckless hate. Perhaps, in a final twist of irony, we shall be consumed by a force that feels no enmity at all, merely a cold and insatiable hunger.'
>
> *- Farseer Zonayen of Alaitoc*

HIVE FLEET ADAPTATIONS

BEHEMOTH: HYPER-AGGRESSION

Driven by a frenzied hunger, Hive Fleet Behemoth unleashes the full might of its swarms in an overwhelming frontal assault.

You can re-roll failed charge rolls for units with this adaptation.

KRAKEN: QUESTING TENDRILS

The Kraken harries and unbalances its foes with lightning-fast flanking attacks, before encircling them for the final, bloody massacre.

When a unit with this adaptation Advances, roll three dice instead of one and pick the highest to add to the Move characteristic of all models in the unit for that Movement phase. In addition, such units can Fall Back and charge in the same turn.

LEVIATHAN: SYNAPTIC IMPERATIVE

Hive Fleet Leviathan's synaptic network is so strong that its organisms can be compelled by the Hive Mind to fight in spite of injuries that should have crippled or slain them outright.

Roll a D6 each time a unit with this adaptation loses a wound whilst it is within 6" of a friendly **SYNAPSE** unit from the same hive fleet. On a 6, the damage is ignored and the unit does not lose a wound. Ignore this adaptation on a unit that is currently affected by the *Catalyst* psychic power.

GORGON: ADAPTIVE TOXINS

The toxins produced by Hive Fleet Gorgon's swarm-creatures adapt with terrifying speed to any foe, agonising and ravaging the bodies of their unfortunate victims.

You can re-roll wound rolls of 1 in the Fight phase for units with this adaptation.

JORMUNGANDR: TUNNEL NETWORKS

The warrior-organisms of Hive Fleet Jormungandr attack from subterranean tunnels, making them extremely difficult to target until it is far too late.

A unit with this adaptation (other than units that can **FLY**) always has the benefit of cover for the purposes of shooting attacks. If the unit Advances or charges, however, it loses the benefit of this adaptation until the start of your next Movement phase.

HYDRA: SWARMING INSTINCTS

Hive Fleet Hydra's super-swarms overwhelm their prey with sheer weight of numbers, drowning them in a tide of chitin, flesh and slashing claws.

You can re-roll hit rolls in the Fight phase for units with this adaptation that target units containing fewer models than their own.

KRONOS: BIO-BARRAGE

Hive Fleet Kronos obliterates its foes at range by unleashing devastating barrages of bio-plasma and living missiles.

You can re-roll hit rolls of 1 for units with this adaptation in your Shooting phase if they did not move in the preceding Movement phase.

STRATAGEMS

If your army is Battle-forged and includes any Tyranids Detachments (excluding Auxiliary Support Detachments), you have access to the Stratagems shown below, meaning you can spend Command Points to activate them. These reflect the unique strategies used by the forces of the Hive Mind on the battlefield.

PSYCHIC BARRAGE
1CP

Tyranids Stratagem

By channelling the power of the Shadow in the Warp, Tyranid psyker-beasts can obliterate the minds of their prey.

Use this Stratagem in your Psychic phase if a Zoanthropes unit from your army consisting of at least 3 models is within 6" of 2 other such units. If you do so, the Zoanthropes cannot take any Psychic tests this phase – instead, select a point on the battlefield within 18" of, and visible to, all three units. Roll a dice for each unit (friend or foe) within 3" of that point. Add 1 to the result if the unit being rolled for has 10 or more models, but subtract 1 if the unit being rolled for is a **Character**. On a 4+ that unit suffers 3D3 mortal wounds.

CAUSTIC BLOOD
1CP

Tyranids Stratagem

Even the act of slaying a Tyranid can prove fatal, as its corpse spews corrosive ichor capable of eating through power armour.

Use this Stratagem at the start of a Fight phase. Select a **Tyranids** unit from your army. Roll a dice whenever a model in that unit is destroyed in this phase. For each roll of 6, the enemy unit that inflicted the final wound on that model suffers a mortal wound after all of their attacks have been resolved.

RAPID REGENERATION
2CP

Tyranids Stratagem

Some Tyranid bioforms possess bizarre organs that allow them to stitch together ruptured flesh and chitin.

Use this Stratagem at the end of your Movement phase. Select a **Tyranids** model from your army. It regains D3 wounds lost earlier in the battle.

SCORCH BUGS
1CP

Tyranids Stratagem

The thoraxes of these bulbous insectoids pulse with caustic chemicals.

Use this Stratagem when a **Tyranids** unit from your army is selected to attack in the Shooting phase. You can add 1 to all wound rolls made for that unit's fleshborer or fleshborer hive attacks in that Shooting phase.

FEEDER TENDRILS
1CP

Tyranids Stratagem

Feeder tendrils drain the victim's skull, siphoning vital knowledge and memories with every scrap of brain matter.

Use this Stratagem when a Genestealer, **Lictor**, Toxicrene or Venomthrope from your army kills a **Character** in the Fight phase. Gain D3 Command Points.

IMPLANT ATTACK
1CP

Tyranids Stratagem

Some bio-weapons seed their victims with a lethal spore-cyst. This bloated parasite rapidly expands and bursts, tearing the unfortunate host apart in an eruption of gore.

Use this Stratagem after a **Tyranids** unit from your army fights in the Fight phase. Roll a dice for each enemy model (other than a **Vehicle**) that was wounded by any of this unit's attacks and not slain. On a 2+ the model suffers a mortal wound.

BOUNTY OF THE HIVE FLEET
1CP/3CP

Tyranids Stratagem

Each hive fleet can create a number of powerful bio-artefacts and unique weapon symbiotes, to be grafted to its synapse beasts if its supremacy is threatened.

Use this Stratagem before the battle. Your army can have one extra Bio-artefact for 1 CP, or two extra Bio-artefacts for 3 CPs. All of the Bio-artefacts that you include must be different and be given to different **Tyranids Characters**. You can only use this Stratagem once per battle.

METABOLIC OVERDRIVE
1CP

Tyranids Stratagem

Potent chemicals pump through the bodies of the hive fleet's warriors, granting them formidable reserves of stamina at the risk of total cellular breakdown.

Use this Stratagem in your Movement phase, after moving a **Tyranids** unit from your army. You can make a second move with that unit (including Advancing, if you wish), but when you do so you must roll a dice for each model in the unit. For each roll of 1, inflict a mortal wound on the unit. The unit cannot shoot or make a charge move this turn.

SINGLE-MINDED ANNIHILATION
2CP

Tyranids Stratagem

The Hive Mind invests its warrior-forms with but a single imperative: kill.

Use this Stratagem at the end of your Shooting phase. Select a **TYRANIDS INFANTRY** unit from your army – that unit can immediately shoot again.

GRISLY FEAST
1CP

Tyranids Stratagem

The sight of a comrade being devoured even as they fall can break the spirit of the hardiest warrior.

Use this Stratagem in the Morale phase. Select a unit of Ripper Swarms or Haruspex from your army. Your opponent must add 1 to any Morale tests taken for enemy units that are within 6" of that unit in this phase.

PATHOGENIC SLIME
2CP

Tyranids Stratagem

Tyranid biological ammunition is often doused in a pathogenic mucus, which seeps into wounds and devours flesh.

Use this Stratagem in your Shooting phase. Select a **TYRANIDS MONSTER** from your army. Increase the Damage of its attacks by 1 for this phase.

SPOREFIELD
3CP

Tyranids Stratagem

Ahead of its invasion swarms, the hive fleet sows the prey world with vast clouds of living mines.

Use this Stratagem after both armies have deployed but before the battle begins. You can add up to two units of Spore Mines to your army as reinforcements and set them up anywhere on the battlefield that is more than 12" from enemy models.

INVISIBLE HUNTER
1CP

Tyranids Stratagem

Tyranid assassin organisms can melt away before the astonished faces of their foes, only to strike suddenly from an unexpected direction.

Use this Stratagem in your Movement phase. Select a **LICTOR** from your army that is within 1" of an enemy unit. That model can Fall Back, shoot and charge in this turn.

POWER OF THE HIVE MIND
1CP

Tyranids Stratagem

The gestalt consciousness of the Hive Mind possesses a psychic might beyond mortal comprehension.

Use this Stratagem at the end of your Psychic phase. Select a **TYRANIDS PSYKER** unit from your army that manifested a psychic power this turn. It can immediately attempt to manifest one additional psychic power this turn.

PHEROMONE TRAIL
1CP

Tyranids Stratagem

Lictors release a trail of potent pheromones that guide fresh waves of bioforms to the slaughter.

Use this Stratagem when a **TYRANIDS INFANTRY** unit from your army is set up on the battlefield as reinforcements if there is already a **LICTOR** from your army on the battlefield. You can set up the unit wholly within 6" of the **LICTOR** and more than 9" from any enemy models, rather than following the normal rules for setting up the unit.

DEATH FRENZY
2CP

Tyranids Stratagem

Tyranids care nothing for self-preservation, and will fight on even when riven with mortal wounds.

Use this Stratagem when a **TYRANIDS CHARACTER** from your army is slain; the Hive Mind compels it to one final attack, and it can immediately either shoot as if it were your Shooting phase, or fight as if it were your Fight phase before it is removed from the battlefield.

OVERRUN
1CP

Tyranids Stratagem

A Tyranid assault maintains a fearsome momentum. No sooner is one foe butchered than the swarm moves on to the next kill.

Use this Stratagem when a **TYRANIDS** unit from your army destroys a unit in the Fight phase, and is not within 3" of an enemy unit. Instead of consolidating, that unit can move (and Advance) as if it were your Movement phase (it cannot move within 1" of any enemy models).

VORACIOUS APPETITE
1CP

Tyranids Stratagem

The hunger of the Tyranids can never be satiated.

Use this Stratagem in the Fight phase when a **TYRANIDS MONSTER** or **CHARACTER** from your army is chosen to attack. You can re-roll all failed wound rolls for that model until the end of the phase.

THE ENEMY BELOW
Jormungandr Stratagem
The Great Serpent attacks from below, bursting out from subterranean tunnels in the midst of its prey.

1CP

Use this Stratagem when you set up a **JORMUNGANDR INFANTRY** unit during deployment. It is set up within tunnels bored before battle. Whenever you set up a unit of Raveners, a Mawloc, Trygon or a Trygon Prime at the end of your Movement phase (a burrowing unit), you can also set up any number of units you set up within the tunnels. Set up the unit wholly within 3" of the burrowing unit and more than 9" from any enemy units. Any models you cannot set up in this way when you do so are destroyed.

BRUTE FORCE
Behemoth Stratagem
Behemoth's charge crushes all in its path to bloody paste.

1CP

Use this Stratagem when a **BEHEMOTH** unit from your army completes a charge move. Roll a dice for each model in the charging unit that is within 1" of an enemy unit. For each roll of 6 (or 2+ for a **MONSTER**), inflict one mortal wound on an enemy unit within 1".

WAR ON ALL FRONTS
Leviathan Stratagem
Hive Fleet Leviathan brings death from land, sea and sky.

1CP

Use this Stratagem in the Fight phase. Select an enemy unit that is within 1" of at least one **LEVIATHAN** unit from your army that can **FLY** and at least one that cannot. You can re-roll hit and wound rolls of 1 in this phase for attacks for **LEVIATHAN** units that target that enemy unit.

CALL THE BROOD
Tyranids Stratagem
Bounding from the dark corners of the battlefield come hulking figures with razor claws and ravenous eyes.

3CP

Use this Stratagem at the end of your Movement phase. Add a new unit of up to 5 Genestealers to your army and set them up as reinforcements wholly within 6" of a Broodlord or infestation node from your army and more than 9" from any enemy models.

ADRENALINE SURGE
Tyranids Stratagem
Tyranids will not cease their butchery until every living thing in their path has been torn to bloody shreds.

3CP

Use this Stratagem at the end of the Fight phase. Select a **TYRANIDS** unit from your army – that unit can immediately fight again.

THE DEEPEST SHADOW
Kronos Stratagem
Around the swarms of Hive Fleet Kronos, the Shadow in the Warp is at its most suffocatingly powerful.

1CP

Use this Stratagem when an enemy **PSYKER** attempts to manifest a psychic power within 24" of a **KRONOS** unit from your army. Your opponent can only roll a single dice for the Psychic test.

HYPER-TOXICITY
Gorgon Stratagem
There is no defence against the toxins of Hive Fleet Gorgon.

1CP

Use this Stratagem in the Fight phase. Choose a **GORGON** unit from your army that has the toxin sacs biomorph. For the duration of the phase, the toxin sacs biomorph causes 1 additional damage on wound rolls of 5+ (rather than 6+) for attacks made by that unit.

ENDLESS SWARM
Tyranids Stratagem
The swarms of the Hydra are numberless. Kill one organism, and two more will take its place.

2CP

Use this Stratagem at the end of your Movement phase. Select a unit of Termagants, Hormagaunts or Gargoyles (or any **HYDRA INFANTRY** unit) from your army that has been completely destroyed. Add an identical unit to your army, and set it up as reinforcements wholly within 6" of any board edge, more than 9" from enemy models.

OPPORTUNISTIC ADVANCE
Kraken Stratagem
Before the prey can even react, Hive Fleet Kraken's swarms are already amongst them.

1CP

Use this Stratagem in your Movement phase when you roll the dice for an Advancing **KRAKEN** unit (other than a unit that can **FLY**). You can double the number you roll and add that total to their Move characteristic for that Movement phase, rather than following the normal rules for Advancing.

DIGESTIVE DENIAL
Tyranids Stratagem
The process of digestion has already begun, and corrosive mucal slime is already turning this planet's biospheres to boiling slurry.

2CP

Use this Stratagem after deployment but before the first battle round begins. Choose a piece of terrain (other than a Fortification). Units fully within or on this piece of terrain do not gain any bonus to their saving throws for being in cover.

HIVE MIND DISCIPLINE

Tyranid psyker-beasts draw their horrific powers from a fragment of the Hive Mind's gestalt will. They can utilise this psychic might to empower their lesser kin, or obliterate the minds of their opponents with skull-shattering force.

Before the battle, generate the psychic powers for **PSYKERS** that can use powers from the Hive Mind discipline using the table below. You can either roll a D6 to generate their powers randomly (re-roll any duplicate results), or you can select the psychic powers you wish the psyker to have.

D6 RESULT

1 DOMINION

The Tyranid uses its prodigious psychic strength to channel and amplify the will of the Hive Mind.

Dominion has a warp charge value of 5. If manifested, select a friendly **TYRANIDS** unit within 36" of the psyker that has the Instinctive Behaviour ability. Until the end of your next Psychic phase, that unit ignores its Instinctive Behaviour ability and automatically passes Morale tests.

2 CATALYST

Through its synaptic conduits, the Hive Mind reaches out to infuse the organisms under its control, invigorating their metabolisms with such unnatural vitality that they can ignore the most grievous of wounds.

Catalyst has a warp charge value of 6. If manifested, select a friendly **TYRANIDS** unit within 18" of the psyker. Until the start of your next Psychic phase, each time that unit loses a wound, roll a D6; on a 5+, the damage is ignored and the unit does not lose that wound.

3 THE HORROR

The terrifying psychic presence of the Hive Mind radiates from the synapse creature, flooding the minds of the Tyranids' enemies and causing them to quail and panic.

The Horror has a warp charge value of 6. If manifested, select a unit within 24" that is visible to the psyker. Until the start of your next Psychic phase, that unit must subtract 1 from their hit rolls and Leadership characteristic.

'Brother Khulitar stood
before the xenos, wielding the
fury of the storm. Aetheric
lightning struck the creature's
hide, and it hissed in fury.
That hiss rose to a shriek
that tore at my mind and
blasted us from our feet. I saw
Khulitar stagger backwards,
hands clutching his helm –
then his head burst apart.'

*- Brother Temur, White Scars
3rd Company*

4 ONSLAUGHT

The synapse creature reaches out its mind and seizes control of the lesser creatures' weapon symbiotes, guiding their fire whilst simultaneously driving the swarms towards the enemy at a breakneck pace.

Onslaught has a warp charge value of 6. If manifested, select a friendly **TYRANIDS** unit within 18" of the psyker. That unit can shoot this turn (even if it Advanced) without suffering any penalties to its hit rolls for moving and shooting Heavy weapons, or Advancing and shooting Assault weapons. In addition, that unit can charge this turn even if it Advanced (though not if it Fell Back).

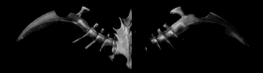

5 PAROXYSM

The Hive Mind debilitates its enemies by triggering every nerve and pain receptor in their bodies, overwhelming their senses with wracking fits of agony.

Paroxysm has a warp charge value of 5. If manifested, choose an enemy unit within 18" of the psyker. Until your next Psychic phase, that unit cannot fight in the Fight phase until all other units that are able to have done so. If the target unit has an ability that allows it to fight first in the Fight phase, it instead fights as if it didn't have this ability. If both players have units that cannot fight until all other units have done so, then alternate choosing which of those units to fight with, starting with the player whose turn is taking place.

6 PSYCHIC SCREAM

Through its vassal, the Hive Mind unleashes a piercing shriek of undiluted psychic energy that shreds the minds of those caught in its wake.

Psychic Scream has a warp charge value of 5. If manifested, the nearest enemy unit within 18" suffers D3 mortal wounds. In addition, if that unit is a **PSYKER**, roll two dice. If the result is higher than their Leadership characteristic, randomly select one of their psychic powers. They can no longer use that psychic power.

BIO-ARTEFACTS OF THE TYRANIDS

The bio-artefacts of the Tyranids are symbiotic organisms of astonishing complexity and rarity, objects of shattering power that can turn the tide of battle in an instant. Spawned by the Hive Mind for the sole purpose of ensuring the galaxy's doom, each of these dread creations has sown the death of countless worlds.

If your army is led by a TYRANIDS Warlord, you may give one of the following Bio-artefacts to a TYRANIDS CHARACTER in your army. Named characters such as the Swarmlord, Old One Eye, Deathleaper and the Red Terror cannot be given any of the following Bio-artefacts – they have their own unique mutations.

Note that some weapons replace one of the model's existing weapons. Where this is the case, you must, if you are playing a matched play game or are otherwise using points values, still pay the cost of the weapon that is being replaced. Write down any Bio-artefacts your CHARACTERS may have on your army roster.

SCYTHES OF TYRAN

The few remaining records of the fall of Tyran speak of an alpha-beast that led the assault upon Magos Varnak's command bunker, tearing open the facility's vast bulkhead doors with a single slash of its scything forelimbs. So sharp were these monomolecular-edged weapon-growths that several Skitarii defenders were bisected with the alpha-beast's every frenzied swipe.

BEHEMOTH model with monstrous scything talons only. The Scythes of Tyran replaces the model's monstrous scything talons and has the following profile:

WEAPON	RANGE	TYPE	S	AP	D
Scythes of Tyran	Melee	Melee	+1	-3	3

Abilities: This model can make 1 additional attack with this weapon each time it fights. In addition, each time you make a hit roll of 6+ for this weapon, you can make an additional hit roll. These additional hit rolls cannot generate further additional hit rolls.

THE YMGARL FACTOR

The Ymgarl Genestealers have long been a cancerous blight on the worlds of the Imperium. Their insatiable voracity is legend amongst those that have had the misfortune to encounter them and live. Now, dark rumours have surfaced of Tyranid leader-beasts that appear to share the unfathomable adaptability of the Ymgarl Genestealers.

At the beginning of each Fight phase, roll a D3 for this model and apply the following effect for the duration of the phase.

D3	Result
1	+1 Strength
2	+1 Attack
3	+1 Toughness

THE REAPER OF OBLITERAX

The Reaper of Obliterax, first encountered amongst the re-emergent swarms of Hive Fleet Jormungandr, is a sentient blade resembling a bonesword that discharges highly concentrated bursts of destructive energy. Even the lightest blow from this bio-weapon can result in its target being rent asunder.

Model with lash whip and bonesword or lash whip and monstrous bonesword only. Add the following to that weapon's Abilities: 'On a wound roll of 6+, this weapon inflicts double damage.'

CHAMELEONIC MUTATION

This chitinous plate armour is an adaptation of the chameleonic carapace common to the Lictor bioform. Sub-dermal crystals capture and redirect light, projecting an ever-shifting mirage that masks the host creature's movements.

KRAKEN model only. Your opponent must subtract 1 from all hit rolls for ranged weapons that target this model.

HYPER-ADAPTIVE BIOLOGY

Leader-beasts spawned by Hive Fleet Gorgon possess an intricate array of bizarre, transmutative organs, each of which can reform itself in mere moments to respond to any internal trauma.

GORGON model only. From the end of the first phase in which this model suffers any wounds, add 1 to its Toughness for the remainder of the battle.

'These beasts, they do not fear us. They do not run from our axes. When we meet in battle, the carnage is glorious. Blood and ichor pools under our boots, turns the ash desert to a sucking quagmire. Our throats are raw from screaming our praises to the Blood God. And still they come, bounding over hills of butchered corpses to get at us. Truly, Khorne has blessed us with a worthy foe.'

- Lord Kalguthar of the Gorehounds

SLAYER SABRES

At the hilt of each of these enormous, curving blades is a shell of diamond-hard chitin. This houses the brain of the weapon-symbiote, a semi-sentient organism which forms a synaptic link with its bearer. With a mental command, the wielder can generate a powerful surge of psychic energy, a fraction of the fell power of the Shadow in the Warp that incinerates the unfortunate victim from the inside out.

LEVIATHAN model with monstrous boneswords only. The Slayer Sabres replace the model's monstrous boneswords and have the following profile:

WEAPON	RANGE	TYPE	S	AP	D
Slayer Sabres	Melee	Melee	User	-2	3

Abilities: A model armed with the Slayer Sabres can make 1 additional attack with them in the Fight phase. In addition, if an **INFANTRY** or **BIKER** model suffers damage from this weapon but is not slain, roll a D3 at the end of the Fight phase. If the result is greater than that model's remaining number of wounds, it is slain.

SLIMER MAGGOT INFESTATION

Rather than individual organisms, this deathspitter fires a wad of self-replicating slimer maggots. Upon striking their target, these ravenous creatures burrow deep into its flesh before beginning the process of fragmentation and regeneration. Within moments, the host body is devoured from the inside by a wriggling mass of grubs.

HYDRA model with two deathspitters with slimer maggots only. The Slimer Maggot Infestation replaces the model's two deathspitters with slimer maggots and has the following profile:

WEAPON	RANGE	TYPE	S	AP	D
Slimer Maggot Infestation	24"	Assault 6	7	-1	1

Abilities: You can re-roll failed wound rolls for this weapon.

BALETHORN CANNON

This enormous bio-cannon spits out a web of hyper-adaptive micro-filament. Upon contact with the target, this sentient substance begins to contract, its contra-empathic surface identifying and adapting to any defences it encounters, flaring white-hot to burn through kinetic shielding, or sharpening to a monomolecular edge to slice through even the thickest power armour.

KRONOS model with stranglethorn cannon only. The Balethorn Cannon replaces the model's stranglethorn cannon and has the following profile:

WEAPON	RANGE	TYPE	S	AP	D
Balethorn Cannon	36"	Assault D6	7	-1	2

Abilities: You can add 1 to hit rolls for this weapon when attacking a unit with 10 or more models. Invulnerable saves cannot be taken against this weapon.

THE MAW-CLAWS OF THYRAX

During the destruction of Thyrax, the dread beast that spearheaded the assault bore a pair of symbiotic fang-lined pincers. These terrible claws consumed both the bodies and the memories of their victims, passing on the assimilated knowledge to the host creature.

Model with rending claws or monstrous rending claws only. When this model slays an enemy model in the Fight phase, you can re-roll failed hit rolls in all subsequent Fight phases for this model.

THE NORN CROWN

First named by Inquisitor Kryptman, the Norn Crown is a unique parasitic organism that burrows needle-like cerebral bores directly into the brain of its host, forming a neuro-synaptic link that acts as a hyper-conduit for the Hive Mind. Through this abhorrent union, the Hive Mind's indomitable will can pour forth to augment and control the hordes of lesser Tyranids that scuttle in the leader-beast's wake.

Friendly **<HIVE FLEET>** units do not suffer the penalties to their hit rolls and charge rolls incurred from the Instinctive Behaviour ability whilst they are within 30" of this model.

THE MIASMA CANNON

The Tyranids utilise all manner of bio-weapons, but none evoke more dread than the Miasma Cannon. Unlike other venom cannons, this weapon fires gobbets of toxin-laden slime so virulent that it reduces organic targets into shapeless puddles of goo in seconds.

Model with a heavy venom cannon only. The Miasma Cannon replaces the model's heavy venom cannon and has the following profile:

WEAPON	RANGE	TYPE	S	AP	D
Miasma Cannon	36"	Assault D3	9	-2	3

Abilities: This weapon hits automatically if the target unit is within 8", and it always wounds targets (other than **VEHICLES**) on a 2+.

INFRASONIC ROAR

Some Jormungandr bio-colossi utilise a complex arrangement of acoustic organs to unleash fearsome infrasonic bellows. So powerful are these booming sonic emanations that they cause a primal terror and confusion in many sentient species.

JORMUNGANDR MONSTER only. Enemy units within 6" of this model must subtract 1 from their Leadership.

WARLORD TRAITS

Tyranid leader-beasts have experienced centuries of combat, and are reborn upon death with every vestige of their battlefield knowledge intact. Cunning, adaptable and created to sow the destruction of entire worlds, these creatures are truly the stuff of nightmares.

If a **Tyranids Character** is your Warlord, it can generate a Warlord Trait from the following table instead of the one in the *Warhammer 40,000* rulebook. You can either roll on the table below to randomly generate a Warlord Trait, or you can select the one that best suits its background.

D6 RESULT

1 ALIEN CUNNING
This Warlord possesses highly sophisticated neural pathways, allowing it to outwit even the most experienced generals of other races.

At the start of the first battle round but before the first turn begins, you can remove your Warlord from the battlefield and set them up again. If both players have units that can do this, roll off. The player that wins the roll-off decides who sets up their unit(s) first.

2 HEIGHTENED SENSES
Whether through rows of bristling antennae or clusters of glistening compound eyes, this Warlord can sense the location of its prey with unerring accuracy.

Your Warlord never suffers any penalties to their hit rolls (although they still only hit on rolls of 6 when firing Overwatch).

3 SYNAPTIC LYNCHPIN
This Warlord's cerebral cortex pulsates with the irresistible power of the Hive Mind, acting as a blazing synaptic beacon to the lesser creatures of the swarm.

Add 6" to the range of the Warlord's Synapse ability.

4 MIND EATER
This Warlord devours not only the flesh of the prey's leaders but their thoughts as well, so that it may learn of their strategies and direct the movements of the swarm accordingly.

Each time the Warlord slays an enemy **Character** in the Fight phase, choose a friendly <**Hive Fleet**> unit within 3". At the end of the phase, that unit can move (and Advance if you wish) as if it was your Movement phase.

5 INSTINCTIVE KILLER
This Warlord has been bioengineered with genetic memories of how best to slay the myriad species which the Hive Mind calls prey.

At the beginning of the battle but before the first turn begins, choose an enemy unit. You can re-roll failed hit rolls for the Warlord for attacks that target that unit or any unit that has the same datasheet (for example, all Intercessor Squads or all units of Nobz etc.).

6 ADAPTIVE BIOLOGY
The same weapon rarely works against this Warlord twice, as its alien physiology adapts at an astonishing rate to counter the attacks of the foe.

From the end of the first phase in which this Warlord suffers any wounds, for the remainder of the battle when inflicting damage upon the Warlord, reduce the damage of the attack by 1 to a minimum of 1.

'I will not retreat. I will not yield the rightful domain of the Necrontyr to this mindless vermin. Open the vault and unleash the Endless Flame. Let the fires of oblivion consume us all.'

- Last words of Overlord Krozha of the Nhemret Dynasty

HIVE FLEET WARLORD TRAITS

If you wish, you can pick a Hive Fleet Warlord Trait from the list below instead of the Tyranid Warlord Traits to the left, but only if your Warlord is from the relevant hive fleet.

BEHEMOTH: MONSTROUS HUNGER

The Warlord embodies the Hive Mind's eternal hunger, tearing great chunks out of its victims in a feeding frenzy, or even swallowing them whole.

Each time you make a wound roll of 6+ for the Warlord in the Fight phase, that attack inflicts 1 additional damage.

KRAKEN: ONE STEP AHEAD

There is no move the prey can make that this Warlord has not foreseen.

In each Fight phase, you can pick one friendly **KRAKEN** unit within 6" of your Warlord. That unit can fight first in the Fight phase, even if it didn't charge. If the enemy has units that have charged, or that have a similar ability, then alternate choosing units to fight with, starting with the player whose turn is taking place.

LEVIATHAN: PERFECTLY ADAPTED

This Warlord was created for one purpose – to completely eradicate the defenders of this world.

Once per battle round, you can re-roll a single hit roll, wound roll, damage roll, Advance roll, charge roll or saving throw made for your Warlord.

GORGON: LETHAL MIASMA

The air around the Warlord throngs with microscopic organisms that invade the bodies of its foes, devouring them from the inside.

At the end of the Fight phase, roll a D6 for each enemy unit within 1" of the Warlord. On a 4+ that unit suffers a mortal wound.

JORMUNGANDR: INSIDIOUS THREAT

This Warlord has lurked unseen on this world, developing such an intimate knowledge of its terrain that there is nowhere for its prey to hide.

Enemy units never gain any bonus to their saving throws for being in cover for attacks made by the Warlord or friendly **JORMUNGANDR** units within 3" of the Warlord.

HYDRA: ENDLESS REGENERATION

Enemy soldiers are horrified to see the Warlord's severed limbs and shattered plates regrowing before their eyes.

At the beginning of each of your turns, roll a dice for each wound that your Warlord has lost. For each roll of 6, your Warlord regains a wound lost earlier in the battle.

KRONOS: SOUL HUNGER

This Warlord has an insatiable hunger for psykers, and can manipulate the Shadow in the Warp to isolate and overwhelm its prey.

Whenever an enemy **PSYKER** fails a psychic test within 18" of your Warlord, they suffer D3 mortal wounds.

> '*At Sha'draig we faced the Tyranids with eager hearts, sure that no species so crude could stand against the Empire and triumph. I left that world as the sole survivor of my kau'ui, cleansed of my arrogance. We must never underestimate these creatures again. We must learn quicker and adapt faster than they, lest the light of the Greater Good be extinguished forever.*'
>
> *- Shas'o Magami, Sa'cea Sept*

NAMED CHARACTERS AND WARLORD TRAITS

The mightiest creatures spawned by the Hive Mind have each been created with a specific purpose. If one of the following named characters is your Warlord, they must be given the associated Warlord Trait shown below.

NAMED CHARACTER	WARLORD TRAIT
The Swarmlord	Alien Cunning
Old One Eye	Adaptive Biology
Deathleaper	Mind Eater
The Red Terror	Heightened Senses

POINTS VALUES

If you are playing a matched play game, or a game that uses a points limit, you can use the following lists to determine the total points cost of your army. Simply add together the points values of all your models, as well as the weapons and biomorphs they are equipped with, to determine your army's total points value.

UNITS

UNIT	MODELS PER UNIT	POINTS PER MODEL (Does not include weapons)
Biovores	1-3	36
Broodlord	1	162
Carnifexes	1-3	67
Exocrine	1	216
Gargoyles	10-30	6
Genestealers	5-20	10
Harpy	1	121
Haruspex	1	198
Hive Crone	1	153
Hive Guard	3-6	18
Hive Tyrant	1	143
Hive Tyrant with Wings	1	170
Hormagaunts	10-30	5
Lictor	1	41
Maleceptor	1	162
Mawloc	1	104
Mucolid Spores	1-3	20
Neurothrope	1	70
Pyrovores	1-3	38
Raveners	3-9	23
Ripper Swarms	3-9	11
Screamer-Killers	1-3	90
Spore Mines	3-9	10
Sporocyst	1	79
Termagants	10-30	4
Tervigon	1	225
Thornbacks	1-3	70
Toxicrene	1	157
Trygon	1	108
Trygon Prime	1	138
Tyranid Prime	1	100
Tyranid Warriors	3-9	20
Tyrannocyte	1	98
Tyrannofex	1	181
Tyrant Guard	3-6	35
Venomthropes	3-6	30
Zoanthropes	3-6	40

UNITS

UNIT	MODELS PER UNIT	POINTS PER MODEL (Includes weapons)
Deathleaper	1	90
Old One Eye	1	200
The Red Terror	1	75
The Swarmlord	1	300

RANGED WEAPONS

WEAPON	POINTS PER WEAPON
Acid spray	25
Barbed strangler	10
Bio-electric pulse	0
Bio-electric pulse with containment spines	0
Bio-plasma	9
Bio-plasmic cannon	0
Bio-plasmic scream	0
Choking spores	0
Deathspitter	5
Deathspitter with slimer maggots	7
Devourer	4
Devourer with brainleech worms	7
Drool cannon	0
Flamespurt	0
Flesh hooks	2
Fleshborer	0
Fleshborer hive	15
Grasping tongue	0
Heavy venom cannon	25
Impaler cannon	30
Massive toxic lashes	0
Rupture cannon	49
Shockcannon	21
Spine banks	2
Spinefists (Ravener and Tyranid Warrior)	1
Spinefists (Termagant)	0
Spinemaws	2
Spore mine launcher	0
Spore node	0
Stinger salvo	8
Stranglethorn cannon	25
Tentaclids	0
Toxic lashes	0
Venom cannon	20

MELEE WEAPONS

WEAPON	POINTS PER WEAPON
Acid maw	0
Biostatic rattle	0
Blinding venom	0
Bone mace	2
Boneswords	2
Claws and teeth	0
Crushing claws	12
Distensible jaws	0
Grasping talons	0
Lash whip and bonesword	2
Lash whip and monstrous bonesword	15
Massive crushing claws	20
Massive scything talons (Tervigon and Maleceptor)	10
Massive scything talons (two or more pairs) (Trygon and Trygon Prime)	60
Massive toxic lashes	0
Monstrous acid maw	10
Monstrous boneswords	20
Monstrous crushing claws	12
Monstrous rending claws	0
Monstrous scything talons (**Carnifex**)	14
Monstrous scything talons (Hive Tyrant)	15
Monstrous scything talons (two pairs) (**Carnifex**)	15
Monstrous scything talons (two pairs) (Hive Tyrant)	20
Powerful limbs	0
Prehensile pincer tail	0
Ravenous maw	0
Rending claws	2
Shovelling claws	0
Scything talons	0
Scything wings	0
Thresher scythe	7
Toxic lashes	0
Toxinspike	1
Wicked spur	0

BIOMORPHS

BIOMORPH	POINTS PER BIOMORPH
Adrenal glands (**Monsters**)	5
Adrenal glands (other units)	1
Chitin thorns	5
Enhanced senses	10
Extended carapace	2
Spore cysts	10
Toxin sacs (Hormagaunt)	2
Toxin sacs (Hive Guard, Mawloc, Termagant, Tervigon, Tyrant Guard and Tyrannofex)	1
Toxin sacs (Trygon and Trygon Prime)	8
Toxin sacs (**Carnifex**, Genestealer, Hive Tyrant, Tyranid Prime and Tyranid Warrior)	4
Tusks	8

TACTICAL OBJECTIVES

Though their weapons and tactics may vary, every single Tyranid host is driven to fulfil the same primal imperative: the complete and total consumption of all galactic life.

If your army is led by a **TYRANIDS** Warlord, these Tactical Objectives replace the Capture and Control Tactical Objectives (numbers 11-16) in the *Warhammer 40,000* rulebook. If a mission uses Tactical Objectives, players use the normal rules for using Tactical Objectives with the following exception: when a Tyranids player generates a Capture and Control objective (numbers 11-16), they instead generate the corresponding Tyranids Tactical Objective, as shown below. Other Tactical Objectives (numbers 21-66) are generated normally.

D66	TACTICAL OBJECTIVE
1	Swarm
2	Crush
3	Dominate
4	Decapitate
5	Terrify
6	Devour

11 — SWARM — Tyranids

The Tyranids' numbers are unending, their reach seemingly limitless. In time, there is no corner of space that will not suffer the consequences of their ravenous hunger.

Score 1 victory point if you control more objective markers than your opponent at the end of the turn.

14 — DECAPITATE — Tyranids

During its initial incursions into the galaxy, the Hive Mind swiftly learned the value of slaughtering its prey's strongest and most capable leaders, leaving the remainder in frightened confusion.

Score 1 victory point if at least one enemy **CHARACTER** was destroyed this turn. If two or more enemy **CHARACTERS** were destroyed, score D3 victory points instead.

12 — CRUSH — Tyranids

One by one, the Tyranids' foes are overrun and butchered, crushed and hacked into a formless slurry to be consumed by slavering feeder-beasts.

Score 1 victory point if at least one enemy unit was completely destroyed this turn, and the last model in the enemy unit was slain by an attack made by a **TYRANIDS MONSTER** or a **TYRANIDS** unit of more than 10 models.

15 — TERRIFY — Tyranids

Terror only serves the Hive Mind's ends. A panicked enemy has no defence against its relentless onslaught.

Score 1 victory point if at least one enemy unit failed a Morale test this turn. If three or more enemy units failed Morale tests this turn, score D3 victory points instead.

13 — DOMINATE — Tyranids

By harnessing the horrifying psychic immensity of the Hive Mind, the Tyranids will overwhelm and obliterate the prey races.

Score 1 victory point if at least three psychic powers were successfully manifested by friendly **TYRANIDS** units in your Psychic phase.

16 — DEVOUR — Tyranids

Isolate. Slaughter. Consume. This simple, brutal strategy has seen The Great Devourer lay waste to vast swathes of the galaxy.

Score 1 victory point if an enemy unit was destroyed during the Fight phase this turn. If 3 or more enemy units were destroyed during the Fight phase this turn, score D3 victory points instead, and if 6 or more enemy units were destroyed during the Fight phase this turn, score D3+3 victory points instead.

'The war against the Tyranids will not be won with honour, bravery or mighty deeds. To survive we must embrace the ruthless mathematics of attrition. We must be willing to sacrifice a hundred innocent worlds to save a thousand.'

- Inquisitor Kryptman